ESSENTIALS OF
ROASTING

WILLIAMS-SONOMA

ESSENTIALS OF
ROASTING

RECIPES AND TECHNIQUES FOR DELICIOUS OVEN-COOKED MEALS

TEXT
RICK RODGERS

RECIPES
MELANIE BARNARD, BOB AND COLEEN SIMMONS

GENERAL EDITOR
CHUCK WILLIAMS

PHOTOGRAPHY
NOEL BARNHURST

Oxmoor
House.

Contents

No cooking technique fills the home with more mouthwatering aromas than roasting. I always enjoy watching when dinner guests walk through my front door and get that first whiff of roast beef cooking in the oven. Their immediately happy expressions inevitably combine recognition, comfort, and anticipation. Of course, beef is not the only option. Everything from shrimp, chicken, duck, lamb, and pork to potatoes, beets, onions, and even peaches will give off that unmistakable—and irresistible—sweet roasted scent.

In other words, roasting is endlessly adaptable. Is there any meat that does not benefit from the burnished, savory crust that roasting delivers? Countless ways to cook chicken exist, but has anyone improved on that culinary icon, the roast chicken? What is a holiday table without a roast turkey? Is there a more dramatic way to present a whole striped bass or red snapper than roasted in a salt crust? A hot oven can help you turn out a variety of preparations, from a snack of simple spiced nuts to a side dish of hearty root vegetables to a warm and satisfying dessert.

In the past, roasting demanded a commitment of time, with most foods cooked in a slow oven on a long, lazy weekend afternoon. But times have changed. Nowadays, high-temperature roasting is popular, which means that you can roast a meal quickly on any day of the week. Also, more homes than ever are outfitted with convection ovens, modern kitchen wonders that can reduce conventional roasting times by one-third. When you do have the time, however, slow roasting is still the best way to cook such foods as baby back ribs or pork shoulder.

For the most part, the old school of roasting adhered to the principle of one temperature fits all foods. This book shows today's cooks how to roast at three different oven temperatures: high, moderate, and low. You will also discover how to combine two heat levels, such as high and moderate, and how to combine techniques, such as searing and roasting for pan-roasting, to yield the best results for every recipe.

Finally, roasting is for every occasion. Whether you are preparing a simple family weeknight supper or a lavish Saturday dinner for company, roasting sets the stage for memorable eating.

Roasting, Past and Present

For eons, food was cooked outdoors directly over flames. When cooking moved indoors, the centerpiece of the meal was often turned on a spit over an open fire. With the advent of the stove, food moved off the spit and into a pan, and eventually into the heat of an oven.

Historians have not yet dated the domestication of fire, which makes pinpointing the origin of roasting difficult. But the discovery of blackened stones and a crude hearth of woolly mammoth tusks from the Paleolithic era suggests that early humans had already started cooking. The first roasted food was probably an accident: A piece of raw meat inadvertently dropped into a fire was retrieved by a hungry human. Browned by the heat, the meat had strangely changed color and texture. But food was hard to come by and not to be wasted, so it was eaten regardless of the odd appearance. By pulling the meat from the fire, the hungry human became a novice cook. One taste likely convinced this early diner that "roasted" meat tasted better than raw meat, and a cooking technique was born.

Vegetables and fruits, as well as meats, poultry, and seafood, develop a flavorful, evenly browned surface when roasted.

From that point on, humans have continuously improved on this primitive method for making raw food more palatable. The next development was impaling food on a stick and holding it over the fire to cook in the licking flames. This system eventually proved both awkward and labor-intensive. The invention of vessels to contain the meat freed the cook's hands for other work. Although pots certainly proved efficient, the prehistoric cook's appreciation for the flavor of fire-browned meat did not go away.

As the concept of the kitchen developed—moving from the stone-lined cooking pits of prehistoric huts to the raised stone hearths of Pompeii—the stick was modified into a spit suspended and turned over an open fire. Turning the food accomplished two things: it contributed to even browning, and it allowed the melting fat to distribute itself around the slowly twirling meat. Cooks placed a pan under the spit to catch the dripping fat, which was then used to baste the meat (they believed this moistened the meat, a theory that has since been discounted). The drippings in the pan were saved and used to cook other foods.

Roasting on a traditional spit in a hearth was not easy. Before the days of electric motors, the meat had to be turned by hand almost constantly to keep the food from burning. But the English mastered the spit, and by the eighteenth century they were well known beyond their borders for their talent with roasted meats. Indeed, their literature of the day is filled with images of huge, juicy joints

Both whole poultry and parts such as this duck breast (page 152) emerge from the oven with crisp skin enveloping tender flesh.

on groaning tables. The French, perhaps a bit jealous that another nation had trumped them in the kitchen, even now sometimes call the British *rosbifs*. This somewhat condescending name is a nod to their roasting expertise and love for what could be considered the English national dish, standing beef rib roast with Yorkshire pudding (see this book's version on page 177). Nowadays, it is still the custom in some British homes to retrieve the flavorful, if fatty, drippings from the beef's roasting pan and spread them on bread as a snack.

MODERN ROASTING

Today's roasted foods are cooked in a pan in the radiant, dry heat of an enclosed oven, making the technique similar to baking (see Roasting Criteria, opposite), another indispensable cooking method. (When liquid is added and the pan is covered, the food is cooked by moist heat, or braised.) Roasting no longer relies on the variable heat of an open flame. Instead, the oven's thermostat is turned to a specific roasting temperature. To coax the currents of hot air around the food, a rack is often used to lift it off the pan bottom.

It has been about a hundred years since the connection between the deeply browned surface of roasted food and increased flavor became clear. The process of how roasting colors the outside of raw food is called the Maillard reaction, named after the French scientist who discovered the effect.

Simply stated, when the natural sugars in food come in contact with the oven's heat, the sugars break down. Hydrogen and oxygen dissipate, leaving behind sweet carbon compounds similar to caramel. At the same time, the heat slowly penetrates to the center of the food, keeping it juicy. Note that the browned surface does not seal in juices, a common misunderstanding. Browning merely adds flavor. For additional information on the Maillard reaction, see page 21.

The best candidates for roasting meat are tender cuts such as tenderloin, loin, chops, and thick steaks, which are often, although not always, cooked at high temperatures. Tougher cuts, such as ribs or shoulder, have sinew and gristle that must be broken down. Although braising is a popular way of dealing with the problem, long, slow roasting at a moderately low temperature will bring successful results, too. Poultry, cut up or whole—what is a holiday meal without a roast turkey?—fish and shellfish from salmon and sea bass to lobsters and clams, and dozens of vegetables and fruits all take well to roasting.

As the varying thermostat settings for tender and tougher cuts illustrate, not all foods are roasted at the same temperature. This book shows you how to achieve excellent results with low, moderate, and high roasting temperatures—how to use the classic technique of roasting to create foods with richly browned surfaces and complex, concentrated flavors.

Roasting even delicate vegetables like asparagus (page 257) browns their surface and concentrates their flavor, while preserving their color.

Roasting Criteria

What are the differences between roasting and baking? Not surprisingly, the answers to that question vary depending on the source and are far from clear-cut.

One simple distinction is that roasting demands the use of fat while baking does not. For example, a potato cooked in its skin in the oven is baked, but toss it with some oil and put it in the oven at the same temperature and it is called a roasted potato. The addition of fat, however, is not always the defining element of roasting. Many cuts of meat or poultry have sufficient marbling (bits of fat running through the flesh) or a layer of fat under the skin that negates the need to add more. Semantics can

SPIT-ROASTING

Roasting food on a spit is an ancient technique that fell out of favor once the modern oven entered middle-class kitchens. Instead of using the direct, but somewhat random, heat of an open fire, cooks preferred the oven, which allowed the hot air to circulate around the food in an enclosed area, without needing constant attention. While oven roasting proved to be an improvement over rotating a spit by hand for hours over a hot fire, the evenly browned surface of spit-roasted foods remained undeniably delicious and appealing.

Enter the rotisserie to bridge the gap between past and present. The home cook can choose from among three main types: Countertop rotisseries are available in two models, uncovered and completely enclosed. But the third type, an electric spit for an outdoor charcoal grill, allows you to cook over the coals of a wood fire, recapturing the authentic flavor of old-time spit-roasting.

be muddled in practice, too. For instance, no one ever refers to a roasted ham.

Sometimes color is used to distinguish the two methods. Baked foods are usually cooked to an even golden brown, while most roasted foods are ideally dark brown. An uncovered pan is an important criterion of roasting, as it permits hot air to move freely around the food, encouraging even browning and cooking. But baking can be done in either a covered pan or an uncovered pan.

Finally, transforming the pan juices into a sauce is a classic part of roasting. The same process that makes meat brown in the oven also darkens and flavors the juices in the

bottom of the pan. Deglazed with broth, wine, or another flavorful liquid, these browned bits are the beginning of a delicious sauce to accompany the roasted food.

BENEFITS OF ROASTING

Properly roasted food tastes great. But there are many other reasons for roasting.

ROASTING SAVES TIME: Hurried cooks love roasting because many foods are done in under an hour. On the busiest workday, a meal can be put on the table in less time than required by other methods. As a bonus, most leftovers from roasted meat, poultry, and seafood main courses can be turned into other meals. Almost any of the roast chicken recipes, for example, can be transformed into interesting salads or hearty baked dishes.

ROASTING SAVES LABOR: Generally, roasted foods require minimal preparation. Usually a recipe demands little more than adding some oil and seasoning to the food and putting the pan into the oven, where the food cooks without special attention, aside from a glance or two to check the progress or an occasional basting. In many recipes, an accompaniment cooks in the same pan. With some planning, an appetizer or dessert can be cooked at the same time, an energy-saving bonus.

ROASTING ENHANCES FLAVOR: The browned surface of oven-cooked food is only part of the reason for its rich flavor. Roasting also evaporates moisture, concentrating and revealing the true character of foods and adding complexity in the bargain. Roasting evaporates moisture from auxiliary ingredients as well. For example, if a roast is basted with broth, the liquid will reduce down to a flavorful glaze that will make the subsequent sauce all the more delicious.

ROASTING IS IDEAL FOR HEALTHFUL COOKING: True, roasting requires fat, but only enough to

Firm-textured fruits such as apples retain their essential character during roasting and can be served for dessert or with meats or poultry.

moisten the food lightly. Of course, the choice of fat affects the healthfulness of the recipe. Simply put, the consumption of saturated fats should be kept to a minimum. In contrast, the monounsaturated fatty acids found in olive oil and canola oil can positively affect the way the body uses the cholesterol-controlling lipoproteins. Roasting also offers the healthful advantage of many retained nutrients, which can be incorporated into a sauce.

ROASTING IS VERSATILE: Too often, the term roasting conjures only images of golden-skinned whole chickens and big, browned beef rib roasts. But this technique embraces a much broader table, from soup (Smoky Red Pepper Soup, page 59) to nuts (Indian-Spiced Mixed Nuts, page 30). This book also includes starters like Pancetta-Wrapped Figs (page 38) and Lime and Cilantro Shrimp (page 42), main dishes such as Bacon-Wrapped Meat Loaf (page 187) and Veal Loin Chops with Tarragon-Wine Sauce (page 193), and desserts like Apricot Crisp (page 270) and Gingered Rhubarb (page 276)— all of them roasted.

Types of Roasting

Most roasting recipes use moderate temperatures, which ensure a succulent result. High temperatures deliver deep surface browning and an intense roasted flavor. Low temperatures produce less caramelization, but promise evenly cooked meat in exchange.

HIGH-TEMPERATURE ROASTING

High-temperature roasting, which is defined as temperatures of 400°F (200°C) and higher, practically guarantees a tasty, caramelized outer crust and a distinct "meaty" flavor. The pan juices will also be deeper in flavor and color than those produced at lower temperatures, and the resulting sauces will be especially rich and tasty. High temperatures mean that food cooks quickly, too, reducing time in the kitchen.

There are, however, a few drawbacks to high-temperature roasting, but they have simple solutions. Extreme heat quickly evaporates juices in foods, which can cause excessive shrinkage and drying in some cuts of meat. But cooking times are typically short, so this is seldom a problem.

Another caveat is possible overcooking. Foods cook so quickly that it is easy to overshoot optimum doneness temperatures. Also, all roasted meats retain heat and continue to cook outside of the oven, making it particularly important to remove them when they are 5° to 10°F (3° to 6°C) below their ideal doneness temperature. Having a reliable meat thermometer (page 16) is imperative to help prevent overcooking. Do not use a probe thermometer for high-temperature roasting, as the connecting wire can become inoperable at temperatures above 392°F (200°C), although some recent models have solved this problem.

Finally, high-temperature roasting can cause a number of minor cleanup aggravations, such as smoking, splattering, and a dirty oven.

Never use thin-gauge pans. They heat too quickly, shortening the period of time before the pan juices sizzle and smoke. Invest in a heavy-gauge roasting pan, which will absorb the heat gradually and evenly, reducing splattering and smoking. You will also find that efficient kitchen ventilation helps solve the problem of smoke, and a self-cleaning oven takes care of splatters. Even under the best circumstances, many cooks find that the smoke caused by high-temperature roasting sets off the kitchen smoke alarm, so if you decide to remove the batteries while you roast, be sure to reinstall them once you are finished.

High temperatures do not enhance tenderness, so choose lean, tender meats and in general cook them no more than medium-rare to medium. Select uniformly shaped meats as well, so that the heat will penetrate them evenly. Beef Tenderloin with Madeira Sauce (page 171) and Rack of Lamb with Mustard and Thyme (page 202) are two good examples of high-temperature meat roasting. Tender, sphere-shaped poultry—the roundness contributes to even cooking—also takes well to this method, as illustrated by Classic Roast Chicken (page 101), which cooks in a 500°F (260°C) oven. Whole fish sealed inside a protective salt crust (page 87) and roasted in a 400°F (200°C) oven yields moist, tender flesh.

Roasting at high temperature creates an irresistible caramelized crust on foods such as this butterflied chicken (page 108). The resulting pan juices are particularly deep in flavor and color.

Moderate-temperature roasting is well suited to cooking meat such as a cross-rib roast (page 168) and vegetables in the same pan.

A lengthy roasting time at a low temperature produces tomatoes with a rich, concentrated flavor and an almost chewy texture (page 280).

MODERATE-TEMPERATURE ROASTING

Most recipes in this book call for moderate-temperature roasting, that is, oven settings that range from more than 300°F (150°F) up to 400°F (200°C), sometimes combined with a second level of heat to create a so-called hybrid roasting method (page 13). These moderate temperatures keep shrinkage and moisture loss at a modest level. With the gradual, steady application of heat, liquid evaporates more slowly, which means that more juices are retained. You can also usually roast vegetables in the same pan as meat or poultry, or you can cook another course on another oven rack at the same time. Moderate temperatures need less monitoring, allowing you to turn your attention to other kitchen or household tasks.

Keep in mind that the amount of caramelized surface crust will vary according to roasting time. Smaller cuts of meat that cook in under two hours, such as eye of round or rib-eye steaks, will not brown deeply. You can easily

solve the problem by searing the meat in a heavy-gauge frying pan on the stove top before roasting—a simple, easy additional step.

Moderate-temperature roasting works well for a wide range of foods. Relatively tender cuts of meat with a high ratio of fat marbled through the flesh are best; the fat melts slowly during roasting, keeping the meat moist. Stuffed Breast of Veal (page 191), which is often a candidate for braising, is first steamed and then roasted in moderate heat until browned and juicy. Large roasts, such as Crown Roast of Pork with Wild Rice Stuffing (page 215), need moderate heat to cook through without over-browning the outside.

Whole poultry (Lemon-Garlic Chicken, page 102) or parts (Sherry-Glazed Chicken Thighs, page 123) can be cooked by this method without concern for splattering or smoking. Cooking side dishes along with the main course does not need to be limited to meats and poultry, as Cod with Potatoes and Aioli (page 77) so aptly illustrates.

LOW-TEMPERATURE ROASTING

With low-temperature roasting, also known as slow roasting, liquid evaporates slowly, keeping foods juicy and weight loss to a minimum. Temperatures range from 250° to 300°F (120° to 150°C), and cooking times are typically long, two characteristics that effectively melt the fat and break down the tough connective tissues in less expensive cuts of meat.

Roasting can sometimes last for three hours or more, but by choosing the right cut of meat or the proper vegetable, slow roasting can yield great results. Slow-roasted meats will not gain a savory caramelized crust, but many of them promise falling-off-the-bone tenderness, a good trade-off. You can rub the meat with a seasoning mixture of spices or herbs as a tasty substitute for the browned crust (see Slow-Roasted Pork Shoulder, page 208). Pan juices will not darken, so sauces will not be quite as flavorful as those made from meats roasted at higher temperatures. You can, however, place the roasting pan over high heat on the stove top for a few minutes until the juices are reduced and darkened to a nut brown.

Save this method for fatty meats with a high level of sinew and gristle. These connective tissues are mainly collagen, which melts from the heat of the oven and bastes the meat from the inside out, making for a succulent result. Vegetables are also good candidates for low-temperature roasting. Tomatoes (page 280), acquire a dark red color and concentrated flavor after two hours in the oven.

PAN-ROASTING

Most home cooks do not combine cooking techniques. They decide to sauté or roast chops or fillets, for example, but rarely do they sauté *and* roast them. Restaurant chefs, in contrast, regularly employ pan-roasting, a two-level technique that adds browned flavor to thinner cuts of meat and supplies plenty of pan juices for a sauce as well.

First, the meat, poultry, or seafood is seared in a heavy frying pan over high heat to give the outer surface a flavorful light browning. Then the pan is placed into a moderate to hot oven, where the food roasts until it has finished cooking. The food is transferred to a platter or carving board, and the pan juices are deglazed and quickly made into a sauce.

A heavy-gauge, ovenproof frying pan is a must for pan-roasting. Flimsy pans or pans with plastic handles will not stand up to the high heat of the stove top or the moderate to high temperatures of the oven. Good-quality kitchenware absorbs and retains heat well and also encourages deeper browning of the pan juices for superior sauces.

Pan-roasting is best for chops, steaks, and other relatively thin cuts of meat, various poultry cuts such as chicken breasts, and fish fillets and steaks. If these cuts were roasted without an initial searing, they would never develop sufficient surface browning before they finished cooking, and a lesser flavor would be the result.

HYBRID ROASTING METHODS

Whenever you combine two roasting temperature levels, you have even more control over the outcome of the finished dish. For example, the high-temperature roasting method may be appealing because it is sure to give meat a tasty crust, but a particularly hot oven can also cause excessive shrinkage and/or splattering. The solution is to give meat an initial roasting at a high temperature to start the browning process, and then reduce the heat to moderate to finish the cooking.

Or try the reverse: Cook the meat at a moderate temperature, thereby reducing shrinkage and promoting juiciness, until it registers about 15°F (7°C) shy of doneness on a thermometer. Then increase the temperature to high and roast the meat until it is browned and registers about 5°F (3°C) less than desired doneness. (Remember, the internal temperature of the meat will continue to rise a few degrees after being removed from the oven.)

Leg of Lamb with Bread Crumb Crust (page 196) is a good example of two-temperature-level roasting. First, the boneless leg is roasted at a high temperature (425°F/220°C) for 30 minutes to brown and flavor the outer surface. Once this is accomplished, the meat is coated with an herbed bread crumb mixture and returned to the oven, and the temperature is reduced to 350°F (180°C) to avoid burning the crust as the lamb roasts. A classic standing rib roast (page 177) is another excellent example. The meat goes into a 450°F (230°C) oven to brown for 20 minutes, then the temperature is reduced to a much cooler 300°F (150°C) to finish.

Searing small cuts like pork chops (page 222) adds flavor before they are roasted in the oven.

Equipment for Roasting

You need only an oven and a few essential pans and tools to roast almost any food. Gas, electric, and convection ovens are equally efficient. Most roasting equipment is versatile, moving easily into the worlds of baking and other cooking techniques.

Ovens

The oven is the most important cooking component in roasting. The accuracy of your oven's temperature is critical, and you cannot assume the precision of its thermostat. It is common for ovens to vary 25°F (12°C) hotter or cooler than the thermostat setting indicates.

An oven thermometer is an invaluable tool for checking your oven's correctness. (For more information on thermometers, see page 16.) Some thermometers are slow to register the temperature. To save time, place the thermometer on the rack on which the food will be roasted before you turn on the oven to preheat it. This way, when the oven is opened to add the food, you can the check the temperature. Allow at least 15 minutes to preheat a moderate oven, longer for high temperatures. If you find that the temperature of your oven fluctuates dramatically and unpredictably, you will want to have the thermostat serviced and the oven professionally calibrated.

The oven must be large enough to hold the food to be cooked with some space to spare. If the sides of the oven crowd the pan, the hot air will not circulate around the food properly, inhibiting even cooking and browning. If the pan is too close to the heat source (especially in electric ovens with top-heating elements), the food can burn.

Some ovens have hot spots that can cause food to cook erratically or even burn. To check for hot spots, place an oven rack in the center of the oven and preheat the oven to 400°F (200°C). Line a large baking sheet with parchment (baking) paper and place in the oven. Wait for 15 minutes, then check the paper for areas that are more browned than others. The deeper color indicates the locations of hot spots. If you have hot spots, you can compensate for them by turning the pan occasionally during roasting.

Be sure that your oven is clean, especially when roasting at high temperatures, which can cause smoking and splattering. For easy cleanup, place a purchased foil liner on the bottom of the oven, or use a sheet of heavy-duty aluminum foil. Also, adequate ventilation, preferably an efficient range fan, is important for whisking away smoke and odors.

Before preheating the oven, be sure the oven rack is in the correct position. Recipes in this book specify only the upper or lower third of the oven. When no position is indicated in a recipe, the rack should be placed in the middle. If the rack is in the top third of the space, foods will be browned by the reflected heat from the roof of the oven, although this is not as powerful as broiling, which uses a top heating element. Placed in the middle, foods are browned from all sides and will cook evenly, especially over long periods of time. In the lower third of the oven, foods are heated and cooked from below, somewhat like sautéing.

Convection ovens use a fan to circulate the hot air rapidly around the food, which decreases the cooking time, improves browning, and reduces the chance of hot spots. In general, reduce the oven temperature in a recipe by 25°F (12°C) when using a convection oven. Because of the circulating air, the food can be placed on any convenient oven rack.

Left to right: CONFIRMING ACCURACY OF OVEN TEMPERATURE; CHECKING PAN SIZE AND OVEN CAPACITY; DETERMINING HOT SPOTS IN OVEN

Left to right: ROASTING PAN; BAKING DISHES FOR ACIDIC FOODS; RIMMED BAKING SHEETS

Roasting Pans

The best materials for roasting pans are heavy-gauge stainless steel, anodized or enameled aluminum, or enameled steel or cast iron. These metals ensure even cooking and keep the bottom of the food and the pan drippings from burning. Also, heavy-gauge metals allow stove-top searing and deglazing of pan juices to create sauces. Plain, untreated aluminum is not a good choice for roasting pans because it can react with acidic ingredients, such as tomatoes, vinegar, and wine, resulting in discolored food with a metallic flavor.

Glass, ceramic, or earthenware baking dishes are particularly good for roasting fruits. If a recipe includes directions for deglazing the dish on the stove top, be sure that it is flame-proof, or it will crack or shatter over direct heat. You can use rimmed baking sheets for smaller pieces of food, such as chicken thighs and breasts, quail or other small whole birds, scallops, shrimp, and cut-up fruits and vegetables. Avoid using baking sheets for any recipe that calls for substantial liquid or yields considerable pan juices, both of which could easily spill. Ovenproof frying pans, key equipment for pan-roasting (page 13), can also be used for cooking small roasts or poultry.

Roasting pans with nonstick surfaces, which are easy to clean, are also an option. Their dark surfaces readily absorb heat, creating pan sauces with particularly deep color and flavor. By comparison, roasting pans with untreated surfaces have the advantage of causing browned bits to cling to the bottom, which can then be released by deglazing with liquid and a wooden spatula for making sauces. Flat-bottomed pans are preferred over pans with raised patterns on the bottom. The latter are designed to lift the food without the addition of a rack, but the ridges make the pan difficult to deglaze for sauces and to clean.

Look for pans with relatively low sides (no more than 3 inches/7.5 cm) to permit the oven heat to move freely around the food and to catch pan drippings. If the pans are too shallow, drippings will splatter beyond the rim. If they are too tall, the food will steam rather than brown.

The correct pan size is crucial as well. If a pan is too large, the drippings can evaporate too quickly and burn. If a pan is much too small, food will not brown properly. The food should fit somewhat snugly in the roasting pan or baking dish, but with enough room to encourage good air circulation.

A well-equipped kitchen has three roasting pans: small, medium, and large. Large pans, measuring 18 by 13 by 3 inches (45 by 33 by 7.5 cm), are used for large turkeys and particularly large cuts of meat, such as a crown roast of pork or a standing rib roast. Measure the interior of your oven to be sure it will hold a pan of this size. Medium-sized pans, measuring 14 by 12 by 2 inches (35 by 30 by 5 cm), are ideal for moderately sized meats and poultry, while small pans, measuring 12 by 8 by 1½ inches (30 by 20 by 4 cm), are good for modest quantities and compact roasts. Good handles for gripping are important. Look for heavy-duty, upright handles that are riveted to the body of the pan.

Disposable aluminum pans are a poor choice for roasting for a number of reasons. Their thin construction makes them ill-advised on the stove top, removing the option of searing the food before it goes in the oven. It is nearly impossible to scrape up the browned bits from a disposable pan for sauces. The largest pans have tall sides that trap steam around the food and discourage browning. Finally, these pans can buckle under the weight of large roasts, inviting the disaster of a dropped turkey or other centerpiece of a meal.

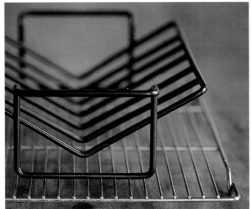  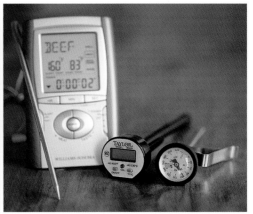

Left to right: ROASTING RACKS; OVEN MITTS AND SILICONE POT HOLDERS; THERMOMETERS (LEFT TO RIGHT): DIGITAL PROBE AND INSTANT READ

Roasting Racks

A well-designed roasting rack elevates the food above the bottom of the pan, promoting even roasting by allowing the heat to reach all sides of the food. (Some cooks prefer not to use racks; others also turn some meats and poultry to ensure uniform browning.) A rack also prevents the food from stewing in its own juices and permits melting fat to drip into the pan.

Roasting racks come in a range of designs. A flat-bottomed rack adapts to a variety of foods, especially the hinged models that fold up to secure round foods that might otherwise roll. Fixed V-shaped racks are best for cylinder-shaped foods, such as boneless pork loins or beef tenderloins. U-shaped racks have flat bottoms, but flare at the sides to hold turkeys and other broad items. Nonstick racks are ideal for long-cooked or glazed foods that might stick to racks without treated surfaces. Look for racks with handles to ease the transfer of food from the pan to a carving board.

You can also create a rack with cut-up aromatic vegetables, such as the onions used in the roast turkey recipe on page 127. Or you might use some appropriate bones—the neck from a turkey, a few beef bones—to fashion a rack. Such racks will do double duty, elevating the food and flavoring the pan juices. With long roasting times these ingredients could scorch. If they threaten to do so, add a little broth or water to the pan to moisten them.

Oven Mitts

Thick oven mitts provide indispensable protection when you lift hot roasting pans from the oven. High-temperature roasting can result in splattering fat and juices, too, so mitts that reach a few inches up your forearms are an even safer choice. Pot holders, another option, come in quilted fabric, leather, and silicone, all of which can offer sufficient protection. Be sure that they are sturdy enough to be effective and are not just decorative.

Thermometers

There are two kinds of thermometers. Liquid-filled thermometers, considered the most accurate, have a heat-sensitive liquid (formerly mercury, but now most commonly alcohol) enclosed in a glass tube. As the liquid heats and expands, it rises up the scale. Spring-action thermometers contain a spring made from two metals with different expansion rates. As the metals heat, they unwind and point to the appropriate temperature on the scale. They are easier to read than most liquid thermometers, but be alert to possible inaccuracy, even with new purchases.

Old-fashioned meat thermometers, both liquid-filled and spring-action models, have a thick stem that is inserted into the food before cooking. This creates a hole in the food that can release juices, however, making them less than ideal. Late-model thermometers with thin stems are a much-appreciated improvement.

Instant-read thermometers, made in spring-action and battery-powered digital versions, are inserted into the food toward the end of the cooking period to determine the temperature. Do not leave these thermometers in the food for longer than 20 seconds, or the plastic dial face could melt.

Digital probe thermometers have a long, slender sensor that remains in the food throughout the entire roasting period. The sensor is attached to an armored wire that runs out of the oven into a readout unit on the kitchen counter (there are cordless models, too). With a glance, you can see the internal temperature of the food, taking much of the guesswork out of roasting. Most models can be set to sound an alarm when the thermometer reaches the desired temperature.

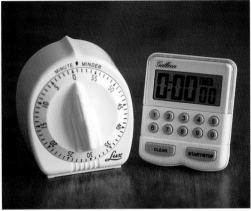

Left to right: KITCHEN STRING AND POULTRY SHEARS; TIMERS; CARVING BOARD AND CARVING TOOLS

No matter what type of meat thermometer you use, it must be correctly positioned. Insert the thermometer halfway through the meat, avoiding bone and fat, both of which heat more quickly than muscle and will cause an inaccurate reading. To determine if your meat thermometer is precise, place it in a saucepan of boiling water; it should read 212°F (100°C) at sea level. If the thermometer is off, compensate for the difference, or buy a new one.

An ideal oven thermometer (photo, page 14) has a flat bottom to help it remain stable on an oven rack and a hook for hanging. Because the thermometer should be placed as closely as possible to the food in the oven, the option of standing or hanging the thermometer is helpful. The numbers on the thermometer should be large and legible, allowing you to read them easily.

Kitchen String

Many recipes require that the meat be tied or the poultry be trussed to create a uniformly shaped roast for even cooking. Stuffed birds or boneless stuffed roasts also depend on kitchen string to keep the stuffing in place. Linen kitchen string, made for use in the oven, does not burn easily and is perfect for these jobs.

Poultry Shears

Cutting up whole poultry (page 282) is more economical than buying individual parts, plus it allows you to personalize the process. For example, you may want chicken breasts with wings attached for a larger portion than the typical breast half. The shears can also be used to carve roasted poultry into serving pieces. Working with shears can be faster than cutting with a knife. Extra heft is needed to cut through bones, so choose relatively heavy shears with a sturdy safety lock for securing the blades closed during storage. Some blades have a slight curve, to negotiate curved chicken bones.

Timers

To allow for countless variables, it is better to rely on the actual temperature of the cooked food rather than on cooking time. Nonetheless, always set a timer to be sure that you do not forget to check on the roasting food. Underdone food can be cooked for a few minutes more, but overcooked food cannot be corrected. Mistakes can be costly. Look for a battery-powered digital model or dial model with large, legible numerals and controls that are easy to manipulate. Some timers can be set for up to four dishes simultaneously, which can

be helpful during a dinner party with multiple courses. The alarm should sound for at least 30 seconds and be loud enough to be heard in rooms adjacent to the kitchen.

Carving Boards

A wooden carving board with grooves and a trough to catch juices is often the best choice for carving. Look for a solid, heavy board with rubber feet to prevent slippage. Respected research has shown that wood surfaces do not readily transfer bacteria to other items, so plastic is not necessarily safer.

Carving Knife and Fork

A carving knife should be long and slender enough to crosscut large roasts with one or two slicing motions. A slicing knife, well suited for carving whole fish and poultry, has a flexible blade that can be maneuvered easily around poultry bones. A knife with a serrated blade is desirable for carving ham and other meats that might stick to an ordinary blade. Always realign the blade of your knife on a stone or hone it on a steel before using. A carving fork should have long, sharp prongs and a comfortable handle that permits you to hold the meat steady with ease.

Roasting Basics

Roasting requires three basic steps: preparing the food, roasting the food, and finishing a recipe after the food is removed from the oven. This section, which walks you through each stage, explains how the approach used in this book's recipes can be applied to all foods.

PREPARING TO ROAST

Most of the work takes place before cooking begins, making roasting the perfect choice for entertaining. A roast can be seasoned and refrigerated well before it goes into the oven. During cooking, the kitchen will fill with tantalizing aromas that perform as the ultimate appetite arousers. Once the meat is done, the host needs only a few minutes away from the guests to make a pan sauce. Most meats and poultry need to rest before carving, which allows time to put side dishes in the oven for reheating or even to serve a previously prepared first course.

Roasting is also a fine option for everyday meals. With the high-temperature technique, you can cut the traditional roasting times of many foods almost in half. If you are busy, you will appreciate recipes cooked at moderate temperatures, as many of them allow you to create a main course and a side dish in the same pan. Low-temperature roasting is perfect for leisurely, mostly unattended cooking on weekends. Every temperature level includes some dishes that yield leftovers, which will save you even more time in the kitchen.

Plan ahead, if possible, and allow particu-larly large cuts of meat, such as a whole beef tenderloin or a big turkey, to stand at room temperature for about 1 hour before roasting, or a whole chicken for about 30 minutes. This stabilizes the temperature of the food and encourages even roasting. Refrigerator-cold food will take longer to cook, because the oven heat must struggle to penetrate the chilled surfaces.

Each recipe indicates which temperature level to use, but the same guidelines in this section can be applied to foods outside these pages. In general, the high-temperature tech-nique is used for deeply browned meats; the moderate-temperature technique is for large cuts, especially those that will be cooked with other ingredients, such as vegetables and potatoes; and the low-temperature technique is for tougher, fatty meats that will become

How to Prepare a Roast

1 Trim meat, such as eye of round (page 167), of most surface fat. For whole poultry, trim and truss as directed in individual recipes. Some meat cuts are tied into a compact shape.

2 Brush or rub an oil such as olive or canola on all surfaces if directed in the recipe or if the roast is particularly lean. Season evenly with salt and pepper, herbs, spices, or a dry rub.

3 Select a roasting pan just large enough to hold the roast. Place a rack in the pan so that heat will circulate around the roast. Set the seasoned roast on the rack.

tender with long, slow cooking. Pan-roasting (page 13) is reserved for relatively thin pieces of meat, poultry, or fish—a butterflied chicken, a thick veal chop, a hefty salmon fillet—that need to be browned before roasting, as they are in the oven too briefly to develop a tasty outer crust.

Position the rack at the appropriate level, keeping in mind that the higher the rack, the more readily the food will brown, and then preheat the oven to the temperature indicated in the recipe, or according to the temperature technique you have chosen. Allow plenty of time for the oven to reach the desired temperature, which will be about 15 minutes for most ovens, or allow a little longer for temperatures above 400°F (200°C). This preheating period often gives you sufficient time to prepare the food for the oven.

Next, choose a properly sized roasting pan. If the food is crowded, it will steam and not brown. Nor should it be dwarfed by a large pan, as the pan drippings could evaporate too quickly and burn. Heavy-gauge metal pans will reduce the chance of splattering and smoking, especially when using the high-temperature roasting method.

"The better the raw product, the better the finished dish will be" is a culinary maxim. But it is never as true as with roasting, for the Maillard reaction (page 21) intensifies surface flavors. This is the opportunity to use prime-grade meats, free-range poultry, the freshest fish, and the finest produce from the farmers' market, especially when guests will be at the table.

Gather the ingredients, rinsing and trimming as needed. Use a long, thin flexible knife—a carving knife is ideal—to trim away some of the surface fat from roasts. Do not trim away too much, as some fat is necessary to help keep the food moist. But an excess will only melt and

Soaking poultry and lean white meats in water and salt before roasting enhances flavor and moistness.

TO BASTE OR NOT TO BASTE

A classic image associated with roasting is of the cook carefully basting a roast to browned perfection. But the jury is out on the value of basting.

Opponents say basting washes away seasonings (but they are reapplied if the cook bastes with the pan drippings). They also believe that the basting liquid softens poultry skin and discourages browning (a problem only when the liquid does not contain melted butter). And they warn that opening the oven door too often makes the oven temperature plunge, increasing the cooking time and leading to dry meat (no argument there).

Proponents insist that basting promotes surface browning, especially if the basting liquid contains butter (whose milk solids caramelize easily) or any sweet ingredient (which can be a little sugar, sweet wine, or fruit juice). Basting also helps keep lean meats moist and flavorful. The liquid will not penetrate poultry skin, but basting helps brown and flavor the skin, which itself is beneficial. The more fat naturally present in the food, the less basting is needed.

If you decide to baste food as it roasts, do so only every 30 minutes, and work quickly to keep the oven temperature stable. An efficient bulb baster with a glass or metal siphon is indispensable. Plastic versions can melt when they come into contact with hot fat and pans.

collect in the roasting pan, causing messy splatters. If working with poultry, be sure to remove any clumps of fat from the tail area.

Many foods are patted dry with paper towels before roasting. A moist outer surface can create steam and hinder browning. When foods are marinated, however, the liquid is inevitably drained off, but the food is often not patted dry. This allows the marinade to continue to flavor the food while it roasts. For the crispest poultry skin, an optional drying step is recommended: refrigerate the uncovered poultry overnight, which dries the skin and opens the pores to release extra fat during roasting (see Lacquered Duck, page 149).

At this point, the food is ready for seasoning. Proper attention to seasoning is one of the most important aspects of good cooking. Seasoning can be as simple as sprinkling with salt and pepper (Rib-Eye Steaks Marchands de Vin, page 181) or more complex, such as the application of a spice rub (Caribbean-Spiced Chicken, page 111) or herbs (Halibut Fillets with Herbes de Provence, page 69).

If you have the time, marinating is also a good way to add a layer of flavor. If the marinade includes an acidic ingredient, such as the plain yogurt in Chicken Legs, Tandoori Style (page 120), it can have a tenderizing effect as well. Soaking lean white meat or poultry in a brine will add flavor and moisture to these foods, which can dry out in the oven. Prime candidates for brining include turkey (Brined Turkey, page 133) and pork (Pork Chops with Cranberry-Orange Stuffing, page 225).

Vegetables can also be used to season meat, poultry, and fish. A layer of vegetables in the bottom of the roasting pan not only will act as a rack to elevate the food off the bottom, but will also flavor the sauce, as in Beef Tenderloin with Madeira Sauce (page 171). When in doubt, use a *mirepoix*, the classic combination

Bacon placed on poultry or meat, a traditional technique called barding, keeps food moist during roasting.

of coarsely chopped onion, carrot, and celery (the proportions are traditionally one-half onion and one-fourth each carrot and celery). It is an adaptable mixture that will enhance almost any meat, poultry, or fish dish that has its roots in Western cuisine.

Leaner roasted meats sometimes need extra fat to keep them moist in the oven. Two time-honored methods are barding and larding. For barding, thin sheets of pork fat or bacon slices are laid on meat or poultry and melt and baste the covered food during roasting, as in Bacon-Wrapped Butterflied Quail (page 138). Larding, which calls for inserting thin strips of pork fat into a lean cut of meat by using a special tool called a larding needle, is a less commonly used technique.

Modern cooks rub foods with oil or place flavored butters under poultry skin to perform a similar function. Chicken with Rosemary and Sweet Potatoes (page 106) is a good example of this technique. Vegetables are typically tossed with oil to keep them from sticking to the pan and scorching. Olive oil is often the choice because it both lubricates and adds flavor. Melted unsalted butter or a flavorless oil is used to coat fruits before roasting.

DURING ROASTING

The relationship between browning and the unique flavor of roasted foods is explained by a phenomenon called the Maillard reaction. In 1911 in Paris, while conducting experiments on the relationship between the presence of amino acids and the formation of proteins, Dr. Louis Camille Maillard found that when he heated amino acids and sugars together, the mixture turned brown.

More than thirty years later, American soldiers fighting in World War II were unhappy that their powdered eggs became an unappe-

Baby back ribs (page 219) are basted only before a final brief roasting at 400°F (200°C).

tizing brown before they were ever cooked, and when the eggs were cooked, they had an unpleasant flavor. After the war, while researching ways to solve the problem of darkening dried eggs, scientists discovered that a high concentration of amino acids and sugars was enough to provoke the browning, or Maillard reaction, without the eggs even being exposed to heat. Further research showed that the Maillard reaction caused a number of positive flavors and aromas to develop whenever food, from a standing rib roast to a bran muffin, is browned.

The Maillard reaction occurs most readily at temperatures above 300°F (150°F). The natural sugars in the food react with the amino acids in the proteins, turning the food brown and producing flavors that taste similar to caramel. This explains why roasted foods seem slightly sweet even without added sugar. Heat also moves the juices toward the center of the food,

which affects the final juiciness. If the food is browning too quickly, you can turn the heat down or cover the food loosely with aluminum foil, which slows the penetration of heat.

Do not open the door too often to check on the progress of roasting food. This will lower the temperature and lengthen the cooking time. If you do open the oven, work quickly, as the temperature can drop dramatically in a short period. When a recipe calls for basting, follow carefully the directions for the frequency of basting the food as it roasts. With experience, you will eventually learn to depend on the heady aromas and sizzling sounds coming from the oven as one way to determine the doneness of food.

Finally, be careful not to overcook roasted foods, especially meats. When the meat is removed from the oven, the retained heat will continue to cook it, a process that is called carryover cooking.

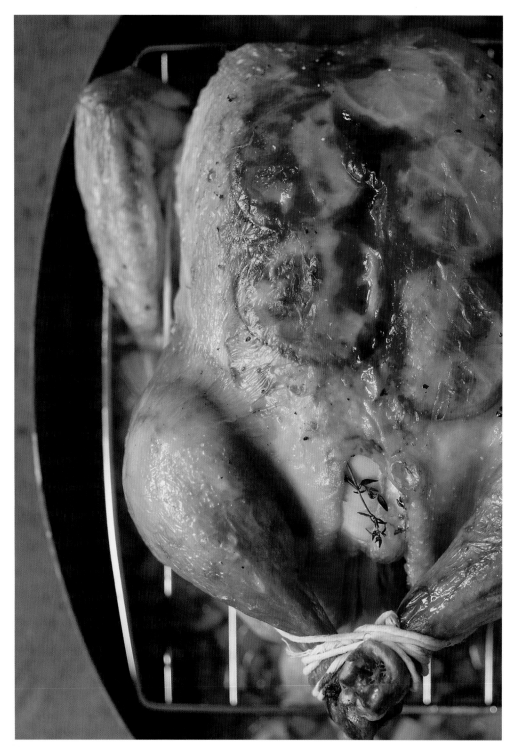

On being removed from the oven, whole poultry and large roasts should be tented with aluminum foil and allowed to rest before carving so that the juices concentrated in the center will redistribute.

AFTER ROASTING

The aroma of roasted food just out of the oven will undoubtedly make you anxious to serve it immediately, but instead you will want to wait. Many foods, especially large roasts, need to rest before carving. There are two significant reasons why patience is truly a virtue when it comes to roasting.

The first is carryover cooking. Outside the oven, roasted food will retain enough heat to continue cooking. During the resting stage, the internal temperature will rise, changing the degree of doneness. The larger the food item, the greater the amount of retained heat, and the more the internal temperature will change.

For example, during a 20-minute resting period, the internal temperature of an 8-pound (4-kg) standing rib roast that has been roasted to a rare 120° to 125°F (49° to 52°C) could rise 10°F (6°C) to a medium-rare to medium 130° to 135°F (54° to 57°C). On the other hand, a 3-pound (1.5-kg) pork loin roasted to 140°F (60°C) may only rise 5°F (3°C).

To avoid overcooking, always remove meat roasts of more than 5 pounds (2.5 kg) from the oven 10°F before the optimum temperature for doneness, and smaller roasts of 3 to 5 pounds (1.5 to 2.5 kg) 5°F before the optimum temperature is reached.

The chart on page 164 gives the temperatures at which beef, veal, lamb, and pork should be removed from the oven for various levels of doneness before the roasted meat is allowed to rest. For a detailed discussion of doneness temperatures and resting times for poultry, see page 99. Like meats and poultry, whole fish and large pieces of fish such as salmon (page 81) and monkfish (page 78) are also set aside to rest before serving. Tips for determining the doneness of fish and shellfish are covered on page 65.

Letting meat, poultry, or whole fish rest before carving also promotes juiciness. The oven temperature heats the proteins, forcing the juices from the heated surfaces toward the center of the roast. As the meat rests, it cools, and the juices redistribute throughout the mass. If the meat is cut too soon, it may look rawer than expected. But more important, the juices collected in the center of the roast will be released and run out with the first slice.

Loosely tenting roasted foods with aluminum foil during resting to keep in some of the heat is common practice. Some experts caution against tenting poultry, believing that it softens the skin, but many others discount this concern. Each recipe in this book in which a resting time is indicated specifies the number of minutes you need to wait before picking up the carving set.

Making Pan Sauces and Gravies

Creating savory sauces from pan juices is just one of the benefits of roasting. Releasing the browned bits in a roasting pan or frying pan with a flavorful liquid is called deglazing. Even if you are not making a sauce to serve with the finished dish, it is a good idea to deglaze the pan, following the steps below but using water, to speed cleanup.

Pan sauces are based on *jus*, the deglazed natural juices of roasted meat or poultry. These juices alone can be served as a sauce, as in Standing Rib Roast with Yorkshire Pudding (page 177) and Cross-Rib Roast with Roasted Root Vegetables (page 168). The *jus* for the cross-rib roast, which also includes the juices from the platter that holds the resting roast, is seasoned simply with salt and pepper and then is spooned over the slices of meat for serving.

Often, the deglazed juices are supplemented with a little broth or wine. To complement the roast, the cook would ideally use broth made from the same main ingredient, such as beef broth for roast beef *jus*. However, high-quality reduced-sodium chicken broth is a versatile option that works well with nearly any meat or poultry. Wines might range from a dry white, such as Sauvignon Blanc, or a dry red, such as Merlot, to dry vermouth, dry or cream sherry, or semisweet Madeira or Port.

A *jus lie* is made by lightly thickening a broth- or wine-enhanced *jus* with a slurry, a mixture of a little cornstarch (cornflour), arrowroot, potato starch, or another thickener dissolved in a small amount of liquid, usually water or broth. The mixture is then stirred into the pan juices to thicken them. Cornstarch is the most common thickener, but it results in a

How to Deglaze

1 Pour off the fat and juices in the pan, leaving the browned bits stuck to the bottom. Skim off any clear fat that rises to the top of the juices; discard or reserve as directed. Reserve the juices unless otherwise instructed.

2 Place the pan on the stove top over medium heat and warm any fat remaining in the pan so it melts. If the pan is especially large, place it over two burners. Be careful not to scorch or burn the bits in the bottom of the pan.

3 Return the juices to the pan and then add liquid and other flavorings as directed. Raise the heat to medium-high and bring to a boil, vigorously scraping up the browned bits on the pan bottom with a wooden spoon.

How to Thicken Sauces

USING CORNSTARCH

1 Combine about 1 tablespoon cornstarch (cornflour) and about 2 tablespoons water in a small bowl. Stir the mixture thoroughly to dissolve the cornstarch in the water and remove any lumps.

2 Bring the sauce to a boil and gradually pour in the cornstarch mixture, whisking constantly to combine. Simmer, stirring occasionally, until the sauce is thickened as desired.

USING A BEURRE MANIÉ

1 To make a beurre manié, combine about 2 tablespoons unsalted butter, at room temperature, and about 2 tablespoons all-purpose (plain) flour in a small bowl. Mix until well blended.

2 Bring the sauce to a simmer and add the beurre manié a little at a time to the sauce, whisking well after each addition. Simmer the sauce, whisking occasionally, until thickened as desired.

USING A ROUX

1 Place about 3 tablespoons fat skimmed from the pan juices (page 23) or butter into a saucepan over medium heat. Add about 3 tablespoons all-purpose flour and whisk until blended with the butter, to make a roux. Cook until the roux turns light brown.

2 Slowly add broth or pan juices, whisking to prevent lumps from forming. Cook, whisking constantly, until the sauce is smooth and thickens as desired.

slightly cloudy sauce. If you do use cornstarch, keep in mind that it does not realize its full thickening capacity until the sauce reaches a boil, so you must wait until that point to judge if it has achieved proper thickness. Arrowroot and potato starch yield clearer sauces than cornstarch does and thicken at lower temperatures. However, they lose their binding power if overheated or held at serving temperature for too long.

You can also thicken a pan sauce with a beurre manié, a mixture of room-temperature butter worked together with an equal amount of flour to make a soft paste, as for the sauces served with Brined Turkey (page 133), Leg of Lamb with Garlic and Rosemary (page 195), and Beef Tenderloin with Madeira Sauce (page 171). Whisked into a simmering *jus*, the butter enriches the juices as the flour thickens them, making a particularly opaque and flavorful sauce. The sauce should be simmered for a few minutes after the beurre manié is added, not only to thicken it but also to cook away any raw flour taste.

Pan gravy, an American classic, is made from the pan drippings from roasted meat or poultry, as in the gravies served with Classic Roast Turkey with Dressing (page 127) and Lemon-Thyme Capon (page 124). A roux, a lightly cooked combination of fat from the roast (or sometimes butter) and flour, is used to thicken the gravy, which is usually made with broth and can be enhanced with cream or wine.

Making a pan sauce is not limited to roasted meats or poultry. The heat of the oven causes the natural sugars of pears, apples, and other fruits to caramelize and draws out juices ideal for creating a sauce. The dish in which the fruits were roasted can be deglazed using heavy (double) cream or a fruit juice or liqueur that complements the main ingredient.

SAFETY ISSUES

When roasting, as with all cooking techniques, a little common sense goes a long way. It is important to remember that you are dealing with hot surfaces and hot air, both of which can burn you.

When opening the oven door, avert your head and wait for a moment or two to avoid the rush of hot, steamy air. If you wear glasses, you should be doubly cautious, as the heat and steam could fog up the lenses and therefore reduce visibility.

If an excessive amount of fat is accumulating in the roasting pan, use a bulb baster (page 20) to remove it, thus reducing the likelihood of fire. Do this only when absolutely necessary, and never more often than every 30 minutes, or the oven temperature will drop dramatically and affect the outcome of the dish.

To help reduce the smoke from a roasting pan, add just enough broth or water to cover the bottom. If that fails, reduce the oven temperature by 25°F (12°C). High-temperature roasting can create enough smoke to set off a smoke alarm (working with a clean oven and a heavy-gauge roasting pan will lessen the chances of this happening). If you deactivate the alarm, remember to reinsert the batteries after cooking.

Food Safety

The high temperature of the oven will kill surface bacteria on roasted food, but care must be taken in handling the food before and after roasting. Bacteria is most likely to grow at temperatures between 40° and 140°F (20° and 60°C). Keep food out this "danger zone" by making sure cold food is cold and hot food is hot. Never leave food at room temperature for longer than 2 hours.

Defrost meats, poultry, and fish in the refrig-

Washing boards and utensils thoroughly after preparing raw meat, poultry, and fish helps prevent bacterial contamination.

erator and not at room temperature. If you use a microwave, choose a very low setting and turn the food often so that it thaws without cooking. Do not refreeze thawed food.

To avoid cross-contamination, wash carving boards with plenty of hot, soapy water immediately after use. Never return a roast to an already-used board without washing it first.

Follow the guidelines for doneness for various meats and poultry in their respective chapters. Keep in mind that if you choose to cook your meat to temperatures lower than the suggested USDA guidelines, you may be exposing yourself to food-borne diseases.

Some cooks choose to cook poultry stuffing outside the bird, but stuffed poultry can be roasted safely. If you stuff poultry, be sure that all raw ingredients are thoroughly cooked before the stuffing goes in the bird. The stuffing will only be warmed in the body cavity, not cooked. Also, always make the stuffing and fill the bird just before cooking, and never refrigerate a stuffed bird before cooking.

Starters and Small Plates

About Starters and Small Plates

Every savvy party host and successful caterer knows that roasting makes quick work of a wealth of starters and small plates. In this chapter's recipes, a minimum of preparation and relatively short roasting times bring out big flavors in a broad range of seasonal fresh ingredients.

Variety is a defining element in this chapter. A pantryful of different foods is used, from vegetables and nuts to meats, seafood, and poultry. Some dishes are classics, such as a hearty French onion soup, while others are contemporary, such as plump shrimp coated with a rustic arugula (rocket) pesto. In addition, the recipes, which include finger foods, plated first courses, and snacks, boast flavors from around the globe.

The busy host will especially appreciate how roasting can speed the preparation of many starters. For example, Sesame Chicken Wings (page 39), which are marinated for as little as 30 minutes, spend less than 15 minutes in the oven. Indian-Spiced Mixed Nuts (page 30) are nearly as quick, roasting for 20 minutes.

Roasting can also help you manage the overall cooking time of a recipe by allowing part of it to be prepared in advance. The mushrooms for the Mushroom Toasts (page 33) can be cooked up to several hours ahead and reheated just before serving. Having a portion of a dish already prepared frees you to concentrate on other parts of the meal.

ADDING FLAVOR AND RICHNESS

Even if the whole dish is not roasted, roasting individual ingredients can deliver an enormous amount of flavor in a short amount of time. For the French Onion Soup (page 55), yellow onions are deeply caramelized in the oven instead of on the stove top. Roasting the ingredients for a puréed soup, such as Apple, Leek, and Butternut Squash Soup (page 56), deepens their natural sugars and flavors. After being processed to a smooth finish and combined with broth, the soup is reheated only briefly on the stove top before serving.

Intense oven heat combined with seasonings also brings heightened flavor and richness to dishes. For the Mushroom Toasts, the mushrooms are tossed in a generous mixture of butter, shallots, garlic, and wine before roasting, and then finished off with a touch of Cognac during the last few minutes in the oven—just enough time to marry the Cognac with the other flavors. Likewise, the meat for the Pork Tenderloin Canapés (page 40) is coated with a heady blend of mustard, citrus, garlic, and fennel before it goes into a high-temperature oven.

This chapter also showcases a bounty of distinctively—and generously—seasoned shellfish recipes. Shellfish are ideal for starters and small plates in part because they are typically of a size that makes portioning easy. For example, you might serve four or five extra-large shrimp or sea scallops or half a dozen oysters to each diner.

Even the shells of these deep-sea denizens are appreciated, and for good reason: they make practical "containers" for the prepared shellfish and they look charmingly rustic on a serving tray. Clams and Sausage, Portuguese Style (page 51) and Oysters with Toppings (page 48) illustrate both advantages. Also, when the shells are left on shrimp (prawns), they help keep the flesh moist and tender. You can still flavor the meat beforehand by gently loosening the shells and surrounding the meat with seasonings, as in Shrimp with Arugula Pesto (page 43). Another way to add flavor and preserve moisture is to toss the shrimp, with the shells still loosely attached, in a light oil-based coating, as in Salt-Roasted Shrimp with Tomato-Horseradish Sauce (page 45).

If you prefer to roast shrimp without their shells, keep the tail segments intact for easier eating and marinate the shrimp to keep the meat moist, as in Lime and Cilantro Shrimp (page 42). Scallops, like shrimp, cook quickly in high heat, and even a brief marinating will help keep them succulent. In Prosciutto-Wrapped Scallops (page 47), thin slices of prosciutto protect the delicate flesh from drying out in the oven's high heat, borrowing from a technique known as barding (page 21).

EASY ENTERTAINING

All of these seafood dishes, as well as the other recipes, are suitable for entertaining, whether you are hosting a casual get-together or an elegant company dinner. The recipes follow a natural progression within the chapter, from finger foods to plated first courses.

The first few recipes, including Roasted Chestnuts (page 31) and Herbed Potato Chips (page 32), are ideal for setting out in bowls for guests to nibble on before dinner. Pancetta-Wrapped Figs (page 38) and Rainbow Pepper Bruschetta (page 34) are good for passing on trays. Smoky Red Pepper Soup (page 59) and Endive Salad with Roasted Pears and Walnuts (page 52) are among the recipes that make excellent sit-down first courses.

You can even assemble two or three of these starters to make a light meal: begin with one of the soups, then follow it with Pizza Topped with Mediterranean Vegetables (page 37) and a mixed green salad.

Indian-Spiced Mixed Nuts

2 cups (8 oz/250 g) lightly salted mixed nuts

1 tablespoon unsalted butter, melted

1 tablespoon finely chopped, peeled fresh ginger

1 teaspoon garam masala

1/2 teaspoon ground cumin

1/8 –1/4 teaspoon cayenne pepper

Mixed nuts offer the most choices for your guests, but if a single nut—cashews, peanuts, or almonds—is your favorite, roast it alone with the same spice mixture. In every case, be sure the nuts are fresh. Vacuum-packed tins labeled with expiration dates are usually good guarantees of freshness, as are nuts sold in bulk at a market with a high turnover. The nuts are roasted at a relatively low temperature to avoid burning and to give them time to absorb the fragrant spices.

Preheat the oven to 300°F (150°C). Line a rimmed baking sheet with aluminum foil or parchment (baking) paper.

In a bowl, toss together the nuts, butter, ginger, garam masala, cumin, and cayenne until the nuts are evenly coated with the spice mixture. Spread the nuts out in a single layer on the prepared baking sheet.

Roast the nuts, stirring 1 or 2 times, until golden and fragrant, 20–22 minutes. Immediately transfer the nuts to a bowl and serve warm or at room temperature. You can also roast the nuts up to 24 hours ahead of time and store them, tightly covered, at room temperature. To serve them warm, spread them on a baking sheet and reheat in a 350°F (180°C) oven for about 5 minutes.

VARIATIONS

Chili-Spiced Nuts

Omit the ginger. Add 1 tablespoon chili powder and increase the cumin to 1 teaspoon.

Italian-Spiced Nuts

Substitute hazelnuts (filberts) for the mixed nuts, if desired. Omit the ginger, garam masala, and cumin. Add 1 tablespoon chopped fresh rosemary, 1 teaspoon grated lemon zest, and 1/2 teaspoon finely chopped garlic.

Roasted Chestnuts

Look for firm, shiny chestnuts, signs of both freshness and good taste. A long-handled chestnut-roasting pan and a curved-bladed chestnut knife are traditional tools for roasting chestnuts in a fireplace, but you will need only a baking sheet and a paring knife for cooking them in an oven. Peeled roasted chestnuts are delicious on their own and can also be chopped and added to poultry dressing or rice pilaf.

Preheat the oven to 425°F (220°C). Using a small, sharp knife, make an X on the flat side of each nut, cutting all the way down to the nut meat. Do not skip this step, or the nuts probably will explode in the oven. The cross also makes the nuts easier to peel without the use of tools. Spread the nuts out in a single layer on a rimmed baking sheet.

Roast the chestnuts, turning 2 or 3 times, until they are very fragrant, a shade darker in color, and the edges of each X have curled back, 10–15 minutes.

Remove the pan from the oven, let the chestnuts cool slightly in the pan, and then transfer them to a napkin-lined basket. Serve warm, and let everyone peel his or her own chestnuts.

1 lb (500 g) chestnuts in the shell

Herbed Potato Chips

1 lb (500 g) russet potatoes, unpeeled

2 tablespoons canola oil or extra-virgin olive oil

Kosher salt and freshly ground pepper

2 tablespoons chopped fresh tarragon, or 2 teaspoons dried tarragon

1–2 teaspoons malt or cider vinegar (optional)

Preheat the oven to 425°F (220°C). Cut the potatoes crosswise into slices $^1/_8$ inch (3 mm) thick. Spread the slices out in a single layer on a large baking sheet. Drizzle evenly with the oil, toss to coat, and then spread out again in a single layer. Sprinkle with 1 teaspoon salt, $^1/_2$ teaspoon pepper, and the tarragon.

Roast the potato slices until the bottoms are golden, about 10 minutes. Remove the pan from the oven, turn the slices, and continue to roast until golden and crisp on both sides, 7–10 minutes longer.

Remove the pan from the oven and sprinkle the slices with additional salt to taste, then drizzle with the vinegar, if using. Transfer to a napkin-lined basket and serve at once.

If you have a mandoline, cutting the potatoes is easy. If you are working with a large, sharp knife and a cutting board, try for consistent thickness so the chips will roast evenly. In Great Britain it is traditional to sprinkle french fries, known as "chips," with malt vinegar, while in the Pennsylvania Amish country cider vinegar is often the choice. Here, the vinegar adds zest to potatoes that are sliced crosswise. You can substitute mint, rosemary, or oregano for the tarragon.

Mushroom Toasts

Any combination of flavorful mushrooms is delicious on these toasts. Since some varieties can be quite expensive, use a blend of full-bodied shiitake, morel, chanterelle, and oyster mushrooms with less costly and milder white or brown button mushrooms. The roasted mushrooms can also be served as a topping for grilled steak or slices of roast beef, or as a filling for tiny pastry tartlets.

Preheat the oven to 450°F (230°C). Brush the mushrooms clean and remove any tough stems. Cut the mushrooms into thick slices. Place the mushrooms and garlic on a rimmed baking sheet. Cut the butter into small pieces and add to the pan with the shallots, wine, and $1/2$ teaspoon each salt and pepper. Toss until well mixed. Spread the mixture out evenly on the pan.

Roast the mushrooms, stirring every 5 minutes, until tender, 20–25 minutes. Stir in the Cognac and continue to roast until the Cognac is slightly reduced, about 5 minutes longer. Remove from the oven, taste, and adjust the seasoning. (Use immediately, or let cool, cover, and refrigerate for up to 6 hours, then reheat in a saucepan over low heat for 5–10 minutes.)

Increase the oven temperature to 500°F (260°C). Place the bread slices directly on the oven rack or on a baking sheet. Toast until pale golden on one side, about 2 minutes. Turn the slices and toast until pale golden on the second side, 1–2 minutes longer.

Divide the mushroom mixture evenly among the toasts and serve at once.

$1^1/_2$ lb (750 g) mixed fresh mushrooms (see note)

3 large cloves garlic, thinly sliced

$1/_4$ cup (2 oz/60 g) unsalted butter

$1/_4$ cup (1 oz/30 g) chopped shallots or green (spring) onions

$1/_4$ cup (2 fl oz/60 ml) dry red or white wine

Kosher salt and freshly ground pepper

2 tablespoons Cognac or brandy

16 baguette slices

Rainbow Pepper Bruschetta

2 yellow or orange bell peppers (capsicums)

2 red bell peppers (capsicums)

¹/₄ lb (125 g) garlic-and-herb-seasoned fresh cheese such as Boursin or Rondele

16 baguette slices, each ³/₄ inch (2 cm) thick

2 tablespoons extra-virgin olive oil

2 tablespoons slivered fresh basil

Freshly coarse-ground pepper

In Italy, bruschetta—from the Italian *bruscare*, or "roasted over coals"—is traditionally grilled bread that is brushed with olive oil and sometimes rubbed with garlic. But the bread often gets a more elaborate treatment elsewhere. Here, it is topped with roasted bell peppers, but nearly any roasted vegetable—zucchini (courgette), leek, tomato, fennel, eggplant (aubergine)—alone or in combination, can be used. If you like, rub the toasted bread with a cut garlic clove before topping the slices with the vegetables.

Preheat the oven to 500°F (260°C). Arrange the bell peppers on a baking sheet.

Roast the peppers, turning as needed, until blackened and blistered on all sides, 20–30 minutes. Remove the pan from the oven, drape the peppers loosely with aluminum foil, and let cool for 10 minutes. Leave the oven set at 500°F. Using your fingers, and holding the peppers over a bowl to capture the juices, peel away the skins, then cut in half lengthwise and remove the stems, seeds, and ribs. (The peppers can be roasted up to 1 day ahead, covered, and refrigerated.)

Cut the yellow peppers and 1 red pepper lengthwise into narrow strips and set aside. Cut the remaining red pepper into chunks, place in a food processor, add about 1 tablespoon of the captured juices, and process until nearly smooth. Then add the cheese and process until well blended and nearly smooth.

Brush both sides of each bread slice lightly with the olive oil. Place the bread directly on the oven rack or on a baking sheet. Toast until pale golden on one side, about 2 minutes. Turn the slices and toast until pale golden on the second side, 1–2 minutes longer.

Spread each bread slice with about 1 tablespoon of the cheese mixture. Using the yellow and green pepper strips, make a crisscross pattern on top of each toast. Sprinkle with the basil and ground pepper.

Pizza Topped with Mediterranean Vegetables

Bread flour is higher in gluten than all-purpose (plain) flour, thus producing a chewier, crisper crust, while the addition of a little semolina flour or cornmeal to the dough gives it a rustic character. If you have a baking stone, cook the pizzas directly on it, following the manufacturer's instructions for preheating it. Whether you use a baking sheet or baking stone, be sure to sprinkle it with semolina or cornmeal so that the bottom of each pizza crust will crisp and char lightly. You can roast other sliced vegetables in place of the ones here, such as bell peppers (capsicums), mushrooms, and leeks.

In a large bowl, whisk together 1 cup (8 fl oz/250 ml) lukewarm water and the yeast. Let stand until foamy, about 5 minutes. Whisk in 1 cup (5 oz/155 g) of the bread flour and 1 teaspoon salt. Stir in the $1/4$ cup semolina flour and enough of the remaining 1 cup bread flour to form a sticky dough. Turn the dough out onto a well-floured work surface and knead until it is smooth and satiny, 5–10 minutes. If the dough is too sticky, add a little more flour; if it is too dry, add a few drops of water. Brush a large bowl with 1 tablespoon of the olive oil. Form the dough into a ball, place in the oiled bowl, and turn the dough to coat the top with oil. Cover the bowl with a kitchen towel and let the dough rise at room temperature until doubled in bulk, $1^{1}/2$–2 hours.

Meanwhile, preheat the oven to 450°F (230°C). Cut the onion, eggplants, tomatoes, zucchini, and crookneck squash into slices about $1/4$ inch (6 mm) thick. Brush a large rimmed baking sheet with 1 tablespoon of the oil. Arrange all the sliced vegetables and the garlic in a single layer or only slightly overlapping on the prepared pan. Brush with 2 tablespoons of the oil, then season with salt and pepper.

Roast the vegetables, turning 1 or 2 times, until nearly tender, about 10 minutes. Remove the pan from the oven and let the vegetables stand at room temperature. Leave the oven set at 450°F.

Brush 1 very large or 2 regular-sized baking sheets with about $1^{1}/2$ teaspoons of the oil. Sprinkle with the 1 tablespoon semolina flour. Punch down the dough and turn it out onto a floured work surface. Divide into 6 equal portions. Roll or pat out each portion into a round about $1/4$ inch (6 mm) thick. Place the rounds at least 2 inches (5 cm) apart on the prepared baking sheet(s). Brush the surface of the rounds with the remaining $1^{1}/2$ teaspoons oil.

If using 2 baking sheets, place them on separate racks in the oven. Bake the pizza crusts until they begin to color and set, about 5 minutes. Remove from the oven and arrange the vegetables on the partially baked crusts, dividing them evenly. Sprinkle evenly with the mint, basil, oregano, and feta cheese. If using 2 baking sheets, switch the position of the sheets. Continue to bake until the crusts are a rich golden brown and crisp, and the vegetables and cheese are tinged with brown, 5–8 minutes. Remove the pizzas from the oven and serve at once.

1 package (2 $1/2$ teaspoons) active dry yeast

2 cups (10 oz/315 g) bread flour

Kosher salt and freshly ground pepper

$1/4$ cup (1 $1/2$ oz/45 g) semolina flour or yellow cornmeal, plus 1 tablespoon

5 tablespoons (2 $1/2$ fl oz/ 75 ml) extra-virgin olive oil

1 yellow onion

2 baby Italian eggplants (aubergines) or small Japanese or Chinese eggplants

2 plum (Roma) tomatoes

1 zucchini (courgette)

1 yellow crookneck squash

2 large cloves garlic, thinly sliced

$1/4$ cup ($1/3$ oz/10 g) shredded fresh mint

2 tablespoons chopped fresh basil

2 tablespoons chopped fresh oregano

$1/2$ cup (2 $1/2$ oz /75 g) crumbled feta cheese

Pancetta-Wrapped Figs

8 figs such as Mission or Adriatic

2 oz (60 g) thin pancetta slices, unrolled

16 small fresh sage leaves, plus sprigs for garnish

1 tablespoon extra-virgin olive oil

Lemon wedges

Preheat the oven to 475°F (245°C). Cut each fig in half through the stem end. Cut the pancetta into 16 strips, each 3–4 inches (7.5–10 cm) long.

Place a sage leaf on the cut side of each fig half, then wrap the fig in a pancetta strip. It is not important that the strips be exactly even. Arrange the wrapped figs, cut side up, in a single layer on a rimmed baking sheet. Brush lightly with the olive oil.

Roast the figs until the pancetta is crisp and the figs are soft, 5–8 minutes. Meanwhile, make a bed of sage sprigs on a platter.

Remove the pan from the oven and arrange the warm figs on the sage sprigs. Serve with lemon wedges for squeezing over the figs.

Figs have two seasons, a short one with a small harvest from early June into July and a longer one with a more substantial harvest from late summer to midautumn. In both cases, the figs must be picked just as they ripen; they do not ripen further once off the tree. They should also be eaten as soon as possible after picking or purchase, or they will spoil. Wrapped in fresh sage leaves and paper-thin pancetta slices, roasted figs are a delicacy often found on antipasto platters. For roasting, choose unblemished figs that yield to pressure but are not soft.

Sesame Chicken Wings

Instead of whole wings, whose bony tips burn easily in a hot oven and which are hard to handle for stand-up eating, this recipe uses the largest, meatiest sections of the wings. The marinade, a mild, yet complex mix of Asian flavors, is also good on baby back ribs or chicken breasts or legs.

Cut the wing tips from the wings. Reserve for another use (such as making stock) or discard. Cut through the joint between the remaining sections to separate each wing into 2 pieces. In a shallow, nonreactive dish, combine the sesame oil, soy sauce, vinegar, garlic, and ginger. Add the chicken pieces to the bowl, turn to coat, cover, and refrigerate for at least 30 minutes or for up to 2 hours.

Preheat the oven to 500°F (260°C). Remove the chicken pieces from the marinade and discard the marinade. Sprinkle on all sides with the sesame seeds. Arrange the pieces in a single layer on a rimmed baking sheet.

Roast the chicken pieces, turning once, until crispy and browned on the outside and opaque throughout when tested with a knife, 10–14 minutes total.

Remove the pan from the oven and transfer the chicken to a platter. Serve warm or at room temperature.

6–8 chicken wings, about
1 3/4 lb (875 g) total weight

2 tablespoons Asian
sesame oil

2 tablespoons soy sauce

2 tablespoons rice vinegar

1 tablespoon chopped garlic

1 tablespoon finely chopped,
peeled fresh ginger

2 tablespoons sesame seeds

Pork Tenderloin Canapés

1 pork tenderloin,
about ³/₄ lb (375 g)

Kosher salt and freshly
ground pepper

2 tablespoons extra-virgin
olive oil

2 tablespoons Dijon mustard

2 teaspoons grated lemon
zest

2 cloves garlic, minced

2 teaspoons fennel seeds

24 baguette slices

1 red bell pepper (capsicum),
roasted, peeled, and seeded
(page 294), then cut into
strips 1¹/₂ inches (4 cm) long
by ¹/₄ inch (6 mm) wide
(48 strips total)

2 oz (60 g) Manchego or
Parmesan cheese

Preheat the oven to 450°F (230°C). Season the tenderloin lightly with salt and pepper. In a small bowl, stir together 1 tablespoon of the olive oil and 1 table-spoon of the mustard. Stir in the lemon zest and garlic. Rub the mixture evenly over the tenderloin, coating it on all sides. Sprinkle the meat on all sides with the fennel seeds. Place the tenderloin in a small roasting pan, tucking the tail end under to make a roast of more even thickness.

Roast the tenderloin, turning once, until browned on the exterior and barely pink on the interior, 25–30 minutes. A thermometer (page 16) inserted into the center of the tenderloin should register 135°–140°F (57°–60°C) for medium (page 164). Remove from the oven, transfer the tenderloin to a carving board, and tent with aluminum foil. Let rest for 5–10 minutes. Do not turn off the oven.

Meanwhile, in a small bowl, stir together the remaining 1 tablespoon olive oil and 1 tablespoon mustard. Arrange the bread slices in a single layer on a baking sheet and spread an equal amount of the mustard mixture on each slice. Toast in the oven just until golden, 5–8 minutes.

To assemble the canapés, slice the meat crosswise into 24 pieces. Place 1 slice on each toasted bread slice. Crisscross 2 roasted pepper strips on each pork slice. Using a vegetable peeler, shave the cheese evenly over the canapés. Arrange on a platter and serve at once.

Pork tenderloin, like its beef counterpart, is buttery tender, but it is also so low in fat that it quickly dries out and tough-ens if improperly cooked. Here, the meat is coated with mustard and oil, to flavor and protect it. Roasting at high heat quickly caramelizes the exterior for superior taste and texture. Thinly sliced, the pork makes a sophisticated, easy-to-assemble canapé.

Lime and Cilantro Shrimp

3 tablespoons extra-virgin olive oil

3 tablespoons chopped fresh cilantro (fresh coriander)

1 tablespoon fresh lime juice

1 teaspoon grated lime zest

$1/4$ teaspoon hot-pepper sauce

Kosher salt

16–20 extra-large shrimp (prawns), about 1 lb (500 g) total weight, peeled and deveined with tail segment intact

Preheat the oven to 450°F (230°C). In a shallow, nonreactive bowl, combine the olive oil, 2 tablespoons of the cilantro, the lime juice and zest, the hot-pepper sauce, and $1/4$ teaspoon salt. Add the shrimp and turn to coat. Let stand for 10 minutes at room temperature.

Remove the shrimp from the marinade and discard the marinade. Arrange the shrimp in a single layer on a rimmed baking sheet. Roast the shrimp, turning once, until they are cooked through and tinged with brown, 5–6 minutes total.

Remove the pan from the oven, transfer the hot shrimp to a warmed platter, and sprinkle with the remaining 1 tablespoon cilantro. Serve at once.

Nearly everyone likes shrimp, so you may want to double or triple this recipe. Leaving the tail on the shellfish provides a little "handle" for easier eating. The high heat cooks the shrimp quickly and seals in the juices. To preserve the texture of the shrimp, take care not to overcook them. Boneless chicken breast strips can be prepared in the same way, then served with toothpicks or small skewers. Depending on the brand of hot-pepper sauce you use, you may need more or less than the amount indicated.

Shrimp with Arugula Pesto

Large shrimp are easy to devein and stuff, so use jumbo shrimp, 11 to 15 per pound (500 g), or extra-large shrimp, 16 to 20 per pound, for this recipe. If only large or medium shrimp (21 to 35 per pound) are available, loosen the shells and devein the shrimp in the same way as the larger shrimp, and then pour the pesto over the shrimp, massaging them a little to force some of the pesto under the shells. They will cook in only 4–5 minutes. These shrimp are definitely finger food, so provide plenty of napkins.

Preheat the oven to 450°F (230°C). Line a rimmed baking sheet with aluminum foil and place a lightly oiled flat rack in the pan. Working with 1 shrimp at a time and using a pair of sharp kitchen scissors, cut down along the back of the shell. Gently loosen the shell from both sides of the shrimp, but leave the shell in place. With a knife tip, lift out and discard the dark, veinlike intestinal tract. Rinse the shrimp under cold water. Pat dry with paper towels and set aside.

Engage the motor of a food processor, drop the garlic cloves through the feed tube, and process for a few seconds to chop. Scrape down the sides of the bowl with a spatula. Add the arugula and pine nuts and process until finely chopped. With the motor running, slowly pour in the olive oil and lemon juice and process until the mixture forms a paste. Spoon the pesto into a small bowl and season with the hot-pepper sauce, 1/2 teaspoon salt, and ground pepper to taste. Taste and adjust the seasoning.

Using a small knife or spoon, push a little of the pesto under both sides of the shell of each shrimp and press the shells closed. It is fine if the pesto coats the outside of the shells as well. Arrange the shrimp on the prepared rack in the pan. Roast the shrimp until they are opaque throughout, 5–6 minutes. Remove from the oven. Serve warm, divided among individual warmed plates.

1 lb (500 g) jumbo or extra-large shrimp (prawns) in the shell (see note)

2 large cloves garlic

2 cups (2 oz/60 g) lightly packed small arugula (rocket) leaves

2 tablespoons pine nuts or slivered almonds, toasted

5 tablespoons (2$^{1}/_{2}$ fl oz/ 75 ml) extra-virgin olive oil

1 tablespoon fresh lemon juice

4 or 5 drops hot-pepper sauce

Kosher salt and freshly ground pepper

Salt-Roasted Shrimp
with Tomato-Horseradish Sauce

Shrimp in their shells roasted on a bed of salt are succulent but not salty, as the purpose of the salt is to transfer the heat rather than flavor the shrimp. Kosher or other coarse salt can be used in place of the rock salt. Fresh horseradish adds a bright, piquant flavor. It is quite pungent, so take care as you grate; it can make your eyes water and take your breath away. Prepared horseradish can be used in the absence of the fresh root. The sauce can be made a day or two ahead and refrigerated until serving. Give your guests plenty of paper napkins and put out bowls for the shells.

To make the sauce, in a bowl, stir together the chili sauce, mayonnaise, horseradish, and lemon juice. Divide the sauce among individual dipping bowls and set aside.

Preheat the oven to 450°F (230°C). Select a roasting pan just large enough to hold the shrimp in a single layer. Pour in enough salt to create a layer $3/4$ inch (2 cm) deep. Place in the preheating oven for 20–25 minutes. The pan and the salt should be very hot.

While the pan is heating, devein the shrimp: Working with 1 shrimp at a time and using a pair of sharp kitchen scissors, cut down along the back of the shell, but leave the shell in place. With a knife tip, lift out and discard the dark, veinlike intestinal tract. Rinse the shrimp under cold water and pat dry with paper towels.

In a shallow, nonreactive bowl, combine the olive oil and wine. Add the shrimp and toss in the oil mixture, allowing a little of the liquid to seep beneath the shells of the shrimp.

When the hot pan of salt is ready, carefully remove it from the oven and lay the shrimp on the salt. Roast the shrimp for 3 minutes, then turn the shrimp and continue to roast until they are opaque throughout, about 2 minutes longer.

Remove the pan from the oven. Using tongs, transfer the shrimp to a serving plate. Allow each person to peel his or her own shrimp. Offer each diner a small bowl of the dipping sauce.

For the Tomato-Horseradish Sauce

$3/4$ cup (6 fl oz/180 ml) prepared mild chili sauce

1 tablespoon mayonnaise

1 tablespoon finely grated, peeled fresh horseradish

2 teaspoons fresh lemon juice

$2^1/2$ lb (1.25 kg) rock salt

1 lb (500 g) extra-large shrimp (prawns) in the shell (16–20)

2 tablespoons extra-virgin olive oil

1 tablespoon dry white wine or dry vermouth

Citrus Sea Scallops

1 yellow or pink grapefruit

**1 lb (500 g) large
sea scallops (about 18)**

**2 tablespoons unsalted
butter, melted**

**2 tablespoons chopped
fresh tarragon**

**1 tablespoon Pernod or other
anise liqueur**

**Kosher salt and freshly
ground pepper**

Preheat the oven to 450°F (230°C). Cut a thick slice off the top and bottom of each grapefruit to reveal the flesh. Stand the grapefruit upright on a cutting board, and, following the contour of the fruit and rotating it with each cut, slice downward to remove the peel, pith, and membrane. Holding the fruit over a bowl, cut along each side of the membrane between the sections, letting each freed section drop into the bowl. Cut away the small, tough muscle on the side of each scallop, then rinse the scallops in cold water. Pat dry with paper towels.

In a shallow, nonreactive bowl, combine the butter, 1 tablespoon of the tarragon, the Pernod, and ¼ teaspoon each salt and pepper. Add the scallops and grapefruit sections and their juice and turn to coat. Let stand for 10 minutes at room temperature.

Remove the scallops and grapefruit sections from the marinade, reserving the marinade. Arrange the scallops and grapefruit in a single layer on a rimmed baking sheet and drizzle with the marinade. Roast the scallops and grapefruit, without turning, until opaque throughout, 5–6 minutes. Remove the pan from the oven. Arrange the scallops and grapefruit on a warmed platter, and sprinkle with the remaining 1 tablespoon tarragon. Serve at once.

The inherent sweetness of these plump shellfish pairs beautifully with tart grapefruit and the licorice flavors of tarragon and Pernod. Look for diver, or day-boat, scallops, which are caught by divers on boats that return to shore every day. If you cannot find them, select the best-looking, freshest-smelling scallops available. For a first-course salad, toss baby arugula (rocket) or spinach in citrus vinaigrette, divide among 6 plates, and top with the scallops and grapefruit.

Prosciutto-Wrapped Scallops

These scallops can be served informally as finger food (without the toothpicks), or with a little Aioli (page 77) or other dipping sauce. For a first course, arrange a few scallops on a salad plate with some lightly dressed arugula or other small, tender greens.

Preheat the oven to 500°F (260°C). Line a rimmed baking sheet with heavy-duty aluminum foil and place a lightly oiled flat rack in the pan. Cut away the small, tough muscle on the side of each scallop, then rinse the scallops in cold water and pat dry with paper towels. In a shallow, nonreactive bowl, stir together the lemon juice, the cayenne, and 1 tablespoon of the olive oil. Add the scallops, turn to coat, and let marinate for 10–15 minutes, turning them several times.

Cut each prosciutto slice lengthwise into strips just wide enough to wrap around the scallop edges. Lay the strips on a work surface. Place 2 basil leaf halves on each strip. On a small plate, arrange the zest and black pepper in parallel lines. Remove the scallops from the marinade. Roll one-half of each scallop edge in a little zest and the other half in a little black pepper. Stand the scallop on its edge at one end of a prosciutto strip and roll up, wrapping the prosciutto completely around the scallop. Secure with a toothpick pushed through the center of the scallop. Brush the scallops on both sides with the remaining 1 tablespoon olive oil. Place on the rack in the pan.

Roast the scallops for 4 minutes. Turn the scallops and roast until opaque throughout, about 3 minutes. Remove the pan from the oven. Transfer the scallops to a platter, remove the toothpicks, and serve warm or at room temperature.

1 lb (500 g) sea scallops (15–20)

2 tablespoons fresh lemon juice

Pinch of cayenne pepper

2 tablespoons extra-virgin olive oil

10 thin slices prosciutto

15–20 fresh basil or small arugula leaves, cut in half lengthwise

Grated zest of 1 lemon

Freshly ground black pepper

Oysters with Toppings

24 small or medium oysters in the shell, well scrubbed

5 lb (2.5 kg) rock salt

For the Bacon Topping

1 slice bacon

1 large shallot, minced

2 tablespoons dry white wine

1 teaspoon white wine vinegar

3 or 4 drops hot-pepper sauce

1/3 cup (3/4 oz/20 g) fresh bread crumbs

Kosher salt and freshly ground pepper

2 tablespoons minced fresh flat-leaf (Italian) parsley

For the Spinach Topping

2 cups (2 oz/60 g) lightly packed spinach leaves

2 or 3 green (spring) onions

4 tablespoons (2 oz/60 g) chilled unsalted butter, cut into small pieces

1 tablespoon pastis or Pernod

1/2 teaspoon grated lemon zest

1/8 teaspoon celery seeds

3 or 4 drops hot-pepper sauce

Kosher salt and freshly ground pepper

To open each oyster, place it, rounded side down, on a heavy kitchen towel. Insert the tip of an oyster knife near the hinged end and twist. Run the knife parallel to the top shell to release the oyster, then remove and discard the top shell. Slide the knife under the oyster to free it from the bottom shell, then cut the oyster into 3 or 4 pieces and return to the shell. Pour off any juice, strain through 2 layers of dampened cheesecloth (muslin), and reserve. Place the oysters in their shells on a large tray in the refrigerator. Measure out 1 tablespoon of the oyster liquor to use in the bacon topping and set aside.

Preheat the oven to 450°F (230°C). Line 1 or 2 rimmed baking sheets with heavy-duty aluminum foil. Pour in enough rock salt to make a layer about 1/4 inch (6 mm) deep. Place the pan(s) in the oven and heat for 15–20 minutes.

Meanwhile, make the bacon topping: Cut the bacon slice into 1/2-inch (12-mm) pieces. In a frying pan over medium heat, sauté the bacon until almost crisp, 8–10 minutes. Add the minced shallot and sauté until softened, 3–4 minutes. Raise the heat to medium-high, add the wine, vinegar, and hot-pepper sauce, and cook until almost all the liquid has evaporated, about 2 minutes. Add the bread crumbs, sprinkle with salt and pepper, and sauté until the bread crumbs are lightly toasted, 2–3 minutes. Stir in the parsley and the reserved oyster liquor. Remove from the heat and set aside.

To make the spinach topping, place the spinach, with the rinsing water still clinging to the leaves, in a large frying pan over medium-high heat and cook until the spinach wilts, 3–4 minutes. Transfer to a sieve and rinse with cold water to stop the cooking. When the spinach is cool enough to handle, squeeze as dry as possible with your hands, then blot with a paper towel. Cut the green onions, including about 1 inch (2.5 cm) of green tops, into 1-inch lengths. In a food processor, with the motor running, drop the onions through the feed tube and process until finely chopped. Scrape down the sides of the bowl and add the spinach. Pulse 4 or 5 times to chop the spinach. Add the butter, pastis, lemon zest, celery seeds, and hot-pepper sauce. Process until well combined. Season to taste with salt and pepper. Transfer to a bowl and set aside.

Remove the oysters from the refrigerator. Top half of the oysters with the spinach topping and the remaining half with the bacon topping. Wearing oven mitts, remove the hot pan(s) from the oven and arrange the oysters on the hot rock salt. Roast the oysters just until the topping is lightly browned, 5–6 minutes. Using tongs, transfer the oysters to individual plates. Serve at once.

Roasted oysters served with two different toppings make a particularly festive appetizer. Ask your fishmonger to shuck, or open, the oysters and place them on a flat tray so that you can transport them home with their liquor intact. If you want to open the oysters yourself, you will need an oyster knife, which has a sturdy flat blade with a narrow tip, and a heavy mitt or towel to protect your hand. Oysters in the shell can be kept in the refrigerator for several hours. Put them in a bowl or on a platter and cover them with wet paper towels, or put them on ice in a colander set over a bowl so the melting ice drains away.

Clams and Sausage, Portuguese Style

Littleneck clams are small hard-shelled clams that are often steamed or served raw on the half shell. Here, they are roasted until they open, then the meat is removed from the shells and added to a filling that is returned to the shells before roasting a second time. Buy a few extra clams in case they do not all open. The unopened clams will keep in a bowl covered with a damp paper towel or in a colander on ice for a few hours in the refrigerator. Linguiça is a garlicky smoked Portuguese sausage that gets its warm color from paprika.

Preheat the oven to 500°F (260°C). Line a rimmed baking sheet with heavy-duty aluminum foil and place a flat rack in the pan.

Discard any clams that do not close tightly to the touch. Arrange the clams on the rack in the pan and roast until they open, 8–10 minutes. Remove the open clams and continue to roast any unopened ones. Discard any clams that do not open after 2–3 minutes additional roasting.

When the clams are cool enough to handle, pour any juice from the clam shells and the roasting pan through a fine-mesh sieve lined with damp cheesecloth (muslin) into a small bowl and reserve the juice. Open each clam and reserve the top shell. With a small knife, remove the clams from the bottom shells and transfer to a cutting board. Cut away the muscles from 5 or 6 of the bottom shells so the shells can be used if there is extra filling. Discard the remaining shells. Cut each clam into 3 or 4 pieces and reserve in a bowl. Discard the foil in the roasting pan. Reduce the oven temperature to 450°F (230°C).

To make the stuffing, in a mortar using a pestle, or in a spice grinder, grind together the aniseeds and peppercorns until finely ground. Set aside. In a frying pan over medium heat, melt the butter. Add the sausage and the green onions and sauté until the onions soften, 2–3 minutes. Add the garlic and lemon juice and sauté for 1 minute longer. Add the bread crumbs, lemon zest, and aniseed-pepper mixture and sauté until lightly browned, 4–5 minutes. Pour the mixture into the bowl with the clams. Add the parsley and 3 tablespoons of the reserved clam juice and mix well. (Discard the remaining clam juice.)

Lightly fill the reserved clam shells with the stuffing. (The clams can be prepared up to this point, covered, and refrigerated for up to 3 hours before roasting.) Place the stuffed shells on the rack in the prepared pan.

Roast the stuffed clams until the stuffing is lightly browned and heated through, 6–8 minutes. Remove the pan from the oven and transfer the clams to individual plates. Serve at once.

30 littleneck clams or other hard-shelled clams, each about 1 1/2 inches (4 cm) in diameter, well scrubbed

For the Stuffing

1/8 teaspoon aniseeds

1/4 teaspoon peppercorns

2 tablespoons unsalted butter

1/4 cup (3 oz/90 g) finely diced, skinned linguiça or other cooked sausage

2 or 3 green (spring) onions, including 1 inch (2.5 cm) of tender green tops, finely chopped

1 large clove garlic, minced

1 tablespoon fresh lemon juice

1 1/4 cups (2 1/2 oz/75 g) fresh bread crumbs

2 teaspoons grated lemon zest

1/4 cup (1/3 oz/10 g) chopped fresh flat-leaf (Italian) parsley

Endive Salad with Roasted Pears and Walnuts

¹/₄ cup (1 oz/30 g) walnut pieces

2 red pears such as red Bartlett (Williams'), unpeeled, halved, cored, and cut lengthwise into slices ¹/₂ inch (12 mm) thick

4 small Belgian endives (chicory/witloof), ¹/₂–³/₄ lb (250–375 g) total weight, halved lengthwise

4 tablespoons (2 fl oz/60 ml) walnut oil

¹/₈ teaspoon ground cloves

Kosher salt and freshly ground pepper

1 tablespoon raspberry vinegar

2 teaspoons finely chopped shallot

1 head butter (Boston) lettuce, leaves separated

¹/₄ cup (1 ¹/₂ oz/45 g) crumbled Roquefort or other blue cheese

Preheat the oven to 400°F (200°C). Spread the nuts out on a rimmed baking sheet. Roast the nuts, stirring 1 or 2 times, until they are a shade darker and fragrant, 5–7 minutes. Immediately transfer the nuts to a plate and let cool.

Place the pears and endives in a single layer on the baking sheet. Brush with 2 tablespoons of the walnut oil and sprinkle evenly with the cloves. Season lightly with salt and pepper. Roast the pears and endives, turning once, just until both are softened and tinged with gold, 7–9 minutes.

Meanwhile, in a small bowl, whisk together the remaining 2 tablespoons walnut oil, the vinegar, the shallot, and a pinch each of salt and pepper. Divide the lettuce among individual plates.

Remove the pan from the oven. When the roasted pears and endives are cool enough to handle, arrange them on the lettuce, dividing them evenly. Drizzle evenly with the dressing. Sprinkle with the nuts and cheese, again dividing evenly. Serve at once.

All the major elements in this late fall or winter salad—nuts, pears, endives—are roasted. Most nuts benefit from roasting, which deepens and enriches their natural oils. Belgian endive, a mildly bitter, elegant salad green, is also enhanced by a brief stint in a hot oven; pears caramelize and become even sweeter.

French Onion Soup

Classic French onion soup is made with onions slowly caramelized in a frying pan. Roasting accomplishes the same result, but is even easier and adds more depth to the sweet onion flavor. The garlic roasts along with the onion, and the finished soup is slipped under the broiler to melt the cheese. If you wish a lighter-tasting soup, use chicken broth, or for a vegetarian version, use vegetable broth.

Preheat the oven to 425°F (220°C). On a rimmed baking sheet, melt the butter with the oil in the preheating oven. Watch carefully to prevent burning. Spread the onions, garlic, bay leaves, and 2 tablespoons of the chopped thyme in the melted butter and oil and stir to coat the vegetables. Season lightly with salt and generously with pepper, stir again, and then spread the mixture out evenly on the baking sheet.

Roast the onions, stirring often, until they are golden with blackened edges and very tender, 25–30 minutes. Remove the pan from the oven, stir in the sherry, and return to the oven for 2 minutes to infuse the onions with flavor. Remove from the oven, stir to scrape up any caramelized onion from the pan, and set aside. Place the bread slices directly on the oven rack and toast until pale gold, 5–10 minutes.

Meanwhile, in a saucepan, bring the broth to a simmer over medium-low heat. When the onions are ready, remove the bay leaves from the onions, add the onions to the broth, and simmer, stirring occasionally, for 5 minutes. Stir in the remaining 1 tablespoon chopped thyme.

Turn on the broiler (grill). Divide the soup among flameproof soup bowls. Cut each slice of toast in half, and top each bowl with a half slice. Sprinkle the toasts evenly with the cheese. Broil (grill) 3–4 inches (7.5–10 cm) from the heat source until the cheese is melted, bubbly, and lightly browned, 1–2 minutes.

Serve the soup at once, garnished with the thyme sprigs, if using.

2 tablespoons unsalted butter

1 tablespoon extra-virgin olive or canola oil

3 large yellow onions, about 1 1/2 lb (750 g) total weight, thinly sliced

3 large cloves garlic, thinly sliced

2 bay leaves, broken in half

3 tablespoons chopped fresh thyme, plus 6–8 sprigs for garnish (optional)

Kosher salt and freshly ground pepper

1/4 cup (2 fl oz/60 ml) dry sherry

3 or 4 thick baguette slices

4 cups (32 fl oz/1 l) reduced-sodium beef broth

1/2 cup (2 oz/60 g) shredded Gruyère or Swiss cheese

Apple, Leek, and Butternut Squash Soup

1 or 2 butternut squashes, about 4 lb (2 kg) total weight, halved, seeded, peeled, and cut into 1 1/2-inch (4-cm) chunks

1 lb (500 g) tart apples, peeled, cored, and cut into quarters

1 large or 2 slender leeks, including tender green tops, cut into slices 1 inch (2.5 cm) thick

4 large cloves garlic

2 tablespoons chopped fresh sage, plus whole leaves for garnish (optional)

2 teaspoons ground cumin

Kosher salt and freshly ground pepper

3 tablespoons extra-virgin olive oil

4 cups (32 fl oz/1 l) reduced-sodium chicken broth

1 cup (8 fl oz/250 ml) hard cider or dry white wine

1/2 cup (4 fl oz/125 ml) crème fraîche or sour cream

1 small tart apple, unpeeled, halved, cored, and thinly sliced

Preheat the oven to 425°F (220°C). Arrange the squash chunks, apple quarters, leeks, and garlic in a single layer on a rimmed baking sheet. Sprinkle with 1 tablespoon of the chopped sage and 1 teaspoon of the cumin. Season with salt and pepper. Drizzle with the olive oil, stir to coat, and spread the mixture out in the pan.

Roast the apples and vegetables, stirring 2 or 3 times, until the squash is fork-tender and all the vegetables and apples are tinged with gold, 20–25 minutes. Remove the pan from the oven.

Working in batches if necessary, transfer the roasted mixture to a food processor and process until a coarse purée forms. With the motor running, pour in 1–1 1/2 cups (8–12 fl oz/250–375 ml) of the chicken broth and process until nearly smooth. Transfer the purée to a large saucepan over medium heat. Stir in the remaining broth, the cider, and the remaining 1 tablespoon chopped sage and 1 teaspoon cumin and bring just to a simmer, stirring often. (The soup can be prepared up to this point several hours ahead and then gently reheated.) Taste and adjust the seasoning with salt and pepper.

Ladle the soup into warmed shallow bowls and top each serving with 1 tablespoon crème fraîche. Float a few apple slices in each bowl. Garnish with sage leaves, if using. Serve at once.

Roasting caramelizes the natural sugars and intensifies the flavors of the apples, leeks, and squash, giving this soup a rich character that needs little embellishment. If you do not want to go to the trouble of peeling and seeding the butternut squash, simply buy the prepared chunks sold in the produce section of the market; you will need 2 1/2 lb (1.25 kg) peeled, seeded, and cut-up squash. Hard cider is apple juice that has undergone fermentation, usually resulting in an alcohol content of no more than about 6 percent. Look for it in a wine shop or the wine section of the supermarket.

Smoky Red Pepper Soup

VARIATION

**Cold Smoky
Red Pepper Soup**

Let the soup cool to room temperature, cover, and refrigerate until well chilled, about 4 hours. Taste and adjust the seasoning, then ladle into chilled bowls. Garnish as directed for the hot soup.

Thickened with lightly dried bread crumbs and garnished with capers and anchovies, this coarsely textured puréed soup has a distinctly Spanish leaning—a kind of winter gazpacho. The crumbs are easily made by tearing the bread into pieces and whirling them in a food processor until reduced to coarse crumbs. If you have only fresh bread, dry the slices by placing them in the preheating oven for a few minutes until they barely begin to color. Yellow bell peppers make an equally attractive and flavorful soup. Spanish smoked paprika has a depth of flavor not found in other varieties. It is sold in many markets and also in specialty-food stores. If it is unavailable, substitute the best-quality medium-heat paprika you can find.

Roast, peel, and seed the bell peppers as directed on page 294, capturing the juices in a bowl. Cut the peppers into pieces.

Preheat the oven to 450°F (230°C). Place the onion slices on a rimmed baking sheet. Sprinkle with the garlic, chopped marjoram, and paprika. Season lightly with salt and generously with pepper. Drizzle with the olive oil, then stir to coat the onions completely and spread out on the baking sheet. Roast, stirring often, until the onions are golden and soft, 15–20 minutes.

Working in batches if necessary, combine the roasted peppers and their juices and the onion mixture in a food processor and process until a coarse purée forms. Add the bread crumbs and 2 of the anchovies, then process again just to a coarse purée. Add 2 cups (16 fl oz/500 ml) of the broth and purée again. Pour into a saucepan along with the remaining 2 cups broth and bring to a simmer over medium heat, stirring often. Taste and adjust the seasoning with salt and pepper and simmer for 1–2 minutes to blend the flavors.

Ladle the soup into warmed bowls. Cut the remaining 2 anchovies lengthwise into 4 pieces each and float 1 slice in each bowl of soup. Sprinkle evenly with the capers and garnish each bowl with a marjoram sprig, if using. Serve at once.

**4 red bell peppers
(capsicums)**

1 large yellow onion, sliced

4 large cloves garlic, sliced

1 tablespoon chopped fresh marjoram, plus 8 sprigs for garnish (optional)

1 tablespoon paprika, preferably Spanish smoked paprika (see note)

Kosher salt and freshly ground pepper

3 tablespoons extra-virgin olive oil

1 cup (2 oz/60 g) coarse bread crumbs from day-old French bread, crusts removed

4 olive oil–packed anchovy fillets

4 cups (32 fl oz/1 l) reduced-sodium chicken or vegetable broth

4 teaspoons small capers

Fish and Shellfish

About Fish and Shellfish

Roasting ensures moist, tender fish fillets and steaks, whole fish with crispy skins and delicate interiors, and succulent lobsters and smaller shellfish such as shrimp and mussels. All you need to get started is a reliable fishmonger who carries only the freshest seafood.

Nearly every type of fish and shellfish is suitable for roasting. A whole fish makes for a dramatic presentation, however, as anyone who has ever eaten at a beachfront restaurant knows. Keeping the skin and bones intact seals in the natural flavors and moisture of the fish, which produces a particularly delicious result. Tell your fishmonger how you will be cooking the fish and ask for help in making the best selection from what is available.

Flavoring the flesh and keeping it moist are top priorities. In Salt-Roasted Whole Fish (page 87), the fish is encased in a mixture of coarse salt, egg whites, and water. The salty barrier hardens during roasting and must be cracked open after cooking to release the fish, which emerges juicy and flavorful.

In Stuffed Trout Wrapped in Grape Leaves (page 82), brined vine leaves are used not only to prevent the delicate fish from drying out in the oven or from breaking apart as they are handled, but also to impart a subtle yet distinctive flavor to the flesh. The trout are given a second flavor boost with the addition of a tasty stuffing of bread crumbs, dried currants, and pine nuts.

Sometimes the cavities are simply seasoned, rather than stuffed, for flavor, much in the same way you would season a chicken cavity before roasting. The fennel fronds, garlic, and other aromatics slipped into the cavity of a whole striped bass (page 85) showcase this technique beautifully.

Meaty fish take particularly well to stuffing, whether whole or a substantial-sized piece. In Salmon with Leek and Rice Stuffing (page 81), a fragrant mixture of rice, leeks, and herbs is put into a large center-cut piece of fish and secured in place with kitchen string.

FISH STEAKS AND FILLETS

Smaller pieces of meaty fish—halibut, swordfish, monkfish, tuna, salmon—in the form of portion-sized steaks or fillets, are good candidates for roasting as well. Searing steaks and fillets on the stove top before briefly roasting them in the intense heat of a hot oven nicely browns their exteriors, which adds a layer of rich flavor.

Salmon Fillets with Sautéed Cucumber and Dill (page 73) and Salmon Steaks with Beurre Rouge (page 67) are excellent examples of how this technique, known as pan-roasting (page 13), works. For the best results, keep in mind that the fillets and steaks must be at least 1 inch (2.5 cm) thick and that they must be uniform in size and shape so that all of them are ready at the same time.

Mild fish in particular can benefit from seasoning with herbs and spices before pan-roasting. For Halibut Fillets with Herbes de Provence (page 69), the steaks are rubbed with olive oil and sprinkled generously with fresh parsley and the signature dried-herb blend of southern France before they are seared. This easy seasoning method works for other fillets and steaks as well.

Sometimes a protective "crust" is used to keep the flesh of fillets and steaks moist during cooking. For both Monkfish with Red Pepper Sauce (page 78) and Swordfish Steaks with Tangerine, Ginger, and Avocado Salsa (page 70), the fish pieces are lightly floured and seasoned before pan-searing, creating a thin shield that helps prevent the flesh from drying out in the oven.

Fillets and steaks can be roasted along with vegetables, creating a main course and accompaniment at the same time. For Snapper Fillets with Belgian Endive (page 74), the endive (chicory/witloof) serves as a natural roasting rack and imparts its pleasantly bitter edge to the simply seasoned fish. In Cod with Potatoes and Aioli (page 77), the buttery fingerlings roast at the opposite end of the pan.

ROASTING SHELLFISH

The same primary concerns—retaining moisture and adding flavor—that govern roasting fish apply to shellfish. Good choices for roasting featured in this chapter are large shrimp (prawns), mussels, and whole lobster. Scallops, oysters, and clams are appropriate as well and can be found in the chapter devoted to starters and small plates.

A sauce often accompanies small shellfish. In Garlicky Mustard Shrimp (page 88), the sauce, which includes chopped tomatoes, is cooked in the same pan as the fish. For the Mussels in Curry Cream Sauce (page 90), the sauce is prepared separately and flavored with the liquid released by the roasted mussels.

The pairing of lobster and garlic butter (page 93) is familiar and irresistible, but here the crustacean is roasted, rather than boiled, to bring out its purest flavor, and the flesh is basted with the butter to keep it moist in the oven. As with all fish and shellfish recipes, the success of this simple dish depends on a good fishmonger supplying you with only the finest—and freshest—seafood.

Roasting Fish and Shellfish

Fish and shellfish pack protein, vitamins, minerals, and healthful fatty acids in a flavorful package. Delicate seafood and a hot oven might not seem a good match, but roasting actually enhances the flavor of seafood and is a quick way to prepare a satisfying meal.

The flesh of fresh fish should feel firm rather than soft. Avoid tuna and other dark-meat fish with an iridescent sheen.

Unlike meat and poultry, there are no federal standards in the United States for fish inspection, nor is there a grading system. Shellfish, however, are inspected to ensure that they come from clean waters. For the most part, consumers must rely on their own knowledge and sound judgment when it comes to buying fish and shellfish.

The first step to securing the best of what is available is to find a reliable purveyor. A fish market often has a larger and higher quality selection than a supermarket and a better-informed staff. Shopping for fish can be complicated because names and availability can change with locale, so the recipes in this book call for the most popular varieties.

Whenever possible, smell your purchase. Your nose will quickly tell you if it is fresh. If the fish is wrapped in plastic, press it gently. It should feel firm rather than soft. Fresh fish will look moist and glistening, and dark-meat fish steaks, such as tuna, will not have a rainbowlike iridescent sheen.

If you are buying whole fish, avoid those with sunken eyes. Some sources advise to look for clear eyes, but since the eyes of some fish are naturally cloudy, this tip is not always a good indicator of freshness. Ask the fishmonger to show you the gills, which should be bright red, not brick red. Select whole fish that are relatively thick for their length. They will roast better and deliver more

substantial servings. Be sure the fishmonger cleans and scales the fish before wrapping it, two jobs that are messy to do at home.

Mollusks—clams, oysters, mussels—must always be purchased live. Check them carefully; their shells should be free of cracks and be tightly closed, or close tightly to the touch. Discard any mollusks that remain open or feel especially heavy for their size; that extra weight is likely mud and sand. Lobsters must also be purchased live—and must be lively. If they are held in a water tank for longer than 2 weeks, they lose vigor and flavor, so buy them from a source where the turnover is brisk. Also, watch carefully when lobsters are pulled from the tank. If they are noticeably placid, pass on purchasing them.

Shrimp (prawns) should feel firm to the touch and have a clean, fresh smell, just like fish. Black stripes on certain varieties are fine, but black spots on the shell can mean that the shrimp are spoiled. Cook crustaceans (lobster, shrimp, crayfish, crabs) and mollusks on the same day that you purchase them.

Before you purchase fish or shellfish, check with a reliable source to make sure that the

Mussels and other mollusks should be live when purchased. Examine them carefully to make sure that the shells are not cracked and that they close tightly to the touch.

variety is not in danger of extinction due to overfishing or another cause. You can ask your fishmonger, you can research the information on the Internet from such groups as the Audubon Society, or you can call your regional fish and game regulatory agency to check on current status in local waters.

When serving whole fish, allow 1 pound (500 g) per person. You need this large an amount to account for bones and other inedible material. For fish fillets and steaks, allow a 6- to 8-ounce (185- to 250-g) portion for each diner. The amount of shellfish appropriate for each serving varies with the recipe.

PREPARING FISH AND SHELLFISH

Rinse whole fish well inside and out under running cold water. Using kitchen shears, open the gill flaps and clip out the gills, then rinse out the gill area well. Pat the fish completely dry with paper towels before roasting. Any fish less than 5 pounds (2.5 kg) can be roasted at up to 425°F (220°C), but fish above that weight should generally be roasted at 350°F (180°C). Large fish need a lower temperature to ensure that the skin will not burn before the fish is cooked through.

Fish fillets that are relatively thick, such as salmon and cod, are deliciously reliable options for roasting, especially when they are pan-roasted. If fillets are thin and delicate, such as flounder, they can be roasted successfully if they are first folded in half crosswise to make a double thickness. Run your finger across the surface to locate any errant pin bones. If you find any, pull them out with needle-nosed pliers or tweezers, first sterilizing the tips over an open flame.

Before roasting mollusks in their shells, scrub them well under running cold water with

The flesh of roasted salmon should flake when tested with a knife. Other varieties, such as striped bass, halibut, and swordfish, will be uniformly opaque.

a sturdy brush. If you suspect that the clams or mussels may contain a lot of grit, you may want to purge them by soaking them in salted water (2 tablespoons sea salt to 1 gallon water) for an hour or so before cooking.

TESTING FOR DONENESS

The general rule for timing fish in the oven is 10 minutes per inch (2.5 cm) of thickness. If you are roasting a whole fish, measure it at its thickest point, typically the center of the body. Stuffed fish will take a little longer to roast than unstuffed fish, although slipping a few herb sprigs or lemon slices in the body cavity will not affect roasting time. Vegetable side dishes cooked in the same pan as the fish are likely to take longer than the fish, so you may want to give them a head start in the oven.

Whole fish is done when a knife inserted alongside the backbone reveals opaque flesh.

The flesh may or may not flake, depending on the variety. Use the same knife test to check if a fillet or steak is opaque. Keep in mind that tuna and salmon are often served rare to medium-rare and that the flesh of these varieties will not be opaque when cooked to these levels of doneness.

Scallops can be cooked to different degrees of doneness. Pan-roasted scallops tend to be cooked medium-well, which is easily tested by making a small slit with a sharp knife. If you like rare scallops, you should sauté them and reserve roasting for other shellfish. Serve clams and mussels the moment the shells open, discarding any specimens that remain tightly closed. Roast shelled oysters just until the edges of the flesh begin to curl. Shrimp are done as soon as they turn a bright color (red, orange, or pink, according to the variety) and the flesh becomes opaque.

Salmon Steaks with Beurre Rouge

Beurre rouge, which accompanies these quickly roasted salmon steaks, is the red wine version of beurre blanc. This buttery, shallot-infused wine sauce takes about 30 minutes to make, so you will need to put it together before you begin cooking the salmon. Open a light, fruity red wine that is not high in tannin for the sauce, such as Beaujolais, Pinot Noir, or Merlot, and then drink the rest with the finished dish.

To make the sauce, in a deep saucepan over high heat, combine the wine, broth, vinegar, celery, shallot, garlic, thyme, and peppercorns. Bring to a boil and cook until reduced to $1/3$ cup (3 fl oz/80 ml), including the vegetables, 20–25 minutes. Remove from the heat and strain through a fine-mesh sieve placed over a small bowl. Discard the contents of the sieve and return the liquid to the saucepan. Set aside. (The sauce can be made to this point up to 1 hour ahead and allowed to stand at room temperature.)

Preheat the oven to 450°F (230°C). Pat the salmon steaks dry with paper towels and season both sides with salt and pepper. Place a large, heavy ovenproof frying pan over high heat and add just enough olive oil to coat the bottom. When the oil is almost smoking, add the salmon steaks and sear for 2–3 minutes on the first side. Carefully turn the steaks and sear for 1 minute on the second side. Immediately place the pan in the oven and roast the salmon steaks until the flesh flakes when a knife is inserted into the thickest part, about 5 minutes.

While the salmon is in the oven, finish the sauce. Reheat the reserved liquid over high heat until almost boiling, remove from the heat, and whisk in the butter 1 piece at a time until the sauce thickens slightly and all the butter is incorporated. Season to taste with salt and pepper. Keep warm.

When the salmon is ready, remove the pan from the oven and divide the steaks among warmed individual plates. Spoon an equal amount of the sauce over each steak. Serve at once.

For the Sauce

1 cup (8 fl oz/250 ml) dry red wine (see note)

1 cup (8 fl oz/250 ml) reduced-sodium chicken broth

3 tablespoons red wine vinegar

$1/3$ cup ($1^1/2$ oz/45 g) thinly sliced celery

2 tablespoons minced shallot

1 clove garlic, thinly sliced

1 fresh thyme sprig

3 or 4 peppercorns

$1/2$ cup (4 oz/125 g) chilled unsalted butter, cut into 8 equal pieces

Kosher salt and freshly ground pepper

4 salmon steaks, each 8–10 oz (250–315 g) and about 1 inch (2.5 cm) thick

Kosher salt and freshly ground pepper

2–3 teaspoons extra-virgin olive oil

Tuna with Tomato-Caper Sauce

4 albacore or ahi tuna steaks (see note)

Kosher salt and freshly ground pepper

3 tablespoons extra-virgin olive oil

3 tablespoons finely chopped shallot

1¹/₂ cups (9 oz/280 g) peeled, seeded, and chopped tomato

2 tablespoons red wine vinegar

1 tablespoon capers, coarsely chopped

6–8 fresh basil leaves, finely shredded

Preheat the oven to 450°F (230°C).

Heat a large, heavy ovenproof frying pan over high heat until very hot, 3–4 minutes. Meanwhile, pat the tuna dry with paper towels and season both sides with salt and pepper. Add 1 tablespoon of the olive oil to the hot pan and then add the tuna. If using albacore tuna, sear for 1 minute on the first side, carefully turn the fish, sear for 15–30 seconds on the second side, and immediately place the pan in the oven and roast for 2–3 minutes for rare. If using ahi tuna, sear for 30 seconds, then turn and roast in the oven for 45–60 seconds for rare. Ahi is done when the outer ¹/₄ inch (6 mm) of the flesh appears cooked and the center is still red. Remove the pan from the oven, transfer the fish to a warmed platter, and tent with aluminum foil while you make the sauce.

In the same frying pan over medium-low heat, warm the remaining 2 tablespoons oil. Add the shallot and sauté until softened, about 2 minutes. Add the tomato, vinegar, and capers and season with salt and pepper. Sauté until the mixture is hot, about 2 minutes.

Divide the tuna among warmed individual plates. Spoon the sauce over the fish, dividing it evenly. Garnish with the basil and serve at once.

When selecting tuna for this recipe, choose thick pieces, each about 1¹/₄ inches (3 cm) thick and 5–6 ounces (155–185 g), as the fish is best served rare. Look for impeccably fresh albacore tuna, also known as tombo, or the darker-fleshed ahi, often used in sashimi. The albacore should be cooked a little longer than the ahi because it has firmer flesh and a lower fat content, but be careful not to overcook the fish, or it will be dry.

Halibut Fillets with Herbes de Provence

Halibut, a mild, flaky fish, can be paired with a variety of herbs and spices. Here, thick steaks or fillets are flavored with a dusting of aromatic herbes de Provence, typically a simple dried blend of thyme, summer savory, basil, lavender, and fennel seed. Serve the fish on a bed of rice or couscous to absorb the delicious juices.

Preheat the oven to 450°F (230°C).

Pat the halibut fillets dry with paper towels. Lightly brush or rub on both sides with 1 teaspoon of the olive oil. Sprinkle the parsley, the herbes de Provence, and salt evenly over both sides of each fillet, and press firmly into the flesh.

Heat a large, heavy ovenproof frying pan over high heat until very hot, 3–4 minutes. Add the remaining 2 teaspoons oil, then add the fillets and sear for 1–2 minutes on the first side. Carefully turn the halibut fillets and immediately place the pan in the oven. Roast the fish until opaque throughout when tested with a knife, 7–8 minutes. Remove the pan from the oven and transfer the fish to a cutting board.

Cut each fillet into 2 pieces and divide among warmed individual plates. Serve with the lemon wedges.

2 halibut fillets or steaks, each 12–14 oz (375–440 g) and about 1 inch (2.5 cm) thick

1 tablespoon extra-virgin olive oil

2 tablespoons finely chopped fresh flat-leaf (Italian) parsley

2 teaspoons herbes de Provence

Kosher salt

Lemon wedges for serving

Swordfish Steaks with Tangerine, Ginger, and Avocado Salsa

For the Salsa

4 tangerines

1–2 serrano chiles, seeded and minced

1 small ripe avocado, halved, pitted, peeled, and cut into $1/2$-inch (12-mm) dice

1 small red onion, chopped and rinsed under cold water

1 teaspoon honey

$1/2$ teaspoon grated, peeled fresh ginger

1 tablespoon extra-virgin olive oil

1 tablespoon cider vinegar

$1/2$ cup ($3/4$ oz/20 g) firmly packed fresh cilantro (fresh coriander) leaves, coarsely chopped

Kosher salt and freshly ground pepper

2 swordfish steaks, each 10–12 oz (315–375 g) and about 1 inch (2.5 cm) thick

About $1/4$ cup ($1^1/2$ oz/45 g) all-purpose (plain) flour

Kosher salt and freshly ground pepper

2 teaspoons extra-virgin olive oil

Preheat the oven to 450°F (230°C).

To make the salsa, first segment the tangerines: Working with 1 tangerine at a time, and using a sharp knife, cut a slice off both ends of the tangerine to reveal the flesh. Stand the tangerine upright on a cutting board and, using the knife, cut downward to remove the peel and pith, following the contour of the tangerine. Holding the tangerine in one hand over a bowl, cut along both sides of each segment, freeing it from the membrane and capturing the segment and any juices in the bowl. Cut each segment into $1/2$-inch (12-mm) pieces, discarding any seeds and returning the pieces to the bowl. Add the chiles, avocado, onion, honey, ginger, olive oil, vinegar, and cilantro and stir to mix. Season to taste with salt and pepper. Set aside.

Pat the swordfish steaks dry with paper towels. Place the flour in a shallow bowl and season with salt and pepper. Dust the steaks on both sides with the flour, shaking off the excess.

Heat a large, heavy ovenproof frying pan over high heat until very hot, 3–4 minutes. Add the olive oil and then add the swordfish steaks and sear for about 2 minutes. Carefully turn the steaks and immediately place the pan in the oven. Roast the fish until opaque throughout when tested with a knife, 5–6 minutes. Remove the pan from the oven and transfer the fish to a cutting board.

Cut each steak into 2 pieces and divide among warmed individual plates. Spoon one-fourth of the salsa alongside each portion of fish and serve.

Found in temperate waters worldwide, swordfish is a medium-fat fish with firm flesh and a mild flavor. It takes well to pan-roasting and finishing in the oven. If tangerines are not in season, use small oranges in the salsa. The salsa can be prepared 1–2 hours ahead, but it tastes best when served as soon as possible after it is made.

Salmon Fillets with Sautéed Cucumber and Dill

Here, salmon fillets are seared in a hot frying pan on top of the stove and then finished in a hot oven. For the cucumber sauté, look for an English cucumber, which is seedless or nearly so and has a mild flavor. A tomato rice pilaf or unpeeled tiny new potatoes would round out the plate for a delicious company dinner.

Preheat the oven to 450°F (230°C).

Pat the salmon fillets dry with paper towels and season both sides with salt and pepper. Place a large, heavy ovenproof frying pan over high heat and add just enough canola oil to coat the bottom. When the oil is almost smoking, add the salmon fillets, skin side up if the skin is intact, and sear for 2 minutes. Carefully turn the fillets and immediately place the pan in the oven. Roast the salmon until the flesh flakes when a knife is inserted into the thickest part, 6–7 minutes.

Meanwhile, prepare the cucumber: Using a small spoon, scoop out any large, hard seeds from the cucumber halves and discard. Cut each half crosswise into half moons 1/4 inch (6 mm) thick. In a frying pan over high heat, melt the butter. When it begins to foam, add the cucumbers and green onions and season to taste with salt and pepper. Sauté until the cucumbers are just softened, 2–3 minutes. Add the dill, cream, lemon juice, and sugar, stir to combine, and heat through. Taste and adjust the seasoning.

Remove the pan from the oven and transfer the fillets to a plate lined with paper towels. Blot the fillets with paper towels, lift off the skin if present, and place the fillets on warmed individual plates. Divide the cucumbers among the plates. Serve at once.

4 salmon fillets, 6–8 oz (185–250 g) each, with or without skin

Kosher salt and freshly ground pepper

2–3 teaspoons canola oil

For the Sautéed Cucumber

1 English (hothouse) cucumber, 14–16 oz (440–500 g), peeled and halved lengthwise

1 tablespoon unsalted butter

2 green (spring) onions, including 1 inch (2.5 cm) of tender green tops, minced

Kosher salt and freshly ground pepper

2 tablespoons finely chopped fresh dill

3 tablespoons heavy (double) cream

2 teaspoons fresh lemon juice

1 teaspoon sugar

Snapper Fillets with Belgian Endive

6–8 white or red Belgian endives (chicory/witloof), or a combination, 12–14 oz (375–440 g) total weight

2 tablespoons unsalted butter, melted

Kosher salt and freshly ground pepper

$1/4$ cup (2 fl oz/60 ml) reduced-sodium chicken broth

1 tablespoon sherry vinegar

$1/2$ teaspoon sugar

2 skinless red snapper fillets, 10–12 oz (315–375 g) each, or 4 smaller fillets, 5–6 oz (155–185 g) each

Extra-virgin olive oil for coating

Spanish or Hungarian sweet paprika

Preheat the oven to 450°F (230°C).

Cut the endives in half lengthwise, then cut out the hard core and discard. Slice the halves lengthwise into strips about $1/2$ inch (12 mm) wide. Pour the melted butter into a shallow baking dish just large enough to hold the fish. Add the endive strips and toss to coat with the butter. Sprinkle with salt and pepper.

Place the dish in the oven and roast the endives for 10 minutes. Remove from the oven and turn the endive strips with a spatula. Add the broth, vinegar, and sugar. Continue to roast for another 10 minutes.

Meanwhile, pat the snapper fillets dry with paper towels. Lightly brush or rub both sides with olive oil, then season both sides with salt and pepper. Lightly sprinkle one side with paprika.

Remove the dish from the oven and place the fillets, paprika side up, on top of the endive strips. Roast the fish until opaque throughout when tested with a knife, 8–10 minutes. Remove the dish from the oven. If using 2 large fillets, transfer the fish to a cutting board and cut each fillet into 2 pieces.

Spoon the endive strips onto warmed individual plates, dividing them evenly. Top with the fish and serve at once.

Many species of saltwater fish are sold as snapper, but one of the most popular types is the true red snapper with its pink skin and red eyes. It is found primarily along the Atlantic Coast from Florida to Brazil and in the Gulf of Mexico. Rockfish, also known as Pacific snapper, though different from true snapper, is a good substitute in this recipe, as is sea bass, halibut, or tilapia. Belgian endives serve as a natural roasting rack for the fish fillets. Their slight bitterness, which softens during cooking, complements the simply seasoned mild fish. The dusting of paprika adds a color accent.

Cod with Potatoes and Aioli

The many species of cod are lean, white-fleshed, mild fish that flake easily when cooked. They form a classic pairing with potatoes, both of which are complemented by aioli, a garlicky mayonnaise. The aioli can be made up to 1 day in advance and refrigerated until serving. Leftover aioli is delicious with green beans or asparagus, or with cooked shrimp (prawns) or scallops. You will need to start roasting the potatoes about 20 minutes before adding the cod to the roasting pan.

To make the aioli, mince the garlic with $1/2$ teaspoon salt. Place in a food processor. Add the egg, lemon juice, vinegar, mustard, chile sauce, and $1/8$ teaspoon white pepper and process until blended. Combine the canola oil and olive oil in a measuring pitcher with a spout. With the motor running, add the oils in a slow, steady stream until the mixture thickens to the consistency of mayonnaise.

Preheat the oven to 400°F (200°C). Line a large rimmed baking sheet with heavy-duty aluminum foil.

In a bowl, toss together the potatoes and 1 tablespoon olive oil, then sprinkle with salt and pepper. Place the potatoes on one end of the prepared pan. Place in the oven and roast the potatoes until the blade of a knife goes in fairly easily but the potatoes are still a little firm, 20–25 minutes.

Meanwhile, pat the cod fillets dry with paper towels. Lightly brush or rub both sides with olive oil, then season both sides with salt and pepper. Lightly sprinkle one side with paprika.

Remove the pan from the oven and place the fillets, paprika side up, on the uncovered end, opposite the potatoes. Continue to roast, without turning, until the fish starts to flake and pull apart and is opaque at the center when tested with a knife, 8–10 minutes. Remove the pan from the oven and transfer the fish to a cutting board.

Cut each fish fillet into 2 pieces and place on individual plates with the potatoes. Spoon the aioli into individual ramekins and place on each plate. Serve at once.

For the Aioli

3 or 4 cloves garlic

Kosher salt

1 large egg

1 teaspoon fresh lemon juice

1 teaspoon white wine vinegar

1 teaspoon Dijon mustard

2 or 3 drops green jalapeño chile sauce

Freshly ground white pepper

$1/2$ cup (4 fl oz/125 ml) canola oil

$1/4$ cup (2 fl oz/60 ml) extra-virgin olive oil

1 lb (500 g) fingerling or small Yukon gold potatoes, unpeeled

1 tablespoon extra-virgin olive oil, plus extra for coating

Kosher salt and freshly ground pepper

2 cod fillets, each 12–14 oz (375–440 g) and about 1 inch (2.5 cm) thick

Spanish or Hungarian sweet paprika

Monkfish with Red Pepper Sauce

2 monkfish tails, each
8–10 oz (250–315 g) and
about 1¹/₂ inches (4 cm)
thick

About ¹/₄ cup (1¹/₂ oz/45 g)
all-purpose (plain) flour

Kosher salt and freshly
ground pepper

2 tablespoons extra-virgin
olive oil

For the Red Pepper Sauce

1 tablespoon extra-virgin
olive oil

1 small shallot, minced

2 cloves garlic, minced

¹/₄ teaspoon red pepper
flakes, or to taste

2 red bell peppers
(capsicums), roasted, peeled,
and seeded (page 294)

2 tablespoons minced fresh
flat-leaf (Italian) parsley

1 tablespoon balsamic
vinegar

Kosher salt and freshly
ground pepper

The tail of a monkfish resembles a small tenderloin of meat, and it is cooked like a tenderloin in this appealing dish. Select thick pieces, as they will roast more evenly. The fish is quickly browned on the stove top before finishing in the oven, a step that forms a flavorful crust. The zesty sauce goes together quickly if you have roasted red peppers on hand. Serve a green vegetable and rice pilaf or couscous with pine nuts to round out the plate.

Preheat the oven to 425°F (220°C). Oil a flat rack and place it in a roasting pan just large enough to hold the fish.

Pat the monkfish dry with paper towels. Place the flour in a bowl and season with salt and pepper. Dredge the fish in the flour, shaking off the excess.

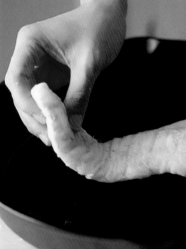

In a large frying pan over high heat, warm the olive oil until very hot. Add the fish and sauté, carefully turning once, until brown and crusty on both sides, about 1¹/₂ minutes on each side. Transfer the fish to the rack in the roasting pan and place in the oven. Roast the fish until opaque throughout when tested with a knife, 12–14 minutes.

While the monkfish is in the oven, make the red pepper sauce: In a small frying pan over medium heat, warm the olive oil. Add the shallot and sauté until softened but not browned, 1–2 minutes. Add the garlic and red pepper flakes, and cook for 1 minute longer. Remove from the heat. In a food processor, combine the shallot mixture, roasted peppers, parsley, and vinegar and process until smooth. Season with ¹/₂ teaspoon salt and pepper to taste.

When the fish is ready, transfer it to a cutting board and tent with aluminum foil. Let rest for 3–4 minutes.

Cut the fish into slices ¹/₂ inch (12 mm) thick. Divide among warmed individual plates. Spoon an equal amount of the sauce over each serving. Serve at once.

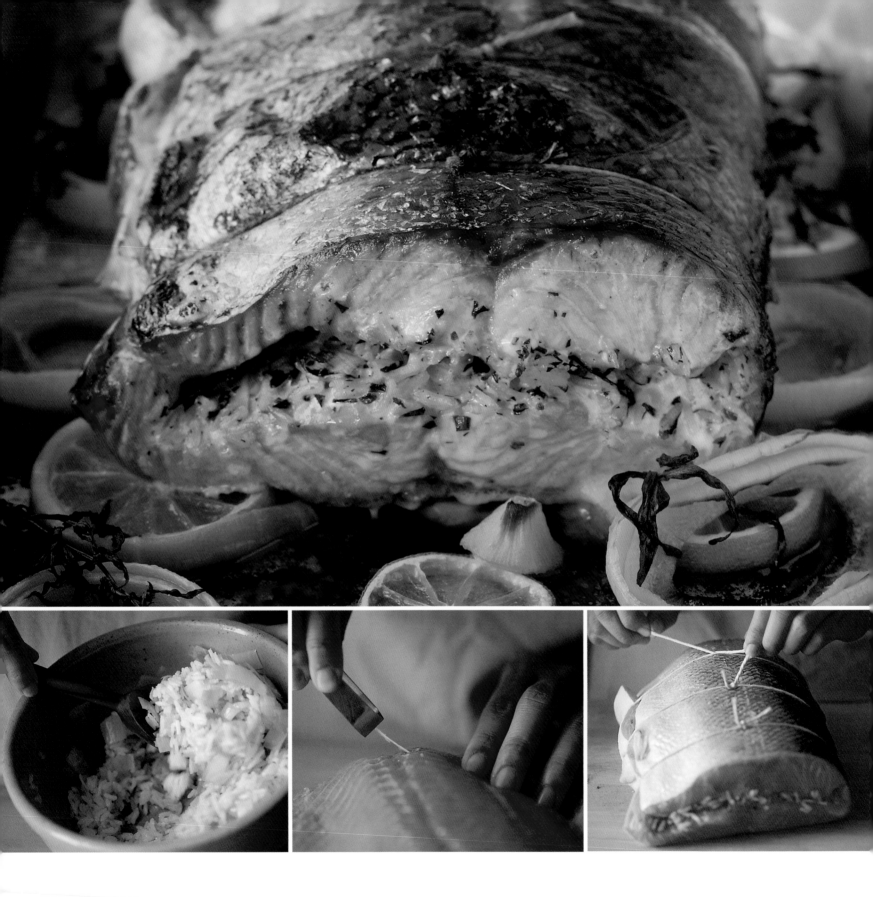

Salmon with Leek and Rice Stuffing

This dish roasts in just under an hour and is delicious served hot straight from the oven, or cold the next day with a lemony homemade mayonnaise or an Italian *salsa verde* (page 279). Pacific king salmon and Atlantic salmon are full-flavored varieties available in large pieces. Ask the fishmonger to remove the scales, fins, and rib bones from the piece of fish, but to leave the backbone, skin, and belly flaps in place.

To make the stuffing, in a small saucepan over high heat, combine the broth and lemon juice and bring to a boil. Add the rice, reduce the heat to low, cover, and cook until the rice is tender and the liquid has been absorbed, about 18 minutes. Remove from the heat and let stand, covered, for 5 minutes.

While the rice is cooking, in a frying pan over medium-low heat, melt the butter. Add the leek and sauté, stirring frequently, until soft, about 5 minutes. Remove from the heat.

When the rice is ready, add it to the leek mixture and mix well. Let cool to room temperature. Stir in the parsley, chives, tarragon, and lemon zest. Season to taste with salt and pepper.

Preheat the oven to 400°F (200°C). Generously oil the bottom of a shallow roasting pan just large enough to hold the fish.

Using tweezers or small, needle-nosed pliers, and running your fingers lightly over the surface of the fish to locate them, remove any pin bones from the fish. Rinse the fish and pat dry with paper towels. Sprinkle the cavity with salt and pepper. Spoon the rice mixture into the cavity, taking care not to pack it too tightly. Tie 3 pieces of kitchen string around the width of the fish, spacing them evenly, to secure the stuffing in place. Brush or rub the skin with olive oil.

Cut the onion into slices ¹⁄₂ inch (12 mm) thick. Thinly slice the lemon. Arrange the onion and lemon slices in the prepared pan. Place the fish on the onion-lemon bed, scatter the tarragon sprigs around the fish, and pour the wine into bottom of the pan.

Roast the fish, basting 1 or 2 times with the pan juices, until a thermometer (page 16) inserted into the thickest part away from the backbone registers 140°F (60°C), or the fish flakes when a knife is inserted into the thickest part, 50–60 minutes. Remove the pan from the oven, transfer the fish to a large platter, and tent with aluminum foil. Let rest for 15 minutes.

To serve, remove the strings. Cut the fish into slices 1 inch (2.5 cm) wide, transfer to warmed individual plates, and serve.

For the Stuffing

¾ cup (6 fl oz/180 ml) plus 2 tablespoons reduced-sodium chicken broth

2 tablespoons fresh lemon juice

¹⁄₂ cup (3¹⁄₂ oz/105 g) medium-grain or long-grained white rice

2 tablespoons unsalted butter

1 leek, white part only, coarsely chopped

¹⁄₄ cup (¹⁄₃ oz/10 g) chopped fresh flat-leaf (Italian) parsley

2 tablespoons chopped fresh chives

1 tablespoon chopped fresh tarragon

Grated zest from 1 lemon

Kosher salt and freshly ground pepper

1 center-cut piece salmon of uniform thickness, about 3 lb (1.5 kg) (see note)

Kosher salt and freshly ground pepper

Extra-virgin olive oil for coating fish

1 large yellow onion

1 large lemon

3 or 4 fresh tarragon sprigs

¹⁄₂ cup (4 fl oz/125 ml) dry white wine

Stuffed Trout Wrapped in Grape Leaves

For the Stuffing

2 tablespoons dried currants

2 teaspoons sherry vinegar

2 tablespoons unsalted butter

1 cup (2 oz/60 g) fresh bread crumbs

2 tablespoons pine nuts, toasted

1 teaspoon grated lemon zest

Kosher salt and freshly ground pepper

4 boneless whole trout, 8–10 oz (250–315 g) each, cleaned

20–24 large brined grape leaves

Kosher salt and freshly ground pepper

1 tablespoon extra-virgin olive oil

Grape leaves work two ways in this recipe: they help the trout retain their moisture and they add a pleasant brined flavor. Any leftover leaves, which keep well in their brine in the refrigerator for up to a month, can be used for wrapping other firm-fleshed fish or chicken breasts for roasting. Each diner is served a whole fish so that he or she can peel back the leaves and savor the aroma as it is released. The leaves can be eaten along with the moist, delicate trout flesh.

To make the stuffing, in a small bowl, combine the currants and vinegar and let soak for 10 minutes. In a frying pan over medium heat, melt the butter. Add the bread crumbs and sauté until lightly browned 3–4 minutes. Drain the currants and add to the pan along with the pine nuts, lemon zest, and salt and pepper to taste. Toss and stir to combine, then remove from the heat.

Preheat the oven to 400°F (200°C). Line a rimmed baking sheet with heavy-duty aluminum foil. Oil a large, flat roasting rack or 2 smaller racks and place in the prepared pan.

Using kitchen shears, remove the fins from the trout and rinse under running cold water. (The head and tail of each fish can be removed, if desired.) Drain and pat dry with paper towels.

Bring a saucepan three-fourths full of water to a boil, add the grape leaves, and blanch for 2 minutes. Drain the leaves, rinse under running cold water, place on paper towels, and pat dry with more towels.

On a work surface, arrange 3 or 4 grape leaves, ribbed side up and overlapping as needed to accommodate the length of a trout. Place a trout on the leaves. Open the trout and season the cavity with salt and pepper. Spoon one-fourth of the stuffing into the cavity, close the fish, and fold the leaves up around it. Place 2 or 3 more leaves on top of the trout if needed to encase the body completely. (It is not important to cover the head and tail completely.) Lightly brush or rub both sides of the wrapped fish with a little of the olive oil. Repeat with the remaining trout, leaves, stuffing, and oil.

Transfer the fish to the rack(s) and roast until firm to the touch, about 25 minutes. Remove the pan from the oven, divide the fish among warmed individual plates, and serve. Let each diner unwrap his or her own fish.

Whole Striped Bass with Fennel and Tomato

A whole roasted fish not only makes a dramatic presentation, but is also particularly flavorful because it is roasted on the bone. Fennel fronds, basil, and garlic are placed in the cavity to perfume the fish as it cooks. Ask your fishmonger to clean and scale the fish, leaving the head on or removing it, as you prefer. If striped bass is unavailable, red snapper, sea bass, or bream is a good substitute. The skin of the cooked fish is edible—and quite tasty—but diners may remove it by lifting it away with a table knife.

Preheat the oven to 425°F (220°C). Generously oil the bottom of a shallow roasting pan just large enough to hold the fish.

Rinse the fish and pat dry with paper towels. Cut 3 or 4 vertical slashes to the bone in each side of the fish. Brush the outside with 1 teaspoon of the olive oil. Sprinkle the outside and the cavity with salt and pepper.

Cut off the fronds from the fennel bulb and place 3 or 4 of them in the cavity. Trim off the stems from the bulb, then cut the bulb in half lengthwise and cut out the tough core portion. Using a food processor fitted with the slicing blade, slice the fennel bulb halves lengthwise paper-thin. Alternatively, cut the fennel with a sharp knife or a mandoline. Place the sliced fennel in a small bowl, add the remaining 3 teaspoons olive oil, and toss to coat evenly. Set aside.

Place 2 or 3 lemon slices, half of the garlic, half of the basil, and half of the parsley in the fish cavity. Lay the fish in the prepared pan and arrange the remaining lemon slices on top. Scatter the reserved fennel slices and the remaining garlic slices around the fish. Drizzle the wine over the vegetables and season with salt and pepper.

Roast the fish for 15 minutes. Remove from the oven and scatter the tomatoes around the fish. Continue to roast until the fish is opaque to the bone when one of the slashes in the thickest part is opened with a fork, about 10 minutes longer. Remove the pan from the oven and, using 2 large spatulas, carefully transfer the fish to a large platter. Discard the lemon slices from the top.

Check the vegetables in the roasting pan to see if the fennel is tender. If it is not, heat the vegetables for a few minutes over medium heat on the stove top. Taste and adjust the seasoning. Spoon the fennel, tomatoes, and garlic around the fish. Coarsely chop the remaining parsley, then finely shred the remaining basil.

Place the platter on the table. Starting near the center of the back, use a thin-bladed knife to loosen the top fillet from the backbone (page 286). Then, using a spatula, transfer it to a warmed individual plate. (If you are dividing the fish into 3 servings, divide the fillet accordingly.) Lift out and discard the backbone, then remove and discard the contents of the cavity. Transfer the remaining fillet to a warmed plate. Scatter the basil and parsley over the vegetables, dividing them evenly among the plates. Serve at once.

1 whole striped bass or sea bass, 1¹/₂–2 lb (750 g–1 kg), cleaned

4 teaspoons extra-virgin olive oil

Kosher salt and freshly ground pepper

1 large fennel bulb, about 1 lb (500 g)

1 lemon, thinly sliced

4–6 cloves garlic, thinly sliced

1 cup (1 oz/30 g) lightly packed fresh basil leaves

¹/₂ cup (¹/₂ oz/15 g) lightly packed flat-leaf (Italian) parsley leaves

2–3 tablespoons dry white wine

2 tomatoes, peeled, seeded, and coarsely chopped

Salt-Roasted Whole Fish

VARIATION

Salt-Roasted Whole Fish with Ginger and Soy

Substitute 2 or 3 thin slices fresh ginger for the fennel fronds and proceed as directed. Just before serving, in a small saucepan over low heat, warm together 3 tablespoons soy sauce and 1 teaspoon Asian sesame oil. Pour the mixture over the fillets, dividing it evenly.

Roasting a whole fish in a salt crust produces a juicy and flavorful result that is also healthful and low in fat. A fish weighing $1^1/_2$ to 2 pounds (750 g–1 kg) is ideal for this preparation and will serve two people generously. Non-oily, firm-fleshed fish such as striped bass are good candidates. The crust is made by mixing together coarse salt, beaten egg whites, and water to form a stiff mixture. Coarse salt varies in density according to brand; look for one with large, flaky crystals. The salt crust gets firm and hard during the roasting, so you will need a mallet or small hammer to crack it in several places before it can be lifted from the fish. Serve the fish with tartar sauce, if desired.

Preheat the oven to 400°F (200°C). Line a rimmed baking sheet with heavy-duty aluminum foil.

Rinse the fish and pat dry with paper towels. Brush or rub the skin with olive oil and sprinkle the cavity with salt. Place the lemon slices, 2 of the bay leaves, the thyme sprigs, the green onion, and the peppercorns in the cavity.

To make the salt crust, pour the salt into a large bowl. In a small bowl, whisk together the egg whites and $1/_3$ cup (3 fl oz/80 ml) water until frothy. Add the egg white mixture to the salt and stir together until the mixture holds together when pressed into a cake, adding a little more water if needed. Form a bed of the salt mixture about $1/_2$ inch (12 mm) thick on the prepared pan, making it just large enough to hold the fish. Lay the remaining 4 bay leaves in a line down the length of the salt, then place the fish on the salt bed. Spoon the remaining salt mixture, a little at a time, onto the fish, pressing down each addition to compact it before adding more. The fish should be covered with salt, although it is not necessary to cover the tail completely.

Roast the fish for 25 minutes. Remove the pan from the oven and allow the fish to rest for 5 minutes. Using a mallet, firmly tap the salt crust to break it into several pieces. Using a heavy knife, cut off the head and the tail. Remove and discard the salt crust. Starting near the center of the back, use a thin-bladed knife to loosen the top fillet from the backbone (page 286). Then, using a spatula, transfer it to a warmed individual plate, skin side up. Remove the skin with a table knife and discard. Lift out and discard the backbone, then remove and discard the contents of the cavity. Transfer the bottom fillet to a second warmed plate, again discarding the skin. Serve at once.

1 whole striped bass, tilapia, or rockfish, about 2 lb (1 kg), cleaned

Extra-virgin olive oil for coating

Kosher salt

4 or 5 thin lemon slices

6 bay leaves

2 or 3 fresh thyme sprigs, or 1 or 2 fresh fennel fronds

1 green (spring) onion, including 3–4 inches (7.5– 10 cm) of green tops, cut into 2-inch (5-cm) lengths

3 or 4 peppercorns

For the Salt Crust

6 cups (2 lb/1 kg) kosher salt

4 large egg whites

Garlicky Mustard Shrimp

1 lb (500 g) jumbo or extra-large shrimp (prawns) in the shell (11–20)

2–3 tablespoons Dijon mustard

Freshly ground pepper

2 tablespoons extra-virgin olive oil

4 cloves garlic, minced

1/4 teaspoon red pepper flakes

1 1/2 cups (9 oz/280 g) peeled, seeded, and chopped tomatoes

Kosher salt

12–15 fresh basil leaves, finely shredded

Preheat the oven to 425°F (220°C).

Working with 1 shrimp at a time and using a pair of sharp kitchen scissors, cut down along the back of the shell, keeping the shell intact. With a knife tip, lift out and discard the dark, veinlike intestinal tract. Rinse the shrimp under cold water and pat dry with paper towels.

Generously brush the shrimp with the Dijon mustard and sprinkle with 1/2 teaspoon ground pepper.

In a large, heavy ovenproof frying pan over medium heat, warm the olive oil. Add the garlic and red pepper flakes and sauté until the garlic softens but is not browned, 1–2 minutes. Add the shrimp and toss to coat with the oil. Add the tomatoes and place the pan in the oven.

Roast the shrimp, turning once about halfway through roasting and stirring the pan contents, until they are opaque throughout, 4–6 minutes. Remove the pan from the oven and season the shrimp to taste with salt.

Divide the shrimp among warmed individual plates and spoon the tomato pieces and any pan liquid over them. Sprinkle with the basil, dividing it evenly, and serve at once along with a stack of napkins for diners to use when peeling away the shrimp shells.

Heating the garlic in the olive oil brings out the fragrance of the garlic and warms the pan before the shrimp are added. Accompany the shrimp with steamed rice or coarse country bread to soak up the garlicky sauce.

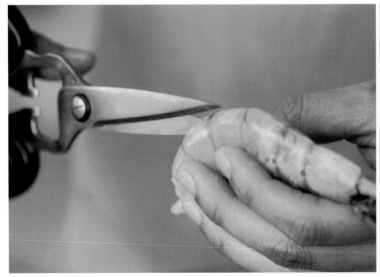

Mussels in Curry Cream Sauce

2 tablespoons unsalted butter

1 shallot, minced

2 cloves garlic, minced

2 teaspoons Madras curry powder

$1/4$ teaspoon red pepper flakes

$1/4$ cup (2 fl oz/60 ml) dry white wine

$1/4$ cup (2 fl oz/60 ml) heavy (double) cream

1 large tomato, peeled, seeded, and chopped

Kosher salt and freshly ground pepper

2 lb (1 kg) mussels (see note)

$1/4$ cup ($1/4$ oz/7 g) finely chopped fresh flat-leaf (Italian) parsley

Preheat the oven to 500°F (260°C). Place a large, heavy ovenproof frying pan in the oven and preheat it for 20 minutes. Meanwhile, in a small saucepan over medium-low heat, melt the butter. Add the shallot, garlic, curry, and red pepper flakes and sauté for 3–4 minutes. Add the wine, raise the heat to medium-high, and cook until the wine is reduced by half, 3–4 minutes. Add the cream and tomato and season to taste with salt and pepper. Set the sauce aside.

Combine the mussels and $1/4$ cup (2 fl oz/60 ml) water in a bowl, discarding any mussels that fail to close to the touch. Remove the hot frying pan from the oven and quickly but carefully pour the mussels and water into it. Roast for 1–2 minutes. Wearing a heavy oven mitt to protect your hand, give the pan a shake. Roast the mussels for another 1–2 minutes. Transfer the opened mussels to a bowl and continue to roast any unopened mussels for another 2 minutes. Add the opened mussels to the bowl and discard any that failed to open. Pour the liquid in the pan through a fine-mesh sieve lined with dampened cheesecloth (muslin) into a measuring pitcher.

Add $1/4$ cup (2 fl oz/60 ml) of the strained liquid to the sauce. (Discard the remaining liquid.) Bring the sauce to a boil over medium-high heat. Reduce the heat to low and simmer for 2–3 minutes. Taste and adjust the seasoning. Place the mussels in individual bowls and pour the hot sauce over them. Sprinkle with the parsley and serve at once.

Before cooking the mussels, give them a brisk scrubbing under cold water with a small, stiff-bristled brush. Many cultivated mussels do not have beards, the wiry threads mussels use to connect to pilings or rocks. If they are present, pull them sharply down toward the hinge of the shell, or scrape or cut them away with a knife. Make sure that all the mussels firmly close to the touch, discarding any that are open. Discard them if they are cracked or are excessively heavy, too, as they may be filled with mud or sand.

Lobster with Garlic Butter

Roasting brings out the wonderful, pure flavor of lobster. The claws take longer to cook and are roasted for a few minutes before the split bodies are added to the pan. If you do not want to boil the lobsters to kill them, lay each lobster on its hard-shell back, insert a heavy knife tip just behind the eyes, and cut down through the spinal cord. Then cut the lobster in half lengthwise, remove the claws, and proceed as directed. Cook live lobsters as soon as possible after purchase. You can store them on seaweed (from the fishmonger who sold you the lobsters) in the crisper section of the refrigerator, covered with damp paper towels, for a few hours.

Bring a large pot three-fourths full of water to a boil. Using tongs, place the lobsters head first into the boiling water. Cover the pot and cook for 2 minutes. Uncover, remove the lobsters from the pot, and let them rest for a few minutes until cool enough to handle.

Preheat the oven to 450°F (230°C). Line a rimmed baking sheet with heavy-duty aluminum foil.

Snap off the 2 large claws and remove any rubber bands or pegs. Using a sharp, heavy knife, split each lobster in half lengthwise. Remove the stomach, the small sac located between the eyes, and the intestinal vein, which runs along the back and can be lifted out with a fork or toothpick, and discard them. If you wish, retain any red roe and the green liver, called the tomalley, which are enjoyed as a delicacy.

In a small saucepan over low heat, melt the butter. Add the garlic cloves and hot-pepper sauce and cook for 2–3 minutes to infuse the butter with the garlic flavor. Remove from the heat and discard the garlic.

Place the lobster claws in the prepared pan and roast for 8 minutes. Remove the pan from the oven and add the split lobster halves, flesh side up. Brush the lobster meat generously with some of the garlic butter. Continue to roast until the flesh is opaque and starting to brown lightly, about 7 minutes.

To serve, crack the claws with a mallet or nutcracker and place the claws on a platter with the lobster halves. Or, give each diner a nutcracker and a shellfish fork and/or pick. Warm the remaining garlic butter and serve in small bowls.

2 live lobsters, 1¹/₄–1¹/₂ lb (625–750 g) each

¹/₂ cup (4 oz/125 g) unsalted butter

3 large cloves garlic, smashed

4 or 5 drops hot-pepper sauce, or to taste

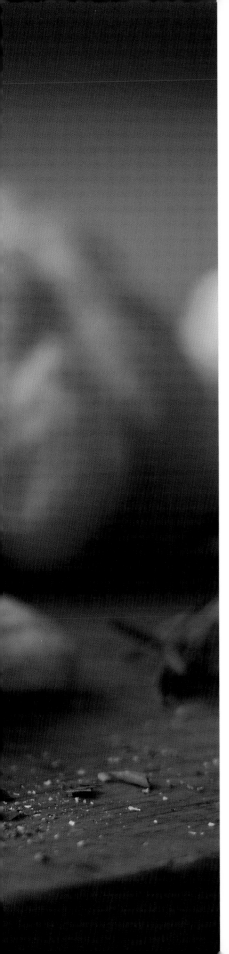

Poultry

About Poultry

A roast chicken is among the most satisfying of all main courses, and its success requires little effort. But chicken is not the only type of poultry good for roasting, as everything from a classic roast turkey to a contemporary chanterelle-stuffed roast squab illustrates.

This generous chapter features a flock of birds, including chicken—both big capons and small poussins—turkey, duck, and goose, as well as single-serving birds, such as Cornish hens, squabs, and quail. Whole birds are particularly well suited for roasting and can be prepared in a variety of ways.

ROASTING WHOLE BIRDS

Classic Roast Chicken (page 101) and Lemon-Garlic Chicken (page 102) use what is perhaps the simplest treatment: the outside of each bird is rubbed with oil and salt and pepper, and the cavity is loaded with onion and herbs. Another tried-and-true technique calls for placing seasonings or a stuffing between the skin and flesh on the breast and legs. For Chicken with Rosemary and Sweet Potatoes (page 106), butter seasoned with roasted garlic and fresh rosemary is spread beneath the skin to moisten and flavor the bird.

Brining is an old-fashioned flavoring technique that is making a welcome comeback. The soaking mixture, which is composed primarily of water and salt and is often infused with other flavorings, helps increase the juiciness of the flesh. Brining works particularly well for chicken, turkey, and goose. One of the recipes in this chapter that showcase the method is Brined Chicken (page 105), which uses a variety of spices, herbs, and aromatics to create its distinctive soaking solution. Similarly, Brined Turkey (page 133) combines basic seasonings with lemon slices, rosemary, coriander seeds, and parsley stems.

Barding, which contributes both flavor and moisture to lean meats, is another old-time technique. Although it is done in a variety of ways, barding poultry invariably calls for tying or draping strips of some type of fatty pork around the bird. Poussins with Watercress (page 144) and Bacon-Wrapped Butterflied Quail (page 138) are notable examples.

Ducks, in contrast, have considerable fat under their skin. One sound way to release some of it, yet still roast the duck to a succulent finish, is to steam the bird first, allow the skin to dry for a few hours, and then finally to roast the duck in a hot oven until the skin is crisp and golden brown. Roast Duck with Turnips (page 146) and Balsamic Duck Legs with Mushrooms (page 151) use this technique with delicious results.

Sometimes a duck or other whole bird is roasted on a "rack" made of vegetables and/or other ingredients. This temporary rack not only keeps the bird from sticking to the pan bottom, but also flavors it and later serves as an accompaniment. For Cornish Hens with Citrus Sauce (page 141), the plump hens roast atop sweet onions and oranges that then join the birds on the dinner plates.

Butterflying a chicken (page 283), which requires a sharp knife to open up and flatten the bird, and some skill to keep it in one piece, helps it roast faster and flavors it nicely, as in Crisp-Skinned Butterflied Chicken (page 108) and Caribbean-Spiced Chicken (page 111). This flattening technique also works well on small birds, such as quail (page 138).

Stuffing a whole bird adds flavor, too, as anyone who has sat down to a big stuffed roast turkey on a holiday dinner table knows. But you can also stuff various types of small poultry, such as squabs (page 142). These smaller birds have the added advantage of cooking quickly, typically in less than an hour.

ROASTING POULTRY PARTS

Some poultry parts can be stuffed as well, especially breasts. Turkey Breast Stuffed with Sage and Pancetta (page 134) and Chicken Breasts Stuffed with Spinach and Porcini (page 119) are two examples. The latter recipe also shows how barding can help keep chicken parts moist and flavorful during roasting, but here the chicken's own skin, rather than bacon or pork fat, is used. Similarly, the skin is wrapped around Sherry-Glazed Chicken Thighs (page 123).

Whenever you are cooking chicken parts, it is always more economical to start with a whole chicken and cut it up using poultry shears or a sharp knife (page 282), rather than simply buy the parts. You can use the same shears to carve a whole bird after roasting.

Marinades span both worlds—whole birds and parts—too. They typically take a minimum of time to prepare and can add flavor and help tenderize the meat before roasting begins, as in Chicken Legs, Tandoori Style (page 120).

Finally, a roasting pan, whether used for a whole bird or parts, nearly always contains flavorful drippings once the poultry has finished roasting. Use this tasty bonus to make a sauce or gravy, usually beginning with deglazing the pan with liquid (page 23), followed by reducing the mixture slightly and perhaps adding a thickener (page 24) and some flavorings. Because the pan juices have been flavored by the recipe's ingredients, the resulting sauce or gravy will complement the roasted poultry.

Roasting Poultry

Easy to prepare, recipes for roast chicken appear in almost every cuisine around the world. Cousins of the popular chicken, both large (turkey and duck) and small (poussin, squab, and quail), are naturals for entertaining or for making an everyday meal special.

Fresh poultry is always preferred over frozen for its superior flavor and texture. Whether you purchase a whole bird or parts, look for meaty, plump specimens, free of bruises, tears, or pin-feathers. Despite the occasional observation to the contrary, do not consider skin color a guide to quality. Color is a product of diet, and yellow skin is merely an indication that yellow ingredients were included in the feed, rather than a sign of nutrition.

Generally speaking, younger birds have more tender meat than older ones. In spite of their name, broiler-fryers, which average 2¹/₂ to 4¹/₂ pounds (1.75 to 2.25 kg), are suitable candidates for roasting. Roasters, which weigh in at 5 to 7 pounds (2.5 to 3.5 kg), are meatier but still tender and yield more servings per pound (500 g) than the smaller broiler-fryer. Stewing hens need moist heat

Temperature is the most reliable test of doneness. The thermometer stem should be inserted into the thickest part of the thigh, without touching bone.

to become tender and should not be roasted.

According to prevailing federal regulations, the term *organic* cannot be used directly on poultry labels, although it may appear on promotional materials. Current law prohibits the use of hormones and growth stimulants in the poultry industry, and producers raising organic birds further guarantee that their products have been nurtured on pesticide-free feed. For a bird to be labeled *natural*, it must have been minimally processed and contain no preservatives or artificial ingredients of any kind, but it may have been administered antibiotics. Any bird labeled *free-range* means that it had access to a relatively spacious, if not wide-open, environment during its lifetime, an advantage that permits exercise, which contributes to firmer, more richly flavored meat.

If you decide to purchase frozen poultry, defrost it in the refrigerator overnight, and never at room temperature (see Safety Issues, page 25). Place the bird in a tray or pan to collect any liquid as it thaws. Thawing times vary from 24 hours for an average-sized chicken up to 4 days for a large turkey. Do not be concerned if you purchase a fresh bird that feels partially frozen. Poultry can be chilled to 26°F (13°C), a temperature that considerably increases its shelf life, and still be sold as fresh.

When serving whole birds, allow about 1 pound (500 g) per person. If you are serving bone-in poultry parts, plan on 1 or 2 pieces for each diner; for boneless parts, such as chicken thighs or breast halves, figure on using about 6 ounces (185 g) for each serving.

Duck breasts, unlike chicken breasts, are done when the meat is pinkish red. The skin should be brown and crisp.

PREPARING POULTRY FOR ROASTING

Rinse all poultry well (including the inside of whole birds) under running cold water before roasting. This will clean and refresh the bird, but not thoroughly remove harmful bacteria. If you splash any water on countertops during this step, promptly wash them with hot, soapy water to prevent bacterial cross-contamination. Also, always wash your hands and any preparation areas and tools, such as carving boards and knives, that may have come into contact with raw poultry. Most recipes call for patting rinsed poultry dry with paper towels before proceeding. Any moisture will inhibit the skin from browning and crisping.

Trussing a whole bird with kitchen string before it goes into the oven will ensure it has a uniform appearance when finished roasting (see page 284 for instructions). For a dinner with guests, trussing will make the most appealing presentation. However, trussing also compacts a bird, which sometimes can create areas, such as the inner thigh joint, that will not receive even heat and thus be underdone when the rest of the bird is ready. Turning the bird two or three times during roasting will increase consistent heat exposure. Not everyone wants to bother with turning the hot, slippery bird, which can be difficult with turkeys and large chickens. Therefore, turning, like many other cooking techniques, is often a matter of personal choice.

TESTING FOR DONENESS

There are considerable differences of opinion surrounding the optimum doneness temperature for roasted whole poultry. It is essential, however, that the temperature be above the point at which salmonella bacteria are killed. Whole turkey and chicken should reach an internal temperature of 170° to 175°F (77° to 80°C), as the dark meat typically needs a little extra time in the oven to become tender. You can protect the breast area of a turkey from drying out by tenting it with aluminum foil during the last hour of roasting.

Whole goose is cooked to 170°F and duck to 170° to 180°F (77° to 82°C), temperatures that ensure that all of the meat is evenly cooked. Individual boneless duck breasts are pan-roasted until medium-rare. The breasts are tested by using a small, sharp knife to make a tiny cut into the center; the flesh should be a pinkish red.

To use a meat thermometer for whole birds, insert the stem into the thickest part of the thigh, underneath the drumstick joint. Be sure that the tip reaches the center of the fleshy area and that it does not touch a bone. The thigh of Cornish hens is not meaty enough to be tested with a thermometer, so take the temperature in the thickest part of the breast; it should register 160°F (70°C).

To test a small bird, such as a poussin or

Small birds such as a poussin are difficult to test with a thermometer. Instead, insert the tip of a knife into the thigh joint. The released juices should be clear rather than pink.

quail, pierce the meat at the thigh joint with the tip of a sharp knife. If the juices run clear (place a bird on a white plate to judge the color accurately), the poultry is done. The same test applies to squab, but because this game bird is best when cooked medium-rare, the juices should have a rose tint.

In all cases, allow the roasted bird to rest in a draft-free place in the kitchen before carving. Cornish hens, squabs, quail, and other small birds need only 5 minutes, while whole chicken and duck and boneless roasts, such as turkey breast, should rest for 10 to 15 minutes. Large turkeys should rest for 15 to 20 minutes. Keep in mind that the internal temperature of whole roasted birds will rise 5° to 10°F (3° to 6°C) during resting (the higher figure is for a turkey), so you need to remove them from the oven when they still register slightly below the desired temperature.

Classic Roast Chicken

Nearly everyone likes roast chicken, whether it is served hot and golden brown right from the oven or it is enjoyed the next day in a sandwich or salad. Roasting the bird at a high temperature produces crispy brown skin and moist meat without having to baste or turn the chicken during cooking. Using a roasting rack also helps crisp the skin on all sides. If you like, you can truss the chicken (page 284). Doing this will increase the roasting time by a few minutes because the bird is held in a more compact mass.

If the giblets and neck are in the chicken cavity, remove them and reserve for another use or discard. Remove and discard any pockets of fat from the cavity. Rinse the chicken and pat dry with paper towels. Brush or rub the chicken all over with olive oil, and season inside and out with salt and pepper. Place the onion, parsley, and thyme in the cavity. Tuck the wing tips under the back. Tie the legs together with kitchen string.

Oil a V-shaped roasting rack and place it in a roasting pan just large enough to hold the chicken. Place the chicken on the rack and allow it to stand at room temperature for 30 minutes. Position an oven rack in the lower third of the oven and preheat to 500°F (260°C).

Roast the chicken until a thermometer (page 16) inserted into the thickest part of a thigh away from the bone registers 170°–175°F (77°–80°C), 50–60 minutes.

Remove the pan from the oven. Slip the handle of a long wooden spoon or a pair of tongs in the chicken cavity and carefully tip the bird, draining the liquid from the cavity into the pan. Transfer the chicken to a platter or carving board, remove the string, and tent with aluminum foil. Let rest for 10–15 minutes.

Discard the contents of the cavity, then carve the chicken (page 285) and serve.

1 chicken, 4¹/₂–5 lb (2.25–2.5 kg)

Extra-virgin olive oil for coating

Kosher salt and freshly ground pepper

¹/₂ small yellow onion, cut into chunks

4 or 5 fresh flat-leaf (Italian) parsley sprigs

4 large fresh thyme sprigs

Lemon-Garlic Chicken

1 chicken, 3$^{1}/_{2}$–4 lb
(1.75–2 kg), with giblets

1 large lemon

Kosher salt and freshly
ground black pepper

8–10 cloves garlic

1 bay leaf

1 yellow onion, coarsely
chopped

2 teaspoons extra-virgin
olive oil

For the Sauce

1 cup (8 fl oz/250 ml)
reduced-sodium chicken
broth

Kosher salt and freshly
ground pepper

1 tablespoon unsalted butter

Remove the giblets and neck from the chicken cavity. Reserve the liver for another use or discard. Refrigerate the neck, gizzard, and heart until needed. Remove and discard any pockets of fat from the cavity. Rinse the chicken and pat dry with paper towels. Cut the lemon in half; squeeze the juice from 1 lemon half and reserve. Cut the lemon shell into 3 or 4 strips and place them inside the chicken cavity. Thinly slice the remaining lemon half and reserve. Sprinkle $^{1}/_{2}$ teaspoon salt and some freshly ground pepper into the cavity. Place 2 or 3 garlic cloves and the bay leaf in the cavity. Tuck the wing tips under the back. Truss as directed on page 284. Rub the chicken all over with 1$^{1}/_{2}$ teaspoons salt. Place the chicken on a plate, cover lightly with plastic wrap, and refrigerate for at least 4–5 hours or for up to overnight.

About 30 minutes before roasting, remove the chicken from the refrigerator. Preheat the oven to 375°F (190°C). Oil a V-shaped roasting rack and place it in a roasting pan just large enough to hold the chicken. Put the reserved giblets and neck in a bowl. Add the lemon slices, onion, olive oil, and remaining garlic cloves and toss to distribute the oil evenly. Spread the mixture in the bottom of the roasting pan. Place the chicken on one side on the rack.

Roast the chicken for 20 minutes. Remove the pan from the oven and, using 2 thick pads of paper towels, carefully turn the chicken on its other side. Continue to roast for 20 minutes longer. Remove from the oven again, turn the chicken breast side up, and pour the reserved lemon juice over it. Continue to roast until a thermometer (page 16) inserted into the thickest part of a thigh away from the bone registers 170°–175°F (77°–80°C), about 25 minutes longer. Remove the pan from the oven. Slip the handle of a long wooden spoon or a pair of tongs in the chicken cavity and carefully tip the bird, draining the liquid from the cavity into the roasting pan. Transfer the chicken to a platter or carving board, remove the trussing strings, and tent with aluminum foil. Let rest for 10–15 minutes.

Meanwhile, make the sauce: Deglaze the roasting pan as directed on page 23, using the broth. Pour the contents of the pan through a coarse-mesh sieve into a small, wide saucepan. Discard the giblets and neck. Then, using a spoon, press on the contents of the sieve to extract as much liquid as possible. Bring to a boil over high heat and cook until reduced by half, 8–10 minutes. Season to taste with salt and pepper. Remove from the heat and whisk in the butter.

Discard the contents of the cavity, then carve the chicken (page 285) and serve. Pour the sauce into a warmed bowl and pass at the table.

Many French cooks lightly salt poultry and meat several hours before roasting to draw out moisture and add flavor. That approach is followed here, then the chicken is roasted in a moderate oven and turned twice to produce even browning and moist meat. Onion, garlic cloves, and lemon slices provide the base for a lemony sauce to serve over the chicken.

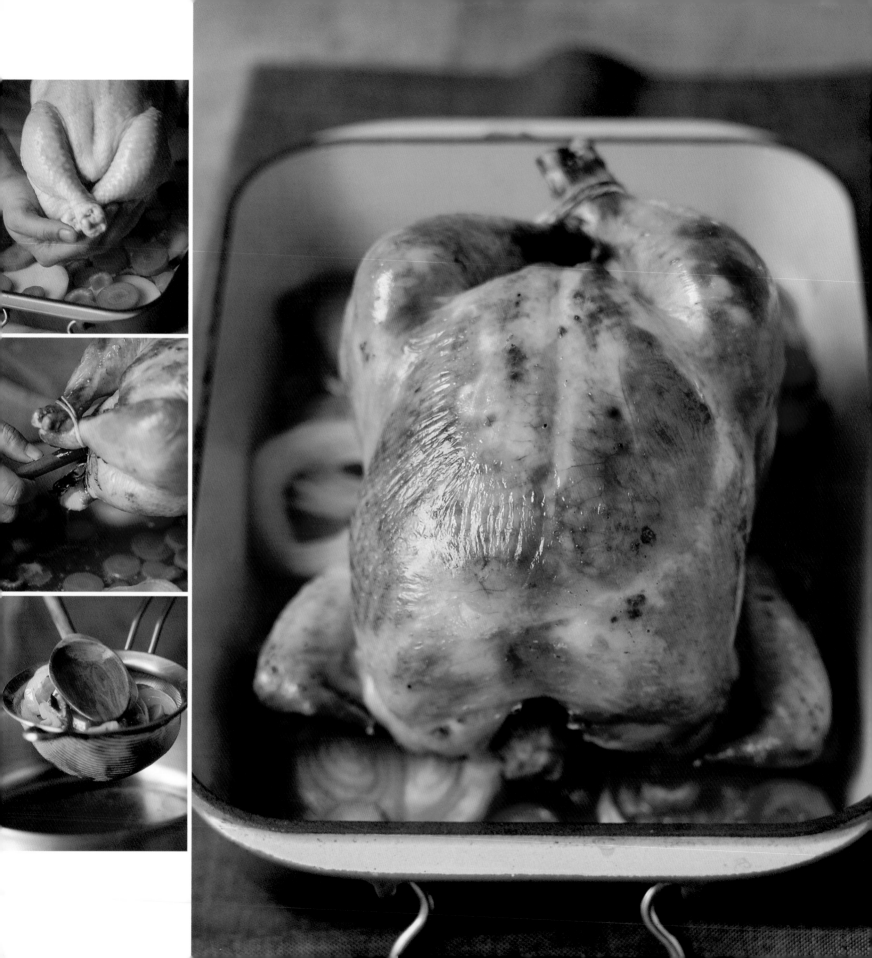

Brined Chicken

Brining, an old-fashioned technique originally used as a method of preserving, has come back into vogue to enhance the flavor and moistness of poultry, such as this whole chicken, and lean cuts of meat. The salt in the brine penetrates the meat quickly and swells the muscle fibers, which allows more water to penetrate, keeping the meat juicier during roasting and seasoning it all the way through. Choose a container about 3 inches (7.5 cm) taller and a little wider than the chicken so that the bird can be totally submerged in the brine. Salt, sugar, herbs, spices, and aromatics make up the basic brine, but there are myriad variations. It is important to dissolve the sugar and salt thoroughly, and for the brine to be at cool room temperature before adding the chicken. Here, vegetables make a natural roasting rack for the chicken.

Combine the salt, sugar, and 2 qt (2 l) room-temperature water in a nonreactive container (see note). Stir until the salt and sugar dissolve. Add the celery seeds, peppercorns, 1-inch tarragon sprigs, leek, and orange zest strips and stir well.

Remove the giblets and neck from the chicken cavity. Reserve the giblets for another use or discard, and reserve the neck for the roasting pan. Remove and discard any pockets of fat from the cavity. Rinse the chicken, then immerse, breast side down, in the brine. If needed, invert a small plate on top of the chicken to keep it submerged. Cover the container with plastic wrap and refrigerate for 24 hours.

Remove the chicken from the brine, rinse, pat dry with paper towels, and let stand at room temperature for 30 minutes before roasting. Preheat the oven to 425°F (220°C). Select a roasting pan just large enough to hold the chicken. Make a layer of the onion, celery, and carrot slices and the neck in the bottom of the pan, forming a natural roasting rack. Place the remaining 4 or 5 tarragon sprigs in the chicken cavity. Tuck the wing tips under the back. Tie the legs together with kitchen string. Place the chicken, breast side up, on top of the vegetables.

Roast the chicken until a thermometer (page 16) inserted into the thickest part of a thigh away from the bone registers 170°–175°F (77°–80°C), about 1 hour. Remove the pan from the oven. Slip the handle of a long wooden spoon or a pair of tongs in the chicken cavity and carefully tip the bird, draining the liquid from the cavity into the roasting pan. Transfer the chicken to a platter or carving board, remove the strings, and tent with aluminum foil. Let rest for 10–15 minutes.

Meanwhile, make the sauce: Deglaze the roasting pan as directed on page 23, using the broth and orange juice and adding the shallot. Pour the contents of the pan through a coarse-mesh sieve into a small, wide saucepan. Discard the neck. Then, using a spoon, press on the contents of the sieve to extract as much liquid as possible. Bring to a boil over high heat and cook until reduced by half, about 8 minutes. Season to taste with salt and white pepper. Remove from the heat and whisk in the butter. Keep warm.

Discard the contents of the cavity, then carve the chicken (page 285) and serve. Pour the sauce into a warmed bowl and pass at the table.

1/3 cup (3 oz/90 g) kosher salt

1/3 cup (2 1/2 oz/75 g) firmly packed brown sugar

2 teaspoons celery seeds

1/2 teaspoon black peppercorns, lightly crushed

4 or 5 fresh tarragon sprigs, cut into 1-inch (2.5-cm) lengths, plus 4 or 5 sprigs

1 leek, white part and about 3 inches (7.5 cm) of green, cut into slices 1/2 inch (12 mm) thick

Zest of 1 orange, removed with a vegetable peeler in long strips

1 chicken, 3 1/2–4 lb (1.75–2 kg), with giblets

1 yellow onion, sliced

1 large celery stalk, thinly sliced

1 large carrot, peeled and thinly sliced

For the Sauce

1 cup (8 fl oz/250 ml) reduced-sodium chicken broth

Juice of 1 orange

1 tablespoon minced shallot

Kosher salt and freshly ground white pepper

2 tablespoons unsalted butter

Chicken with Rosemary and Sweet Potatoes

1 chicken, 3¹/₂–4 lb (1.75–2 kg)

1 head roasted garlic (page 279)

2 tablespoons plus 1 teaspoon unsalted butter, at room temperature

1–2 teaspoons finely chopped fresh rosemary

Kosher salt and freshly ground pepper

2 sweet potatoes, about 1¹/₂ lb (750 g) total, peeled and cut into ³/₄-inch (2-cm) chunks

2 tablespoons extra-virgin olive oil

An aromatic mixture of fresh rosemary, roasted garlic, and butter is stuffed under the skin to flavor the chicken. Chunks of sweet potato are put in the pan alongside the chicken and during roasting are basted by the flavorful chicken juices. Only a salad is necessary to complete the meal.

About 30 minutes before roasting, remove the chicken from the refrigerator. Preheat the oven to 400°F (200°C). Oil a roasting pan just large enough to hold the chicken and potatoes. Oil a V-shaped roasting rack and place it in the prepared pan. If the giblets and neck are in the chicken cavity, remove them and reserve for another use or discard. Remove and discard any pockets of fat from the cavity. Rinse the chicken and pat dry with paper towels.

With the chicken breast side up, and starting at the neck cavity, slip your fingers under the skin and gently separate the skin from the breast meat on both sides, being careful not to tear the skin. Then, starting at the body cavity, gently separate the skin from the thigh and drumstick meat. Separate the roasted garlic cloves and squeeze the softened pulp into a small bowl. Add the 2 tablespoons butter and the rosemary and mash together with a fork. Season with salt and pepper. Push this mixture under the chicken skin, distributing it evenly over the breast and legs. Season the cavity with salt and pepper. Tie the legs together with kitchen string. Tuck the wing tips under the back. Rub the chicken all over with the remaining 1 teaspoon butter. In a bowl, toss together the sweet potato chunks and olive oil and season with salt and pepper. Place the chicken, breast side up, on the rack and scatter the sweet potatoes in the bottom of the pan.

Roast the chicken for 45 minutes. Remove the pan from the oven. If the sweet potato chunks can easily be pierced with a knife, transfer them to a serving dish and keep warm; otherwise, turn them and continue to roast with the chicken until a thermometer (page 16) inserted into the thickest part of a thigh away from the bone registers 170°–175°F (77°–80°C), 15–20 minutes longer. Remove the pan from the oven and transfer any remaining sweet potatoes to the serving dish. Slip the handle of a long wooden spoon or a pair of tongs in the chicken cavity and carefully tip the bird, draining the liquid from the cavity into the roasting pan. Transfer the chicken to a platter or carving board, remove the string, and tent with aluminum foil. Let rest for 10–15 minutes. Carve the chicken (page 285) and serve with the potatoes.

Crisp-Skinned Butterflied Chicken

**1 small chicken, 2¹/₂–3 lb
(1.25–1.5 kg)**

For the Marinade

**2 green (spring) onions,
including tender green tops,
cut into 1-inch (2.5-cm)
pieces**

2 cloves garlic, smashed

**¹/₄ cup (2 fl oz/60 ml) dry
vermouth or dry white wine**

**2 tablespoons extra-virgin
olive oil**

**1 teaspoon fresh thyme
leaves**

**Kosher salt and freshly
ground pepper**

If the giblets and neck are in the chicken cavity, remove them and reserve for another use or discard. Butterfly the chicken as directed on page 283. Rinse the chicken, pat dry with paper towels, and place in a nonreactive dish.

To make the marinade, in a blender or food processor, combine the green onions, garlic, vermouth, olive oil, thyme, and ¹/₂ teaspoon each salt and pepper. Process until well combined.

Pour the marinade into the dish holding the chicken, turn to coat, cover, and refrigerate for 3–4 hours, turning the chicken once or twice.

About 30 minutes before roasting, remove the chicken from the refrigerator and take it out of the dish. Pat the chicken dry with paper towels. Discard the marinade. Preheat the oven to 450°F (230°C). Select a roasting pan just large enough to hold the chicken and line with heavy-duty aluminum foil. Oil a flat roasting rack and place it in the prepared pan. Place the chicken, skin side up, on the rack.

Roast the chicken until a thermometer (page 16) inserted into the thickest part of a thigh away from the bone registers 170°–175°F (77°–80°C), 40–45 minutes. Remove the pan from the oven, transfer the chicken to a platter, and tent with aluminum foil. Let rest for 10 minutes. Cut the chicken in half by cutting along each side of the breastbone with a sharp knife or poultry shears. Serve at once.

A small chicken roasts quickly when butterflied, a technique that involves cutting along the length of both sides of the backbone, removing it, and then flattening the bird to create a uniform thickness for even roasting. This useful technique is also known as spatchcocking, an old culinary term that is believed to have originated in Ireland. Here, the bird goes into a very hot oven, which delivers wonderfully crisp skin and succulent meat for two people in only about 45 minutes. You can also use Cornish hens, which will cook in about 30 minutes.

Caribbean-Spiced Chicken

The marinade for this Caribbean-inspired chicken goes together quickly in a food processor or blender. Traditionally, fiery-hot habanero chiles are among the ingredients, but a little hot-pepper sauce or milder serrano chiles will add piquancy with less fire. Serve the chicken with red beans and rice and a fresh-fruit salsa to make a perfect summer supper fare.

If the giblets and neck are in the chicken cavities, remove them and reserve for another use or discard. Butterfly the chickens as directed on page 283. Rinse the chickens and pat dry with paper towels. Place in a large nonreactive dish.

To make the marinade, in a blender or food processor, combine the canola oil, soy sauce, lime juice, vinegar, yellow onion, green onions, garlic, brown sugar, thyme, hot-pepper sauce, allspice, coriander, ginger, cinnamon, cloves, $^1/_2$ teaspoon salt, and $^1/_4$ teaspoon pepper. Process until smooth.

Pour the marinade into the dish holding the chickens, turn to coat, cover, and refrigerate for 4–6 hours, turning the chickens once or twice.

About 30 minutes before roasting, remove the chickens from the refrigerator and take them out of the dish. Discard the marinade. Preheat the oven to 400°F (200°C). Line a rimmed baking sheet with heavy-duty aluminum foil. Oil a flat rack large enough to hold both chickens side by side and place in the prepared pan. Place the chickens, skin side up, on the rack.

Roast the chickens until a thermometer (page 16) inserted into the thickest part of a thigh away from the bone registers 170°–175°F (77°–80°C), about 50 minutes. Remove the pan from the oven, transfer the chickens to a platter, and tent with aluminum foil. Let rest for 10 minutes.

To serve, cut each chicken in half by cutting along each side of the breastbone with a sharp knife or poultry shears. If desired, cut each half in half again, separating the breast and wing from the thigh and leg. Serve at once.

2 chickens, about 3$^1/_2$ lb (1.75 kg) each

For the Marinade

$^1/_4$ cup (2 fl oz/60 ml) canola oil

$^1/_4$ cup (2 fl oz/60 ml) soy sauce

2 tablespoons fresh lime juice

2 tablespoons cider vinegar

1 small yellow onion, chopped

3 green (spring) onions, including tender green tops, minced

3 cloves garlic, chopped

1 tablespoon firmly packed brown sugar

2 teaspoons fresh thyme leaves

1 teaspoon hot-pepper sauce, preferably with habanero chiles, or 2 serrano chiles, seeded and minced

2 teaspoons ground allspice

1 teaspoon ground coriander

$^1/_2$ teaspoon ground ginger

$^1/_4$ teaspoon ground cinnamon

$^1/_4$ teaspoon ground cloves

Kosher salt and freshly ground pepper

Tuscan-Style Chicken

1 chicken, 3–3¹/₂ lb (1.5–1.75 kg)

For the Marinade

2 tablespoons extra-virgin olive oil

2 tablespoons balsamic vinegar

¹/₂ teaspoon minced fresh oregano

Kosher salt and freshly ground pepper

This is a variation on the classic Tuscan method of cooking chicken under a brick to produce a moist, tender bird with handsome brown, crisp skin. Some versions call for using aluminum foil–wrapped bricks, which are heated and used as weights, but the hot bricks are awkward to handle. A good alternative is to use two large cast-iron frying pans or one heavy ovenproof frying pan (not nonstick) and one cast-iron one and to preheat them thoroughly in a hot oven. Be sure to use heavy oven mitts to handle the hot pans. Cornish game hens are also excellent butterflied and roasted in this manner. They will cook in only 30 minutes.

If the giblets and neck are in the chicken cavity, remove them and reserve for another use or discard. Butterfly the chicken as directed on page 283. Rinse the chicken and pat dry with paper towels.

To make the marinade, in a nonreactive dish large enough to hold the chicken, stir together the olive oil, vinegar, oregano, and ¹/₂ teaspoon each salt and pepper. Add the chicken, turn to coat, cover, and refrigerate for 2–3 hours, turning the chicken once or twice.

About 30 minutes before roasting, remove the chicken from the refrigerator and take it out of the dish. Pat dry with paper towels. Discard the marinade.

Preheat the oven to 500°F (260°C). Place 2 large frying pans (see note) in the oven to heat until very hot, about 20 minutes. Lightly oil one side of a piece of aluminum foil large enough to cover the top of the chicken. When the pans are very hot, carefully place the chicken, skin side down, in one of the hot pans. Place the foil, oiled side down, over the chicken and immediately place the second hot pan on top of the chicken.

Roast the chicken, without turning, until it is browned and crisp, 35–40 minutes. Remove the top pan and the aluminum foil. A thermometer (page 16) inserted into the thickest part of a thigh away from the bone registers 170°–175°F (77°–80°C). Transfer the chicken to a platter, and tent with fresh aluminum foil. Let rest for 10 minutes.

To serve, cut the chicken in half along each side of the breastbone with a sharp knife or poultry shears. If desired, cut each half in half again, separating the breast and wing from the thigh and leg. Serve at once.

Chicken Breasts with Vegetables and White Wine

A simple marinade of olive oil and lemon juice and roasting the chicken with its skin and bone intact add extra flavor and moistness. The rib bones of the breast form a natural roasting rack. Your favorite vegetables can be used in this recipe so long as they are uniformly cut. To ensure that all the vegetables are tender when the chicken is ready, the firmer ones are boiled briefly before they are placed in the oven.

Rinse the chicken breasts and pat dry with paper towels. In a nonreactive dish large enough to hold the breasts, stir together 3 tablespoons of the olive oil, the lemon zest and juice, the red pepper flakes, $1/2$ teaspoon salt, and black pepper to taste. Add the chicken breasts to the marinade, turn to coat, cover, and refrigerate for 2–3 hours, turning the breasts once or twice. About 20 minutes before roasting, remove the chicken from the refrigerator, take it out of the dish, and pat dry with paper towels. Discard the marinade. Preheat the oven to 500°F (260°C). Line a large rimmed baking sheet with heavy-duty aluminum foil.

Bring a saucepan three-fourths full of water to a boil over high heat. Add the potatoes and cook until almost tender, 7–10 minutes. Using a slotted spoon, transfer the potatoes to a plate lined with paper towels and blot dry. Add the carrots to the boiling water and cook until almost tender, about 5 minutes. Transfer the carrots to the same plate. In a large bowl, combine the mushrooms, bell pepper, potatoes, and carrots. Add 3 tablespoons of the oil and the garlic, season with salt and pepper, and toss to coat the vegetables evenly. Add the thyme sprigs. Pour the vegetables onto one end of the prepared pan, spreading them out in a single layer. Place in the oven and roast for 10 minutes.

In a large frying pan over medium-high heat, warm the remaining 2 tablespoons oil. Add the chicken breasts, skin side down, and sauté until the skin is nicely browned, 3–4 minutes. Turn the chicken and cook for about 1 minute longer. Remove the baking sheet from the oven and transfer the chicken breasts to the uncovered end. Reserve the drippings in the frying pan. Roast until the juices run clear when a breast is pierced with a sharp knife, 12–14 minutes.

Meanwhile, deglaze the frying pan as directed on page 23, pouring out and discarding all but 1 tablespoon of the fat and adding the broth and the $1/2$ cup wine. Cook over high heat to evaporate the alcohol and reduce the liquid slightly, 3–4 minutes. Dissolve the arrowroot in 1 tablespoon water. Gradually add the arrowroot mixture and cook until the sauce thickens slightly, about 2 minutes (page 24). If the sauce is too thick, thin with 1 or 2 tablespoons wine. Season to taste with salt and pepper.

Place the chicken breasts on warmed individual plates and spoon a little sauce over each breast. Serve the vegetables alongside.

4 skin-on, bone-in chicken breast halves, about 10 oz (315 g) each

8 tablespoons (4 fl oz/ 125 ml) extra-virgin olive oil

Zest of 1 lemon, grated

2 tablespoons fresh lemon juice

$1/4$ teaspoon red pepper flakes, or to taste

Kosher salt and freshly ground black pepper

1 lb (500 g) Yukon gold potatoes, unpeeled, cut into $1^1/2$-inch (4-cm) cubes

$3/4$ lb (375 g) carrots, peeled and cut into $1^1/2$-inch (4-cm) pieces

$1/2$ lb (250 g) fresh cremini mushrooms, each about 1 inch (2.5 cm) diameter, brushed clean and stemmed

1 large red bell pepper (capsicum), seeded and cut into 1-inch (2.5-cm) squares

2 large cloves garlic, minced

2 or 3 fresh thyme sprigs

$1/2$ cup (4 fl oz/125 ml) reduced-sodium chicken broth

$1/2$ cup (4 fl oz/125 ml) dry white wine, or as needed

1 teaspoon arrowroot

Chicken Breasts Stuffed with Prosciutto, Provolone, and Sage

4 skinless, boneless chicken breast halves, 6–7 oz (185–220 g) each

4 thin slices prosciutto

8 thin slices provolone cheese

8 fresh sage leaves

4 strips roasted red bell pepper (page 294), each about 2$^{1}/_{2}$ inches (6 cm) long and $^{1}/_{2}$ inch (12 mm) wide

2 teaspoons extra-virgin olive oil

Kosher salt and freshly ground pepper

$^{1}/_{4}$ cup (2 fl oz/60 ml) dry Marsala

$^{1}/_{2}$ cup (4 fl oz/125 ml) reduced-sodium chicken broth

Hungarian sweet paprika for sprinkling

Preheat the oven to 400°F (200°C). Oil a roasting pan just large enough to hold the chicken breasts in a single layer.

Rinse the chicken breasts and pat dry with paper towels. Using a sharp knife, and starting at the thickest side of a breast, make a horizontal incision about 1 inch (2.5 cm) long. Cut down the middle of the breast toward the opposite end, turning the knife to enlarge the pocket without cutting through the opposite side. The interior pocket should be about 1$^{1}/_{2}$ inches wide (4 cm) and 3 inches (7.5 cm) long. Repeat with the remaining breasts.

Fold each prosciutto slice in half. Cut 4 of the cheese slices into strips about 1 inch (2.5 cm) wide by 2$^{1}/_{2}$ inches (6 cm) long. Reserve the remaining 4 cheese slices. Place 2 sage leaves on top of each folded prosciutto slice and top with 1 red pepper strip and the strips from 1 cheese slice. Fold the prosciutto around the cheese, forming a compact log, and push it into the pocket of a chicken breast. Stuff the remaining chicken breasts in the same way. Lightly brush or rub the chicken breasts on both sides with the olive oil and season with salt and pepper. Arrange the breasts in the prepared pan and pour in the Marsala and broth.

Roast the chicken breasts for 12 minutes, then place the reserved cheese slices on top of the chicken breasts and sprinkle with paprika. Continue to roast until the cheese melts and the juices run clear when a breast is pierced with a sharp knife, about 5 minutes longer.

Remove the pan from the oven and transfer the chicken to a warmed platter or warmed individual plates. Spoon the pan juices over the chicken. Serve at once.

Stuffing chicken breasts with a savory mixture adds flavor and moistness to the meat. Wrapping the cheese slices and bell pepper strips in prosciutto makes a flavorful package that can easily be slipped into the breasts. The stuffed breasts roast in the oven, basted with Marsala and chicken broth, to make a light sauce.

Chicken Breasts Stuffed with Spinach and Porcini

In this recipe, the skin is removed from each boneless breast, the breast is stuffed and rolled, and then the skin is wrapped around the roll to keep it moist as it roasts. This is a form of barding, which ensures a juicier, more flavorful result. You can serve these rolls hot from the oven as a main dish or cold as an elegant appetizer for eight: cut each roll into slices $1/2$ inch (12 mm) thick, fan out the slices on a plate, and serve with a mayonnaise seasoned with minced fresh herbs and with some multicolor cherry tomatoes.

In a bowl, combine the porcini with hot water just to cover. Let stand for 10 minutes to soften. Remove the mushrooms from the liquid, squeezing out any excess moisture, and chop. Line a fine-mesh sieve with cheesecloth (muslin) and strain the soaking liquid into a measuring pitcher; set aside. Bring a large saucepan three-fourths full of water to a boil, add the spinach leaves, and cook until tender, 3–4 seconds. Drain and rinse until cool. Drain again and squeeze as dry as possible, then blot on paper towels. Finely chop the spinach. In a frying pan over medium-low heat, warm the 1 tablespoon olive oil. Add the shallot and sauté until softened, 2–3 minutes. Raise the heat to medium-high, add the spinach and mushrooms, and cook until the mixture is dry, 2–3 minutes. Add the Pernod and cook for 1 minute longer. Season to taste with salt and pepper. Remove from the heat and let cool to room temperature. Stir in the ricotta.

Preheat the oven to 400°F (200°C). Rinse the chicken breasts and pat dry with paper towels. Remove the skin from each breast and reserve. To butterfly each breast, using a sharp knife, and starting at the thin, long side of the breast, cut it in half horizontally, stopping just short of cutting it all the way through. Open the breast flat, place between 2 sheets of plastic wrap, and pound with a meat pounder until it is an even thickness of about $1/4$ inch (6 mm). Season the top surface of each flattened breast with salt and pepper. Spoon 3–4 tablespoons of the stuffing about $3/4$ inch (2 cm) from one long edge. Roll up the breast, folding in the ends. Wrap the reserved skin around each roll and secure with 2 lengths of kitchen string. Select an ovenproof frying pan just large enough to hold the rolls. Place over medium-high heat and add the 2 teaspoons olive oil. Add the chicken rolls and sear, turning as necessary, until the skin is evenly browned on all sides, 3–4 minutes. Place the pan in the oven and roast the rolls until the juices run clear when a breast is pierced with a sharp knife, about 8 minutes.

In a wide saucepan over high heat, combine $1/4$ cup (2 fl oz/60 ml) of the reserved mushroom soaking liquid, the wine, and the broth. Boil until reduced by about half, 8–10 minutes. Remove the pan from the oven, turn the rolls, and add the sauce to the pan. Roast until the rolls are firm to the touch, 5–6 minutes. Transfer the rolls to a warmed platter, remove the strings, and tent with aluminum foil. Let rest for 5 minutes. Pour the sauce in the frying pan through a medium-mesh sieve into the wide saucepan. Bring to a simmer over low heat, stir in the butter until melted, and season to taste with salt and pepper. Divide the rolls among warmed individual plates, top with the sauce, and serve.

$1/2$ oz (15 g) dried porcino mushrooms

$1/2$ lb (250 g) baby spinach leaves

1 tablespoon extra-virgin olive oil, plus 2 teaspoons

1 large shallot, minced

1 tablespoon Pernod or brandy

Kosher salt and freshly ground pepper

$1/4$ cup (2 oz/60 g) ricotta cheese

4 skin-on, boneless chicken breast halves, about 6 oz (185 g) each

$1/4$ cup (2 fl oz/60 ml) dry white wine

$1/2$ cup (4 fl oz/125 ml) reduced-sodium chicken broth

1 tablespoon unsalted butter

Chicken Legs, Tandoori Style

8 skinless, bone-in chicken legs

Kosher salt

Juice of 1 lemon

For the Marinade

1 cup (8 oz/250 g) plain whole-milk yogurt

1/3 cup (1 1/2 oz/45 g) chopped yellow onion

1–2 serrano chiles, thinly sliced

1 tablespoon grated, peeled fresh ginger

1 large clove garlic, thinly sliced

7 or 8 large fresh mint leaves, cut into ribbons

1 teaspoon ground cumin

1 teaspoon ground coriander

1 teaspoon Hungarian sweet paprika

1 teaspoon garam masala

1/2 teaspoon ground turmeric

Freshly ground pepper

2 tablespoons unsalted butter, melted

2 tablespoons fresh lemon juice

Rinse the chicken legs and pat dry with paper towels. Using a sharp knife, make a cut to the bone around the bottom of the drumstick about 3/4 inch (2 cm) from the end. Remove the flesh and any remaining skin below the cut. In each thigh, cut 2 or 3 slashes about 3/4 inch (2 cm) apart to the bone and cut 1 slash in the meaty part of each drumstick. Sprinkle the chicken with 1 teaspoon salt, pushing some of the salt into the slashes. Rub with the lemon juice, also pushing some into the slashes.

To make the marinade, in a blender or food processor, combine the yogurt, onion, chiles, ginger, garlic, mint, cumin, coriander, paprika, garam masala, turmeric, and 1/4 teaspoon pepper and process until smooth.

Place the chicken legs in a shallow, nonreactive bowl, pour in the marinade, turn to coat, cover, and refrigerate for 12–24 hours, turning occasionally.

About 30 minutes before roasting, remove the chicken from the refrigerator. Take it out of the bowl and wipe off most of the marinade with paper towels. Discard the marinade. Preheat the oven to 500°F (260°C). Line a rimmed baking sheet with heavy-duty aluminum foil. Oil 1 or 2 flat roasting racks and place them in the prepared pan. Place the chicken legs, not touching, on the rack(s).

Roast the chicken until a thermometer (page 16) inserted into the thickest part of the thigh away from the bone registers 170°–175°F (77°–80°C), about 25 minutes.

Meanwhile, in a small bowl, stir together the melted butter and lemon juice. When the chicken is ready, remove it from the oven and immediately baste it with the butter–lemon juice mixture. Transfer the chicken legs to a platter. Serve them hot, warm, or at room temperature.

The traditional clay-lined tandoor oven roasts meats at extremely high temperatures, but a conventional home oven preheated to its highest setting is an excellent substitute. Cutting the flesh from the ends of the drumsticks causes the meat to contract into a nice meaty clump. You need to slash the drumsticks and thighs with a sharp knife so that the marinade of yogurt and spices can penetrate the flesh to flavor and tenderize it. Look for whole-milk yogurt, which is more flavorful than low-fat yogurt.

Sherry-Glazed Chicken Thighs

Chicken thighs are a moist, succulent cut and are great for an easy weeknight dinner. Here, the skin is removed and reserved for barding, or wrapping, the chicken to keep it moist while it roasts. The overnight marination in a mixture of soy and sherry imparts a rich flavor to the meat. You can pack any leftovers in the next day's lunchbox.

Rinse the chicken thighs and pat dry with paper towels. Remove the skin from the thighs and trim any excess fat. Reserve the skin. Place the chicken skin on a plate, cover, and refrigerate.

To make the marinade, in a shallow, nonreactive bowl large enough to hold the chicken, stir together the sugar, soy sauce, sherry, canola oil, garlic, and ginger until the sugar dissolves. Add the chicken to the bowl, turn to coat, cover, and refrigerate for 12–24 hours, turning the chicken occasionally.

About 30 minutes before roasting, remove the chicken from the refrigerator. Preheat the oven to 375°F (190°C). Line a rimmed baking sheet with heavy-duty aluminum foil. Oil a flat roasting rack large enough to hold the chicken thighs without touching and place it in the prepared pan. Remove the chicken from the marinade and arrange, former skin side up, on the rack. Discard the marinade. Drape each thigh with 1 piece of the reserved skin.

Roast the chicken for 25 minutes. Remove the pan from the oven, remove the skin from the chicken pieces, and discard. Continue to roast until the meat starts to pull away from the bone and the juices run clear when a thigh is pierced with a sharp knife, about 20 minutes longer. Transfer the chicken to a warmed platter. Serve warm or at room temperature.

12 skin-on, bone-in chicken thighs

For the Marinade

1/2 cup (4 oz/125 g) sugar

1/2 cup (4 fl oz/125 ml) soy sauce

1/3 cup (3 fl oz/80 ml) cream sherry

1/4 cup (2 fl oz/60 ml) canola oil

1 clove garlic, chopped

1 teaspoon grated, peeled fresh ginger

Lemon-Thyme Capon

1 capon, 7–8 lb (3.5–4 kg), giblets and neck removed from cavity

7 or 8 thin lemon slices

4–6 fresh thyme sprigs

Kosher salt and freshly ground pepper

2 tablespoons unsalted butter, at room temperature

2 carrots, peeled and cut into $1/2$-inch (12-mm) pieces

1 celery stalk, cut into $1/2$-inch (12-mm) pieces

1 small yellow onion, chopped

$1^1/2$ cups (12 fl oz/375 ml) reduced-sodium chicken broth

For the Gravy

Reduced-sodium chicken broth, if needed

3 tablespoons all-purpose (plain) flour

Kosher salt and freshly ground pepper

Capons are male chickens that have been castrated, to produce particularly plump birds with a generous amount of flavorful meat. If a capon is unavailable, use a large 6- to 7-pound (3- to 3.5-kg) roasting hen.

About 30 minutes before roasting, remove the capon from the refrigerator. Preheat the oven to 450°F (230°C). Oil a V-shaped roasting rack and place it in a roasting pan just large enough to hold the capon. Remove and discard any pockets of fat from the cavity. Rinse the capon and pat dry with paper towels. With the capon breast side up, and starting at the neck cavity, slip your fingers under the skin and gently separate the skin from the breast meat on both sides, being careful not to tear the skin. Carefully slide 4 or 5 lemon slices and half of the thyme sprigs under the skin, spacing them evenly. Season the cavity with salt and pepper, and place the remaining lemon slices and thyme in the cavity. Tuck the wing tips under the back. Tie the legs together with kitchen string. Rub the capon all over with the butter. Place the capon, breast side up, on the rack.

Roast the capon for 30 minutes. Remove from the oven and reduce the oven temperature to 325°F (165°C). Add the carrots, celery, onion, and broth to the pan. Continue to roast until a thermometer (page 16) inserted into the thickest part of a thigh away from the bone registers 170°–175°F (77°–80°C), 1–1$1/2$ hours longer. Remove from the oven. Slip the handle of a long wooden spoon or a pair of tongs in the capon cavity and carefully tip the bird, draining the liquid from the cavity into the roasting pan. Transfer the capon to a platter or carving board, remove the string, and tent with aluminum foil. Let rest for 15–20 minutes.

Meanwhile, make the gravy: Scrape up any browned bits from the bottom of the roasting pan and pour the contents of the pan through a medium-mesh sieve into a large measuring pitcher. Using a spoon, press on the contents of the sieve to extract as much liquid as possible. Skim off and reserve 3 tablespoons fat, discarding the remainder. Add broth if needed to the pitcher to total 2 cups (16 fl oz/500 ml). In a saucepan over medium heat, warm the reserved fat. Add the flour to make a roux (page 24) and cook, stirring, until well blended, 2–3 minutes. Slowly stir in the 2 cups liquid. Add any juices from the platter holding the capon. Cook, stirring constantly, until the gravy is smooth and thickens slightly, 3–4 minutes. Season generously with salt and pepper and keep warm.

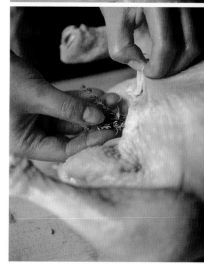

Discard the contents of the capon cavity, then carve the capon as for chicken (page 285). Pour the gravy into a warmed bowl and pass at the table.

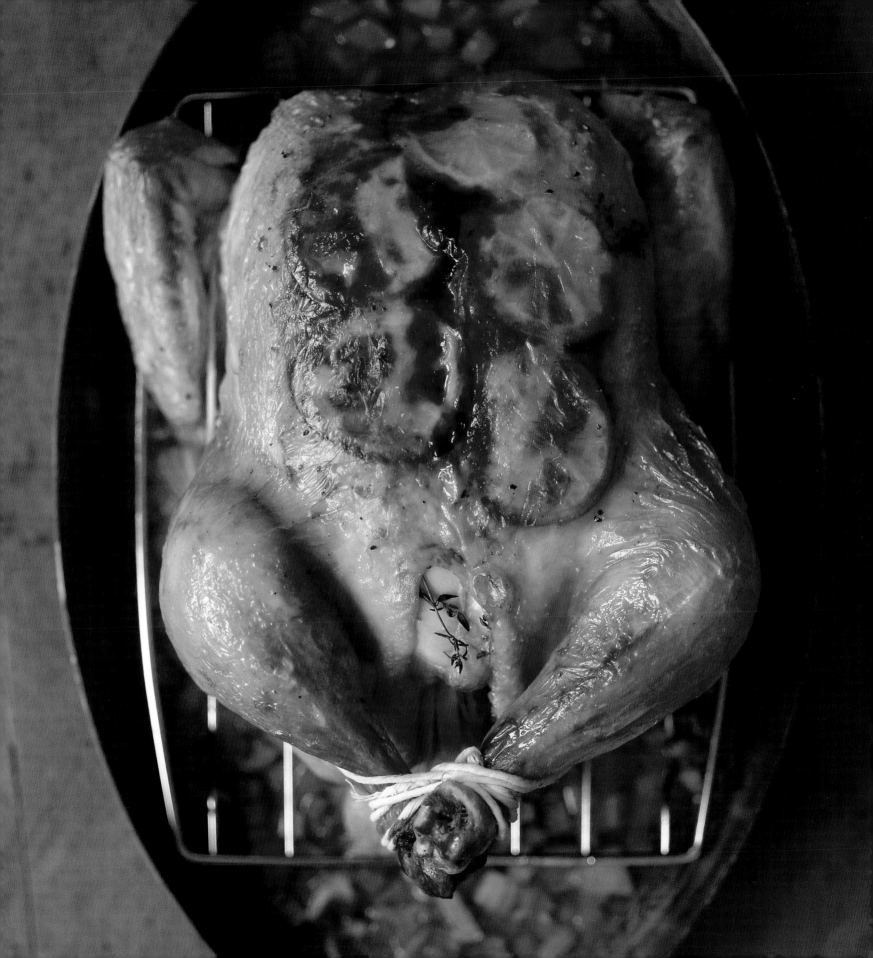

Classic Roast Turkey with Dressing

A whole turkey, roasted until beautifully browned, is the centerpiece for many holiday or special family dinners. Here, the turkey is flavored with sage and onion, rubbed with butter, and then roasted with a piece of dampened cheesecloth placed over the breast to keep it moist and flavorful. Thick onion slices form a natural roasting rack for the bird and flavor the gravy made from the pan drippings. If possible, purchase a fresh turkey. If you can find only a frozen turkey, allow about 4 days for it to thaw slowly in the refrigerator. The bread dressing, studded with dried fruit and sausages, is baked in a separate pan, rather than in the bird. A turkey roasted unstuffed cooks in less time, and the dressing develops an appealing crust and is less soggy. The stock base for the gravy can be made a day ahead, or as soon as the turkey is thawed sufficiently to allow removal of the neck and giblets from the cavity.

About 1 hour before roasting, remove the turkey from the refrigerator. Preheat the oven to 325°F (165°C). Remove the giblets and neck from the turkey cavity. Reserve the liver for another use or discard. Refrigerate the neck, gizzard, and heart until needed for making the broth. Remove and discard any pockets of fat from the cavity. Rinse the turkey and pat dry with paper towels.

Season the cavity with salt and pepper, and add the onion wedges and fresh sage. Tie the legs together with kitchen string. Tuck the wing tips under the back and tie a length of string around the breast to hold the wings close to the body. Rub the butter over the turkey breast. Fold a 24-inch (60-cm) square of cheesecloth (muslin) so it is just large enough to cover the breast. Rinse the cheesecloth in cold water and place over the buttered turkey breast. Select a roasting pan just large enough to hold the turkey. Place the sliced onions in the middle to form a natural roasting rack and position the turkey, breast side up, on top of them.

Roast the turkey until a thermometer (page 16) inserted into the thickest part of a thigh away from the bone registers 170°–175°F (77°–80°C), 3 1/2–4 hours. About 20 minutes before the turkey is done, remove the cheesecloth so that the breast will brown.

Meanwhile, make the broth: In a saucepan over high heat, combine the reserved neck and giblets and the onion, carrot, celery, bay leaf, peppercorns, and water to cover by 5 inches (2 cm). Bring to a boil, skim off any foam from the surface, reduce the heat to low, and simmer, partially covered, for 2 hours, adding more water as needed to keep the giblets and vegetables covered. Remove from the heat and strain through a medium-mesh sieve into a measuring pitcher. Discard the contents of the sieve. You should have about 3 cups (24 fl oz/750 ml) broth. Transfer the broth to a saucepan over high heat, bring to a boil, and boil until reduced by about one-third, 10–15 minutes. Let the broth cool and refrigerate until needed for making the gravy.

(continued on page 128)

1 turkey, 16–18 lb (8–9 kg), with giblets

Kosher salt and freshly ground pepper

1 yellow onion, cut into 6 wedges, plus 3 large yellow onions, cut into slices 1/2 inch (12 mm) thick

8–10 fresh sage leaves

2 tablespoons unsalted butter, at room temperature

For the Broth

1 yellow onion, coarsely chopped

1 small carrot, peeled and coarsely chopped

1 celery stalk, coarsely chopped

1 bay leaf

2 peppercorns

For the Dressing

1¹/₂ lb (750 g) pork link sausages

1–2 tablespoons unsalted butter, melted, if needed

2 yellow onions, chopped

2 large celery stalks, finely chopped

3–4 cups (24–32 fl oz/ 750 ml–1 l) reduced-sodium chicken broth

1 cup (6 oz/185 g) diced dried apricots

²/₃ cup (4 oz/125 g) raisins

²/₃ cup (2 oz/60 g) diced dried apples

12 cups (1¹/₂ lb/750 g) unseasoned dried bread cubes

2 teaspoons dried ground sage

3 large eggs, lightly beaten

Kosher salt and freshly ground pepper

¹/₂ cup (³/₄ oz/30 g) chopped fresh flat-leaf (Italian) parsley

For the Gravy

Melted unsalted butter, if needed

¹/₃ cup (2 oz/60 g) all-purpose (plain) flour

Kosher salt and freshly ground pepper

(Classic Roast Turkey with Dressing, continued)

While the broth simmers, begin making the dressing: In a large frying pan over medium-high heat, combine the sausages with 1 cup (8 fl oz/250 ml) water. Bring to a boil and cook, uncovered, until the water evaporates, about 10 minutes. After the water has evaporated, brown the sausages on all sides, about 5 minutes. Transfer the sausages to a cutting board, reserving the fat in the pan. When the sausages are cool enough to handle, cut into ¹/₂-inch (12-mm) lengths and set aside. Measure the fat in the pan and add melted butter as needed to total ¹/₄ cup (2 fl oz/60 ml). Place over very low heat, add the onions and celery, cover, and cook, stirring occasionally, until softened, about 15 minutes. Add 1 cup (8 fl oz/250 ml) of the chicken broth and the apricots, raisins, and apples, and simmer for 10 minutes to plump the fruit. Remove from the heat.

Butter a 9-by-13-by-2-inch (23-by-33-by-5-cm) baking pan. In a large bowl, combine the bread cubes, ground sage, eggs, 1 teaspoon salt, and ¹/₂ teaspoon pepper. Toss to combine. Add the sausage and the onion-fruit mixture and mix well. Pour in enough of the remaining broth to moisten the mixture evenly. Transfer to the prepared pan and cover the pan with aluminum foil. About 20 minutes before the turkey is done, place the dressing in the oven and bake for about 20 minutes. Remove the foil and continue to bake until the surface is lightly browned and crispy, about 25 minutes longer. If the dressing seems dry, moisten with a little chicken broth. Keep warm until serving time.

When the turkey is done, transfer it to a platter or carving board, remove the strings, and tent with aluminum foil. Let rest for 15–20 minutes.

To make the gravy, deglaze the roasting pan as directed on page 23, using the reserved turkey broth. Pour the contents of the pan through a medium-mesh sieve into a 4-cup (32–fl oz/1-l) measuring pitcher. Spoon off any remaining fat and add to the reserved fat. If there is not enough, add melted butter as needed to total ¹/₃ cup (3 fl oz/80 ml). In a large saucepan over low heat, warm the reserved fat. Add the flour to make a roux (page 24) and cook, stirring, until well blended, 2–3 minutes. Slowly pour the strained juices into the flour mixture, stirring constantly to prevent lumps from forming. Cook, stirring constantly, until the gravy is smooth and thickens slightly, 3–4 minutes. Season to taste with salt and pepper and keep warm.

Discard the contents of the turkey cavity and carve the turkey (page 285). Pour the gravy into a warmed bowl and pass at the table. Spoon the dressing into a warmed bowl and pass at the table.

Turkey with Roasted Garlic and Parsley

1 turkey, about 12 lb (6 kg)

1 large head roasted garlic (page 279)

3 tablespoons unsalted butter, at room temperature

3 tablespoons chopped fresh flat-leaf (Italian) parsley

1/2 teaspoon finely chopped fresh sage

Kosher salt and freshly ground pepper

For the Optional Sauce

2 tablespoons unsalted butter, at room temperature

2 tablespoons all-purpose (plain) flour

2 cups (16 fl oz/500 ml) reduced-sodium chicken broth

1/2 cup (4 fl oz/125 ml) dry white wine

Kosher salt and freshly ground pepper

About 1 hour before roasting, remove the turkey from the refrigerator. Preheat the oven to 325° (165°C). Oil a V-shaped roasting rack and place it in a roasting pan just large enough to hold the turkey. If the giblets and neck are in the turkey cavity, reserve for another use or discard. Remove and discard any pockets of fat from the cavity. Rinse the turkey and pat dry with paper towels.

With the turkey breast side up, and starting at the neck cavity, slip your fingers under the skin and gently separate the skin from the breast meat on both sides, being careful not to tear the skin. Then, starting at the body cavity, gently separate the skin from the thigh and drumstick meat. Separate the garlic cloves and squeeze the softened pulp into a small bowl. Add 2 tablespoons of the butter, the parsley, the sage, 1/2 teaspoon salt, and pepper to taste and mash together with a fork. Push this mixture under the turkey skin, distributing it evenly over the breast and legs. Tuck the wing tips under the back. Truss the turkey as directed on page 284. Rub the turkey all over with the remaining 1 tablespoon butter. Place the turkey on one side on the rack.

Roast the turkey for 45 minutes. Remove the pan from the oven and, using 2 thick pads of paper towels, carefully turn the turkey on its other side. Continue to roast for 45 minutes longer. Remove from the oven again and turn the turkey breast side up. Continue to roast until a thermometer (page 16) inserted into the thickest part of the thigh away from the bone registers 170°–175°F (77°–80°C), about 1 hour longer. Remove the pan from the oven, transfer the turkey to a platter or carving board, and tent with aluminum foil. Let rest for 15–20 minutes.

If a sauce is desired, make it while the bird rests: Place the butter and flour in a small bowl and mix together with a fork, to make a beurre manié. Deglaze the pan as directed on page 23, using the broth and wine. Pour the contents of the pan through a medium-mesh sieve into a small saucepan, bring to a boil, and boil until reduced to about 2 cups (16 fl oz/500 ml), 5–7 minutes. Reduce the heat to low, whisk the beurre manié into the liquid a little at a time, and simmer until slightly thickened, 3–4 minutes (page 24). Season to taste with salt and pepper and keep warm.

Carve the turkey (page 285). If you have made the sauce, pour it into a warmed serving bowl and pass at the table.

A roasted small turkey makes a great main dish for company or family dinners anytime of the year. Leftovers are always welcome for a quick midweek meal or for sandwiches. Small turkeys take only a little bit longer to roast than a large chicken. Here, a flavorful roasted garlic and herb butter is stuffed under the skin. The bird is turned twice during roasting to produce an evenly browned, crisp skin.

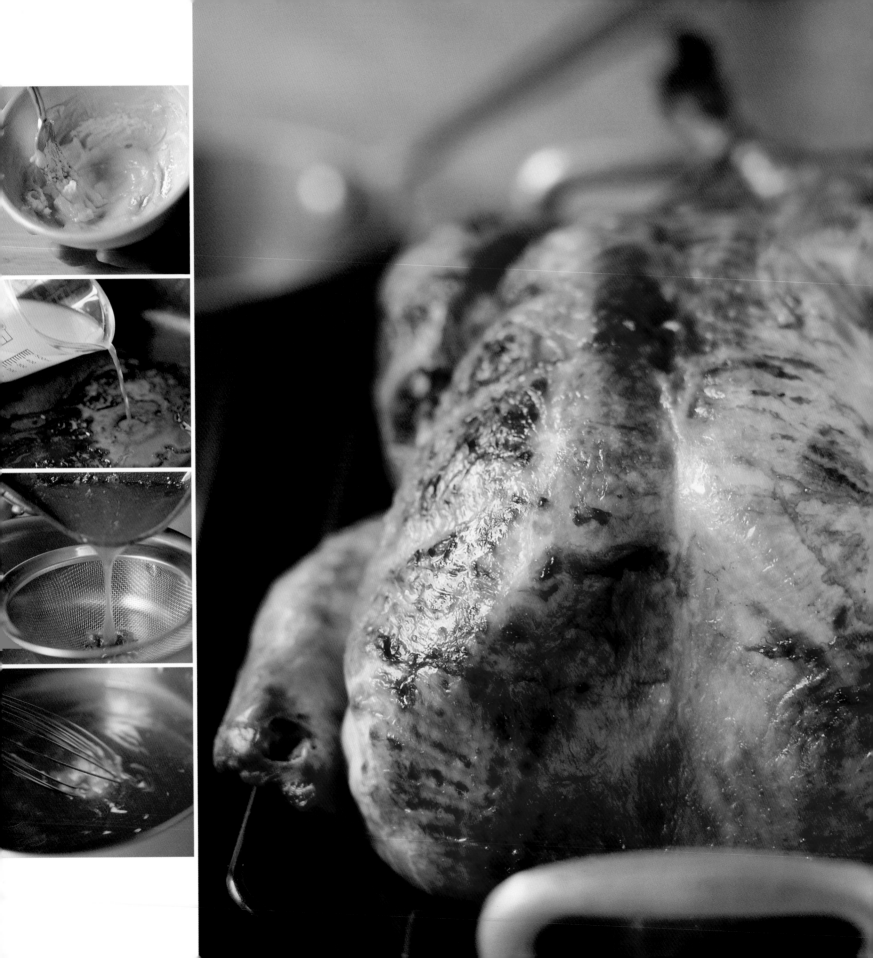

Brined Turkey

Brining creates moist, juicy flesh while enhancing flavor. Brines are primarily made of water and salt, but they can be readily augmented with wine, cider, vinegar, sugar, and spices. Two points are important to remember: choose a pot just large enough to hold the turkey for the brining and be sure to dissolve the sugar and salt completely. This bird is the perfect size to serve six with some leftovers.

Combine the 1 cup salt, the sugar, and 6 qt (6 l) room-temperature water in a nonreactive container about 3 inches (7.5 cm) taller and wider than the turkey. Stir until the salt and sugar dissolve. Add the lemon, the rosemary, the coriander, 8 of the parsley sprigs, 10 of the peppercorns, and 2 of the bay leaves and stir well. Remove the giblets and neck from the turkey cavity; reserve the liver for another use or discard. Refrigerate the neck, gizzard, and heart. Remove and discard any pockets of fat from the cavity. Rinse the turkey, then immerse, breast side down, in the brine. If needed, invert a small plate on top of the turkey to keep it submerged. Cover and refrigerate for 24 hours. Remove the turkey from the brine, rinse, pat dry, tuck the wing tips under the back, and let stand at room temperature for 1 hour before roasting. Preheat the oven to 375°F (190°C). Oil a V-shaped roasting rack and place it in a roasting pan just large enough to hold the turkey.

In a saucepan over high heat, combine the onion, carrot, celery, and remaining 4 parsley sprigs, 6 peppercorns, and bay leaf. Add water to cover by 2 inches (5 cm). Coarsely chop the neck, gizzard, and heart and add to the pan. Bring to a boil, skim off any foam, reduce the heat to low, and simmer, partially covered, for 2 hours, adding more water as needed. Strain into another saucepan. Discard the solids. Spoon the fat from the surface, bring to a boil, and reduce to about 2 cups (16 fl oz/500 ml), 10–15 minutes. Cover and refrigerate.

Rub the turkey all over with 2 tablespoons of the butter. Tie the legs together with kitchen string. Place on one side on the rack. Roast for 45 minutes. Remove the pan from the oven and, using 2 thick pads of paper towels, carefully turn the turkey on its other side. Roast for 45 minutes longer. Remove from the oven again and turn the turkey breast side up. Roast until a thermometer (page 16) inserted into the thickest part of a thigh away from a bone registers 170°–175°F (77°–80°C), 30–40 minutes longer. Transfer the turkey to a platter or carving board and tent with aluminum foil. Let rest for 15–20 minutes.

Meanwhile, place the remaining 2 tablespoons butter and the flour in a small bowl and mix together with a fork, to make a beurre manié. Deglaze the roasting pan as directed on page 23, using about 1 cup (8 fl oz/250 ml) of the reserved broth. Pour through a medium-mesh sieve into a saucepan, add the remaining 1 cup broth and the wine, and bring to a boil. Reduce the heat to low, whisk the beurre manié into the liquid a little at a time, and simmer until slightly thickened, 3–4 minutes (page 24). Season to taste with salt and pepper.

Carve the turkey (page 285). Pass the sauce at the table.

1 cup (8 oz/250 g) kosher salt, plus salt to taste

1 cup (8 oz/250 g) sugar

1 lemon, thinly sliced

1 fresh rosemary sprig

1/2 teaspoon coriander seeds

12 fresh flat-leaf (Italian) parsley sprigs

16 peppercorns

3 bay leaves

1 hen turkey, 9–10 lb (4.5–5 kg), with giblets

1 small yellow onion, quartered

1 small carrot, peeled and cut into slices 1 inch (2.5 cm) thick

1 small celery stalk with leaves, chopped

4 tablespoons (2 oz/60 g) unsalted butter, at room temperature

2 tablespoons all-purpose (plain) flour

1/2 cup (4 fl oz/125 ml) dry white wine

Kosher salt and freshly ground pepper

Turkey Breast Stuffed with Sage and Pancetta

1 tablespoon extra-virgin olive oil

1 yellow onion, finely chopped

1 small clove garlic, minced

3 or 4 slices pancetta, about 2 oz (60 g) total weight, coarsely chopped

$^{1}/_{2}$ cup (4 oz/125 g) ricotta cheese

$^{1}/_{4}$ cup (1 oz/30 g) grated Parmesan cheese

5 tablespoons ($^{1}/_{2}$ oz/15 g) chopped fresh flat-leaf (Italian) parsley

1 tablespoon cider vinegar

1 teaspoon chopped fresh sage, plus 4 or 5 small leaves

Kosher salt and freshly ground pepper

1 skin-on, bone-in turkey breast, 3$^{1}/_{2}$–4 lb (1.75–2 kg)

1 cup (8 fl oz/250 ml) reduced-sodium chicken broth

$^{2}/_{3}$ cup (5 fl oz/150 ml) heavy (double) cream

1 tablespoon cornstarch (cornflour)

Kosher salt and freshly ground pepper

In a frying pan over medium-low heat, warm the olive oil. Add the onion, cover, and cook, stirring occasionally, for 6–7 minutes. Add the garlic and pancetta and cook until the onion is completely soft, 3–4 minutes longer. Remove from the heat and let cool completely. Add the ricotta, Parmesan, parsley, vinegar, and chopped sage. Season to taste with salt and pepper. Set the stuffing aside.

Preheat the oven to 325°F (165°C). Oil a small flat roasting rack and place it in a roasting pan just large enough to hold the turkey breast. To bone the turkey breast, working from one side of the breast, loosen the skin with your fingers and gently pull off in one piece. Using a sharp, flexible knife, cut through the wishbone and then down along one side of the breastbone, scraping the meat from the ribs to free it. Repeat on the other side of the breastbone. Rinse the breast halves and pat dry with paper towels. Place the breast halves cut side up and side by side. Locate the white tendon on each breast half, then remove by holding the tendon and scraping away the meat. Fold out each tenderloin but do not detach.

Lay the skin, inner side up, on the work surface and place one half breast, cut side up, on top of it. Distribute the sage leaves over the meat, then spread the stuffing over the meat. Top with the second turkey breast half, cut side down. Bring up the skin around the 2 halves. Using kitchen string, make parallel ties around the roll at 3 or 4 regular intervals, then tie a long piece of string lengthwise around the roll to form a compact loaf. Place the roll on the rack. Roast until a thermometer (page 16) inserted into the thickest part of the roll registers 160°F (71°C), about 2$^{1}/_{2}$ hours. Transfer the roll to a carving board and tent with aluminum foil. Let rest for 15 minutes.

Meanwhile, deglaze the roasting pan as directed on page 23, using the broth. Strain through a fine-mesh sieve into a small saucepan. Add the cream, place over medium heat, and bring almost to a boil. In a small bowl, dissolve the cornstarch in 2 tablespoons water. Whisk the cornstarch mixture into the cream mixture and cook over medium heat until the sauce thickens slightly, 2–3 minutes (page 24). Season to taste with salt and pepper and keep warm.

To serve the turkey, remove the string. Cut the turkey into slices $^{3}/_{4}$ inch (2 cm) thick and place on warmed individual plates. Spoon some of the sauce over the slices. Pass the remaining sauce at the table.

This roasted boneless turkey breast with a light pan sauce can be carved in the kitchen or at the table, making it a perfect dish for a dinner party. You can ask your butcher to bone the breast for you, or you can do it yourself. In either case, save the bones for the stockpot, and save the skin in one large piece for wrapping around the turkey to keep it moist as it roasts.

Pan-Roasted Turkey Cutlets with Orange Gremolata

Boneless turkey cutlets are regularly stocked in the poultry section of supermarkets. Here, they are dipped in beaten egg, coated with bread crumbs, then browned on the stove top before they are quickly finished in a hot oven. The sauce is inspired by the *gremolata* of northern Italy, a mixture of parsley, lemon zest, and garlic traditionally used on osso buco. Lemon juice and zest may be substituted for the orange juice and zest.

Preheat the oven to 400°F (200°C). Place the flour on a plate and season with salt and pepper. In a pie pan, whisk together the egg, the mustard, and a little salt and pepper. Place the bread crumbs on another plate. Coat each cutlet on both sides with the seasoned flour, then dip both sides in the egg mixture and then finally in the bread crumbs, coating evenly on both sides each time.

In a large, heavy ovenproof frying pan over high heat, melt the butter with the olive oil. When it is very hot, add the cutlets and sauté until the crumbs are crisp and golden, about 2 minutes. Turn the cutlets and place the pan in the oven. Roast until the cutlets are firm to the touch and the bread crumbs are nicely browned, about 5 minutes. Remove the pan from the oven and transfer the cutlets to a warmed platter or warmed individual plates.

To make the sauce, place the pan over medium-high heat and add the orange zest and juice, parsley, garlic, and brandy. Cook, stirring, until slightly reduced, 2–3 minutes. Season to taste with salt and pepper. Spoon an equal amount of the sauce over each cutlet. Serve at once.

²/₃ cup (3¹/₂ oz/105 g) all-purpose (plain) flour

Kosher salt and freshly ground pepper

1 large egg

2 teaspoons Dijon mustard

2¹/₂ cups (5 oz/155 g) fine dried bread crumbs

4 turkey cutlets, each 4–6 oz (125–185 g) and ¹/₂ inch (12 mm) thick

2 tablespoons unsalted butter

2 tablespoons extra-virgin olive oil

For the Sauce

Grated zest of 1 orange

Juice of 1 orange (about ¹/₃ cup/3 fl oz/80 ml)

3 tablespoons finely chopped fresh flat-leaf (Italian) parsley

1 large clove garlic, finely minced

2 tablespoons brandy

Kosher salt and freshly ground pepper

Bacon-Wrapped Butterflied Quail

12 quail, 5–6 oz (155–185 g) each

$^1/_2$ cup (4 oz/125 g) Dijon mustard

1 tablespoon extra-virgin olive oil

1 tablespoon Hungarian sweet paprika

1 teaspoon finely chopped fresh rosemary

$^1/_4$ teaspoon cayenne pepper

Freshly ground black pepper

12 slices bacon, cut in half

Remove the quail from the refrigerator 20–30 minutes before roasting. Preheat the oven to 500°F (260°C). Line a rimmed baking sheet with heavy-duty aluminum foil. Oil a large, flat roasting rack and place it in the pan. Butterfly the quail as directed on page 283. Rinse the quail and pat dry with paper towels.

In a small bowl, stir together the mustard, olive oil, paprika, rosemary, cayenne pepper, and 2 teaspoons black pepper. Rub the mustard mixture all over each quail. Drape 2 half slices of bacon over the breast on each quail. (The quail can be prepared up to this point ahead of time, lightly covered with plastic wrap, and refrigerated for 2–3 hours. Remove from the refrigerator 20–30 minutes before roasting.) Arrange the quail on the oiled rack.

Roast the quail until nicely browned and the juices run clear when a thigh is pierced with a sharp knife, 18–20 minutes. Remove the pan from the oven, transfer the quail to a platter, and tent with aluminum foil. Let rest for 5 minutes.

Leave the quail on the platter or transfer to individual plates. Serve at once.

Quail are dark-meat, full-flavored birds that hold their own when combined with assertive spices and other strong seasonings. They take only a few minutes to roast at high heat and yield sweet, tender meat. Apple-Plum Compote (page 156) makes a delicious accompaniment for a holiday dinner, or you can serve the quail with a mixed green salad.

Cornish Hens with Citrus Sauce

Cornish hens are small birds that are a hybrid of two poultry breeds, the Cornish game cock and the Plymouth Rock hen. They usually weigh under 1 1/2 pounds (750 g) but can weigh as much as 2 pounds (1 kg) or more. The ratio of meat to bone is small, however, so if you are roasting the smaller birds, serve one per person. As with the poussins on page 144, these diminutive birds benefit from salting and refrigerating before roasting to heighten their flavor. The vegetables do double duty here: they serve as a natural rack in the roasting pan and as a delicious bed on each plate.

If the giblets and neck are in the hen cavities, remove and reserve for another use or discard. Remove and discard any pockets of fat from the cavities. Rinse the hens and pat dry with paper towels. Sprinkle the cavity of each bird with salt and pepper. Grate the zest from 1 of the oranges and reserve for the sauce. Using a vegetable peeler, remove the zest from another orange in strips 1/2 inch (12 mm) wide. Using a sharp knife, remove the peel and pith from all 4 oranges. Cut along each side of the membrane between the sections of each orange to free them, then cut into 1/2-inch pieces. Reserve for the roasting pan. Place 3 or 4 strips of zest and 2 garlic clove halves inside each hen. Truss the hens (page 284). Place on a plate, brush or rub with olive oil, season with salt and pepper, cover lightly with plastic wrap, and refrigerate for 3–4 hours.

About 30 minutes before roasting, remove the hens from the refrigerator. Preheat the oven to 425°F (220°C). Oil a roasting pan just large enough to hold the hens.

In a bowl, toss the sliced onions and reserved orange pieces with the 1 1/2 tablespoons olive oil. Transfer to the prepared pan and make a bed in the bottom of the pan. Place the hens, breast side up, on the onions and oranges. Roast the hens until the juices run clear when a thigh is pierced with a sharp knife and a thermometer (page 16) inserted into the thickest part of a breast away from the bone registers 160°F (70°C), 50–60 minutes. Remove the pan from the oven. Slip the handle of a long wooden spoon or a pair of tongs in each hen cavity and carefully tip the bird, draining the liquid from the cavity into the roasting pan. Transfer the hens to a platter, remove the trussing string, and tent with aluminum foil. Let rest for 10 minutes. Using a slotted spoon, transfer the onions and oranges from the roasting pan to a small bowl and keep warm.

Meanwhile, make the sauce: Place the butter and flour in a small bowl and mix together with a fork, to make a beurre manié. Deglaze the roasting pan (page 23), using the broth and wine. Pour through a medium-mesh sieve into a small saucepan, bring to a boil, and reduce slightly, 3–5 minutes. Reduce the heat to low, add the reserved grated zest, whisk the beurre manié into the liquid a little at a time, and simmer until slightly thickened, 3–4 minutes (page 24). Season to taste with salt and pepper.

Divide the onion-orange mixture evenly among warmed individual plates. Place a hen on each bed of vegetables. Spoon a little sauce over the hens, and pass the remaining sauce at the table. Serve at once.

4 Cornish hens, about 1 1/2 lb (750 g) each

Kosher salt and freshly ground pepper

4 oranges

4 cloves garlic, cut in half

Extra-virgin olive oil for coating, plus 1 1/2 tablespoons

4 sweet onions such as Vidalia or Maui, cut into slices 1/4 inch (6 mm) thick

For the Sauce

1 tablespoon unsalted butter, at room temperature

1 tablespoon all-purpose (plain) flour

1 cup (8 fl oz/250 ml) reduced-sodium chicken broth

1/3 cup (3 fl oz/80 ml) dry white wine

Kosher salt and freshly ground pepper

Squabs Stuffed with Chanterelles

For the Stuffing

4 tablespoons (2 oz/60 g) unsalted butter

¹/₂ lb (250 g) fresh chanterelle mushrooms, brushed clean, stems removed, and caps coarsely chopped

1 tablespoon Cognac or Pernod

1 tablespoon minced shallot

2 large cloves garlic, minced

Kosher salt and freshly ground pepper

1¹/₂ cups (3 oz/90 g) fresh bread crumbs

¹/₄ cup (¹/₃ oz/10 g) minced fresh flat-leaf (Italian) parsley

2 tablespoons minced fresh tarragon

4 semi-boneless squabs (see note), about ³/₄ lb (375 g) each

Kosher salt and freshly ground pepper

1 tablespoon unsalted butter, at room temperature

To make the stuffing, in a large frying pan over medium-high heat, melt 3 tablespoons of the butter. When the butter stops foaming, add the mushrooms and sauté until they release their liquid and are lightly browned, 3–4 minutes. Add the Cognac, shallot, and garlic and cook for 1 minute. Season to taste with salt and pepper. Transfer the mushroom mixture to a bowl. Return the frying pan to medium-high heat and add the remaining 1 tablespoon butter. Add the bread crumbs and sauté, stirring frequently, until lightly toasted, 3–4 minutes. Remove from the heat and add the bread crumbs to the mushrooms. Add the parsley and tarragon and mix well. Season to taste with salt and pepper. Let cool completely before stuffing the squabs.

Remove the squabs from the refrigerator 20–30 minutes before roasting. Preheat the oven to 450°F (230°C). Line a rimmed baking sheet with heavy-duty aluminum foil. Oil a flat roasting rack and place it on the pan.

If the giblets are in the squab cavities, remove and discard or reserve for another use. Rinse the squabs and pat dry with paper towels. Season each cavity with salt and pepper. Divide the stuffing evenly among the squabs, filling the cavities and plumping up the breast of each bird by pulling the legs in close to the body. Tie the legs together with kitchen string. Tuck the wing tips under the back. Rub the breast of each squab with the butter, dividing it evenly. Place the squabs, breast side up, on the oiled rack.

Roast the squabs for 20 minutes. Reduce the oven temperature to 350°F (180°C) and continue to roast until nicely browned and the juices have a pale rose tint when a thigh joint is pierced with a knife, about 20 minutes longer. Remove the pan from the oven, transfer the squabs to a platter, and tent with aluminum foil. Let rest for 5 minutes.

Remove the strings. Transfer the squabs to warmed individual plates and serve.

Squabs are small birds, usually weighing less than 1 pound (500 g), with rich, flavorful dark meat. Their size makes them perfect for serving one bird to each diner. Semi-boneless squabs, with only the drumstick and wing bones remaining, can be special-ordered from a butcher, so plan ahead. If chanterelles are unavailable, use any combination of flavorful fresh mushrooms.

Poussins with Watercress

6 poussins, about 1 lb (500 g) each

Kosher salt and freshly ground pepper

1 tablespoon unsalted butter, melted

6 fresh thyme or oregano sprigs

6 slices bacon, cut in half

For the Sauce

¹/₄ cup (2 fl oz/60 ml) dry white wine

1 tablespoon red wine vinegar

¹/₂ teaspoon Dijon mustard

2 large bunches watercress, tough stems removed

Kosher salt and freshly ground pepper

Poussins are young chickens that usually weigh about 1 pound (500 g), and roast to perfection in less than 45 minutes in a hot oven. Small Cornish hens or squabs can be substituted for the poussins. Salting the birds and then refrigerating them for a few hours helps to develop their flavor. If you are unable to find watercress, substitute small arugula (rocket) leaves or other tender leafy greens.

If the neck is still attached to each poussin, remove it with a sharp knife or kitchen shears and reserve for another use or discard. If the giblets and neck are in the cavity, remove them and reserve or discard. Remove and discard any pockets of fat from the cavity. Rinse the poussins and pat dry with paper towels. Tuck the wing tips under the back. Sprinkle the birds inside and out with salt and pepper, cover lightly with plastic wrap, and refrigerate for 3–4 hours.

About 30 minutes before roasting, remove the birds from the refrigerator. Preheat the oven to 450°F (230°C). Oil a flat roasting rack and place it on a rimmed baking sheet.

Brush the poussins with the melted butter and place a thyme sprig inside each cavity. Drape a half slice of bacon over each side of each breast. Tie a length of kitchen string around the breast of each bird to keep the bacon in place. Place the poussins, breast side up and not touching, on the prepared rack.

Roast the poussins for 20 minutes. Remove the pan from the oven, and remove the strings and crisp bacon strips. Reserve the bacon to serve with the birds. Continue to roast until the juices run clear when a thigh is pierced with a sharp knife and the legs move easily, 10–15 minutes longer.

Remove the pan from the oven. Slip the handle of a long wooden spoon or a pair of tongs in each poussin cavity and carefully tip the bird, draining the liquid from the cavity into the roasting pan. Transfer the poussins to a platter and tent with aluminum foil. Let rest for 5 minutes.

Meanwhile, make the sauce: Spoon off any excess fat from the juices in the pan and discard. Pour the pan juices through a medium-mesh sieve into a saucepan. Add the wine, vinegar, and mustard and stir to mix. Bring to a boil and cook until reduced slightly, 2–3 minutes. Season to taste with salt and pepper.

Place the poussins on warmed individual plates and place a small handful of watercress and 2 bacon pieces alongside each bird. Drizzle the birds and the watercress with the sauce, dividing it evenly. Serve at once.

Roast Duck with Turnips

1 Muscovy or Long Island duck, about 5 lb (2.5 kg), with giblets

Kosher salt and freshly ground pepper

1 small celery stalk with leaves, coarsely chopped

1/2 small yellow onion, coarsely chopped

2 cloves garlic, halved

1 fresh thyme sprig

For the Glaze

2 tablespoons orange marmalade, with large pieces of peel finely chopped

1/2 teaspoon Dijon mustard

For the Turnips

4 or 5 small turnips, each 2 inches (5 cm) in diameter, peeled, halved, and each half cut into 4 wedges

2 fresh thyme sprigs

Kosher salt and freshly ground pepper

2 tablespoons Triple Sec or other orange liqueur

Remove the giblets and neck from the duck cavity. Reserve the giblets for another use or discard, and reserve the neck for the steamer. Pull out any pockets of fat from the cavity and discard. Rinse the duck and pat dry with paper towels. Cut off the wing tips and reserve. Holding the blade of a sharp knife almost parallel to the skin, push the tip through the skin to make small slits all over the breast and thighs. Do not penetrate the flesh. Generously salt and pepper the duck inside and out. Place the celery, onion, garlic, and thyme in the cavity. Set up a large pot for steaming (see note). Place the neck and wing tips in the bottom of the pot and add water to a depth of about 2 inches (5 cm). Place the duck, breast side up, on the rack. Bring the water to a boil, cover tightly, and steam the duck until the skin is translucent and most of the fat is rendered, about 45 minutes. Place the duck on a plate. Let cool for 10–15 minutes. Pour the steaming liquid through a fine-mesh sieve into a large measuring pitcher. Skim off most of the fat and reserve it.

Preheat the oven to 425°F (220°C). Place a flat roasting rack in a roasting pan just large enough to hold the duck. Pat the duck dry with paper towels and place, breast side up, on the rack. While the oven is preheating, make the glaze: Pour the reserved steaming liquid into a saucepan and bring to a boil. Boil the liquid until it is reduced to about 1 cup (8 fl oz/250 ml), 10–15 minutes. Remove from the heat, add the marmalade and mustard, and mix well. Set aside.

Roast the duck for 15 minutes. Reduce the oven temperature to 375° (190°C) and baste the duck with the glaze. Continue to roast the duck, basting 2 or 3 times with the glaze, until the skin is brown and crisp and a thermometer (page 16) inserted into the thickest part of a thigh away from the bone registers 170°–180°F (77°–82°C), about 30 minutes longer.

While the duck is roasting, prepare the turnips: In a large frying pan over high heat, combine the turnips, 1 tablespoon of the reserved duck fat, the thyme, and 1/2 cup (4 fl oz/125 ml) water, and season lightly with salt and pepper. Bring to a boil, cover, reduce the heat to low, and simmer for about 15 minutes. Uncover, raise the heat to medium-high, and cook, stirring, until the liquid has almost evaporated, 5–7 minutes. Add the liqueur and cook until the turnips are tender, 3–4 minutes longer. Season with salt and pepper; keep warm.

Transfer the duck to a carving board and tent with aluminum foil. Let rest for 5–10 minutes. Carve as for chicken (page 285), cutting the thighs from the drumsticks and slicing the meat from each thigh in 2 pieces. Serve with the turnips.

Ducks have a generous amount of fat under the skin, which is difficult to render during roasting. Here, the duck is first steamed on the top of the stove to release much of the fat and is then roasted to a golden brown. Steaming, because it is a moist-cooking method, helps keep the duck meat succulent and tender. Select a pot large enough to hold a footed rack at least 2 inches (5 cm) above the bottom of the pot. If needed, you can improvise a footed rack by placing a flat rack on two inverted heat-proof cups or bowls. Ducks do not have as much meat as chickens of the same weight, so a whole duck will yield fewer servings. You can easily increase the servings by preparing two ducks.

Lacquered Duck

A duck with deep golden brown, crispy skin is appealing to the eye and delicious on the palate. This attractive result is achieved by dousing the skin with boiling water, painting it with soy sauce, and then refrigerating the duck for a full day. This dries out the skin, which makes it roast to a crisper finish. If you cannot find pomegranate molasses, which is carried in Middle Eastern markets, you can substitute Chinese hoisin sauce thinned with a little water. Use any leftover duck to make a salad with greens, walnuts, or dried cherries or cranberries, with a scattering of small pieces of crisp duck skin for garnish.

If the giblets and neck are in the duck cavity, remove and reserve for another use or discard. Pull out any pockets of fat from the cavity and discard. Butterfly the duck as directed on page 283. Rinse the duck and pat dry with paper towels. Place the duck, skin side up, on a rack over the sink. Bring about 6 cups (48 fl oz/1.5 l) water to a boil. Pour 1–2 cups (8–16 fl oz/250–500 ml) of the boiling water evenly over the duck. Repeat 2 or 3 times, waiting 2 minutes between dousings. Dry the duck well with paper towels and transfer the duck to a plate or pan just large enough to hold it. Brush the duck skin with the soy sauce. Refrigerate, uncovered, for 24 hours to dry out the skin.

About 30 minutes before roasting, remove the duck from the refrigerator. Preheat the oven to 400°F (200°C). Line a rimmed baking sheet with heavy-duty aluminum foil. Select a flat roasting rack that is tall enough to keep the duck above the liquid that will accumulate in the pan bottom. Oil the rack and place it in the prepared pan.

To make the glaze, in a small bowl, stir together the pomegranate molasses, soy sauce, garlic, ginger, and five-spice powder.

Place the duck, skin side up, on the oiled rack, spreading the legs away from the body to expose more skin. Pour 1 cup (8 fl oz/250 ml) water into the pan. Roast the duck for 30 minutes. Remove the pan from the oven and paint the skin with a light coat of the glaze. Using a small ladle or a bulb baster, carefully remove as much of the accumulated hot liquid as possible from the bottom of the pan. Continue to roast the duck until the skin is brown and crisp and a thermometer (page 16) inserted into the thickest part of thigh away from the bone registers 170°–180°F (77°–82°C), about 30 minutes longer. Remove the pan from the oven, transfer the duck to a carving board, and tent with aluminum foil. Let rest for 10 minutes.

While the duck is resting, pour any remaining glaze into a small saucepan and bring to a boil over high heat. Remove from the heat and set aside.

Using a heavy, sharp knife or poultry shears, cut the duck in half along each side of the breastbone. Cut each half in half again, separating the breast and wing from the thigh and leg. Divide the duck among warmed individual plates. Pour the warm glaze over the duck meat. Serve at once.

1 Muscovy or Long Island duck, 4–5 lb (2–2.5 kg)

2 tablespoons soy sauce

For the Glaze

2 tablespoons pomegranate molasses

2 tablespoons soy sauce

1 clove garlic, finely grated

$1/2$ teaspoon finely grated, peeled fresh ginger

Pinch of five-spice powder

Balsamic Duck Legs with Mushrooms

Duck legs are an economical way to serve duck. The thigh meat tends to be more moist and juicy than breast meat. Banding the drumsticks, that is, cutting the skin from the ends, causes the meat to pull up into a nice meaty clump. The marinated and steamed duck legs can be refrigerated for as long as overnight, then roasted in a hot oven to crisp and brown the skin just before serving.

Rinse the duck and pat dry with paper towels. Working with 1 duck leg at a time, using a sharp knife, make a cut to the bone around the bottom of the drumstick about 3/4 inch (2 cm) from the end. Remove the skin below the cut. In a shallow, nonreactive bowl large enough to hold the duck legs, stir together the olive oil, vinegar, garlic, shallot, thyme, 1/2 teaspoon salt, and a little pepper. Add the duck legs to the bowl, turn to coat, cover, and refrigerate for 3–4 hours, turning the legs 1 or 2 times. Remove the duck legs from the marinade. Pour the marinade into a saucepan, place over high heat, and bring to a boil. Remove from the heat and reserve to use as a glaze.

Select a pot large enough to hold a footed flat rack on which the duck legs will stand at least 2 inches (5 cm) above the bottom of the pot. (If you do not have a footed rack, rest a rack on 2 inverted, small heatproof cups or bowls.) Add water to a depth of about 1 inch (2.5 cm). Place the duck legs, skin side up, on the rack. Bring the water to a boil, cover tightly, and steam the duck until the skin is translucent, about 20 minutes.

While the duck legs are steaming, preheat the oven to 450°F (230°C). Select a roasting pan just large enough to hold the duck legs and line with heavy-duty aluminum foil. Place a flat rack in the pan. When the duck legs are ready, transfer them, skin side up, to the rack in the prepared pan. Brush the skin with some of the glaze. Roast until the skin is brown and crisp and a thermometer (page 16) inserted into the thickest part of a thigh away from the bone registers 170°–180°F (77°–82°C), about 20 minutes. Remove the pan from the oven and brush again with the glaze. Tent with aluminum foil and let rest for 5 minutes.

Meanwhile, prepare the mushrooms: In a large frying pan over medium-high heat, warm the olive oil. Add the mushrooms and green onion and sauté until the mushrooms release their liquid, about 2 minutes. Add the vinegar and thyme and season to taste with salt and pepper. Cook until the mushrooms are soft and most of the liquid has evaporated, 2–3 minutes longer. Transfer the duck legs to warmed individual plates. Spoon the mushrooms alongside the duck legs and serve.

4–6 skin-on, bone-in duck legs, about 6 oz (185 g) each

3 tablespoons extra-virgin olive oil

3 tablespoons balsamic vinegar

2 cloves garlic, thinly sliced

1 small shallot, thinly sliced

3 or 4 fresh thyme sprigs, lightly bruised

Kosher salt and freshly ground pepper

For the Mushrooms

2 tablespoons extra-virgin olive oil

1/2 lb (250 g) fresh cremini mushrooms, brushed clean, stems removed, and caps cut into thick slices

1 green (spring) onion, including tender green tops, thinly sliced

2 tablespoons balsamic vinegar

1/2 teaspoon fresh thyme leaves

Kosher salt and freshly ground pepper

Duck Breasts with Pecan and Dried Cherry Pilaf

2 skin-on, boneless Muscovy duck breast halves, each 12–14 oz (375–440 g)

Kosher salt and freshly ground black pepper

For the Pilaf

1 cup (7 oz/220 g) basmati rice

2 tablespoons unsalted butter

$^1/_3$ cup (2 oz/60 g) minced yellow onion

$^1/_4$ cup (2 fl oz/60 ml) dry vermouth or dry white wine

1$^1/_4$ cups (10 fl oz/315 ml) reduced-sodium chicken broth

$^1/_3$ cup (2 oz/60 g) pitted dried cherries, chopped into pea-sized pieces

$^1/_3$ cup (1$^1/_2$ oz/45 g) pecans, lightly toasted and chopped into pea-sized pieces

Kosher salt and freshly ground black pepper

For the Sauce

$^1/_2$ cup (4 fl oz/125 ml) reduced-sodium chicken broth

$^1/_2$ cup (4 fl oz/125 ml) Port wine or cream sherry

2 teaspoons cornstarch (cornflour)

Freshly ground white pepper

Trim the excess duck skin so it just covers the meat. Using a sharp knife, score the skin, making parallel cuts through the skin, but not into the flesh, at $^3/_8$-inch (1-cm) intervals. Make a second set of cuts at right angles to the first to create $^3/_8$-inch diamonds. Generously season the breasts with salt and pepper. Let stand at room temperature for 30 minutes. Preheat the oven to 400°F (200°C).

While the duck breasts are coming to room temperature, begin cooking the pilaf: In a small bowl, rinse the rice in 3 or 4 changes of cold water until the water runs almost clear. Add fresh water to cover and let the rice soak for 15 minutes, then drain. In a saucepan over low heat, melt the butter. Add the onion, cover, and cook, stirring occasionally, until softened, 5–6 minutes. Add the rice, stir to coat with the butter, and cook until the rice is translucent, 2–3 minutes. Add the wine and cook until the wine has almost evaporated, 2–3 minutes. Add the broth, raise the heat to medium-high, bring to a boil, cover, reduce the heat to the lowest setting, and cook until the liquid is absorbed, about 20 minutes. Remove from the heat, uncover, stir in the chopped cherries, re-cover, and let steam for 5 minutes. Stir in the pecans just before serving and season with salt and pepper.

While the pilaf is cooking, roast the duck: Heat a large, heavy ovenproof frying pan over high heat on the stove top until very hot, about 5 minutes. Place the breasts, skin side down, in the pan and press them down firmly to ensure even contact with the hot pan. Sear for 2 minutes, then pour off the accumulated fat and place the pan in the oven. Roast for 6 minutes. Remove the pan from the oven, turn the breasts, and continue to roast until the skin is quite brown and crisp and the meat is firm but still pinkish red when cut into with a sharp knife, 2–3 minutes. Transfer the breasts to a plate. Let rest for 10 minutes.

To make the sauce, deglaze the pan as directed on page 23, removing and discarding most of the fat from the pan and using the broth. Add the Port and cook over high heat until reduced by one-third, 3–4 minutes. In a small bowl, dissolve the cornstarch in 1 tablespoon water. Reduce the heat to medium, whisk in the cornstarch mixture, and simmer until the sauce thickens slightly, 2–3 minutes (page 24). Season with a pinch of white pepper.

Cut the breasts on the diagonal into thin slices, and place a half breast on each warmed individual plate. Spoon the sauce over the duck, dividing it evenly. Spoon the pilaf beside the duck. Serve at once.

Muscovy duck breasts are generously sized, and those weighing almost 1 pound (500 g) will easily serve two people. If you start with a whole Long Island duck and remove the breasts, you will likely need one whole breast per person, as they tend to be smaller than the breasts from the large Muscovy ducks, which are bred for foie gras. The breasts cook very quickly, so you will need to begin cooking the pilaf before the duck breasts go into the oven. Soaking the long-grain basmati rice before cooking results in light, individual cooked grains.

Christmas Goose
with Apple-Plum Compote

Roast goose is the traditional bird on many Christmas tables. A goose does not yield as much meat as a turkey or capon of equal weight, but it does yield a generous amount of goose fat, which is prized for sautéing potatoes, sausages, or other foods. If you can find only a frozen goose, you will need to allow 2 days for thawing it in the refrigerator. The breast meat tends to dry out during roasting, so brining for 24 hours helps keep it moist and succulent. The dried-fruit compote perfectly complements the rich dark meat of the goose and is also good with roasted pork or quail.

Combine the salt, sugar, and 6 cups (48 fl oz/1.5 l) room-temperature water in a nonreactive container about 3 inches (7.5 cm) taller and a little wider than the goose. Stir until the salt and sugar dissolve. Add the juniper berries, peppercorns, and cinnamon stick and stir well.

Remove the giblets and neck from the goose cavity; reserve the liver for another use or discard. Reserve the neck, gizzard, and heart for the roasting pan. Remove any pockets of fat from the cavity and render for another use (page 295) or discard. Trim the neck skin, leaving just enough to fold over and skewer. Rinse the goose, then immerse, breast side down, in the brine. If needed, invert a small plate on top of the goose to keep it submerged. Cover the container with plastic wrap and refrigerate for 24 hours.

Remove the goose from the brine, rinse, pat dry with paper towels, and let stand at room temperature for 1 hour before roasting. Preheat the oven to 375°F (190°C). Place a V-shaped roasting rack in a roasting pan just large enough to hold the goose.

Holding the blade of a sharp knife almost parallel to the skin, push the tip through the skin to make small slits all over the breast and thighs. Do not penetrate the flesh. Season the cavity with pepper and place the apple and the onion in the cavity. Place 3 metal trussing or poultry pins through the skin from one side of the cavity to the opposite side, making sure they are parallel and evenly spaced. Lace kitchen string around both sides of the pins, as if lacing a shoe, pulling it tight to close the cavity. Knot the string and trim any excess. Tuck the wing tips under the back. Tie string around the legs to hold them together and another piece around the breast and wings. Transfer the goose, breast side up, to the rack. In a saucepan, bring 4 cups (32 fl oz/1 l) water to a boil and pour it into the bottom of the roasting pan. Add the giblets and neck. Cover the pan with aluminum foil.

Place the goose in the oven and steam-roast for 45 minutes. Remove the foil and, using a small ladle, baste the goose with the liquid in the bottom of the pan. Continue to roast the goose uncovered, basting occasionally with the liquid, until a thermometer (page 16) inserted into the thickest part of a thigh registers 170°F (77°C). If the goose is getting too brown, cover the breast with foil.

(continued on page 156)

1¹/₂ cups (12 oz/375 g) kosher salt

³/₄ cup (6 oz/185 g) sugar

10 juniper berries, crushed

10 peppercorns

1 cinnamon stick

1 young goose, about 10 lb (5 kg), with giblets

Freshly ground pepper

1 tart green apple, cored and coarsely chopped

1 small yellow onion, coarsely chopped

For the Compote

2 teaspoons extra-virgin olive oil

1 large shallot, minced

1 1/4 cups (4 oz/125 g) dried apple rings

2/3 cup (4 oz/125 g) dried plums

1/3 cup (2 oz/60 g) pitted dried tart cherries

1/3 cup (2 oz/60 g) golden raisins (sultanas)

1 large strip orange peel, stuck with 2 whole cloves

Juice of 1 orange

1 teaspoon grated, peeled fresh ginger

1/2 teaspoon dry mustard

1/4 teaspoon ground cinnamon

4 cups (32 fl oz/1 l) apple juice

1 1/2 teaspoons cornstarch (cornflour), if needed

For the Sauce

2 cups (16 fl oz/500 ml) reduced-sodium chicken broth

1/3 cup (3 fl oz/80 ml) dry vermouth or dry white wine

1 tablespoon cornstarch (cornflour)

Kosher salt and freshly ground pepper

(Christmas Goose with Apple-Plum Compote, continued)

While the goose is roasting, make the fruit compote: In a small frying pan over medium-low heat, warm the olive oil. Add the shallot and sauté until very soft, 4–5 minutes. Remove from the heat. In a large saucepan, combine the shallot, apples, plums, cherries, raisins, orange peel and juice, ginger, mustard, cinnamon, and apple juice. There should be enough liquid to cover the fruit by 1/2 inch (12 mm) or so. Bring to a boil over high heat, reduce the heat to low, and simmer until the fruit is soft, 20–25 minutes. If there is a lot of unabsorbed liquid, in a small bowl, dissolve the cornstarch in 1 tablespoon water and then stir the mixture into the fruit a little at a time and cook, stirring occasionally, until the juices thicken, 2–3 minutes. Remove from the heat and set aside.

When the goose is done, transfer it to a platter or carving board and tent with aluminum foil. Let rest for 20 minutes.

While the goose is resting, make the sauce: Strain the contents of the roasting pan through a fine-mesh sieve into a saucepan. Spoon off as much fat as possible from the surface and reserve for another use or discard. Add the broth and vermouth to the pan, place over high heat, and bring to a boil. Boil until reduced to about 1 cup (8 fl oz/250 ml), 5–7 minutes. In a small bowl, dissolve the cornstarch in 2 tablespoons water and add to the pan. Continue to cook, stirring occasionally, until the sauce thickens slightly, about 2 minutes (page 24). Season to taste with salt and pepper and keep warm.

Carve the goose as for chicken (page 285), cutting the thighs from the drumsticks and slicing the meat from each thigh. Arrange the goose on a warmed platter, serving as much of the crisp skin as possible. Serve the compote at room temperature or reheat gently. Pass the sauce at the table.

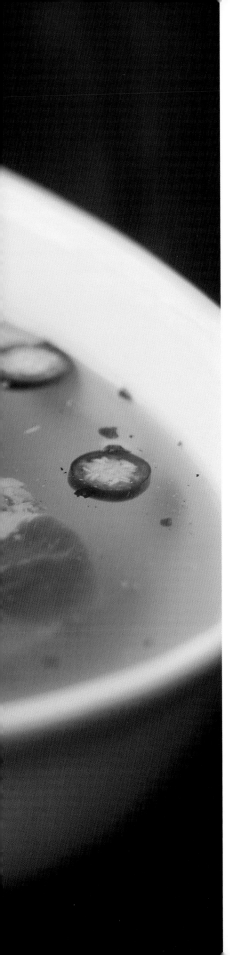

Meats

About Meats

When most people think of roasting meats, a large beef roast is usually what initially comes to mind. This Sunday dinner favorite is the traditional showpiece for this classic cooking technique, but many different kinds of meat and a variety of cuts take well to roasting.

Roasting is ideal for cooking tender cuts of meat, and, in general, the more tender the cut, the shorter the roasting time and the higher the oven temperature. Beef Tenderloin with Madeira Sauce (page 171) and Veal Loin Roast with a Mustard-Shallot Crust (page 188) both follow this simple rule. But roasting is also good for less tender cuts, which are cooked at a lower temperature and for a longer time, as illustrated by Lamb Shoulder Roast with Herbs and Black Olives (page 200) and Slow-Roasted Pork Shoulder (page 208).

Tender cuts come from the less exercised part of the animal. Using beef as an example, that means the short loin, sirloin, and ribs. Tougher cuts, that is, those with more connective tissue, include brisket and chuck roasts. Large pieces of meat are sometimes started at high heat to help brown and caramelize the surface, and then roast at a lower temperature until done. This method, called hybrid roasting (page 13), is used for Leg of Lamb with Bread Crumb Crust (page 196) and a standing rib roast (page 177).

CHOOSING A CUT

Bone-in and boneless meats, such as Fresh Ham with Pineapple-Jicama Salsa (page 211) and Leg of Lamb Stuffed with Roasted Peppers and Onions (page 199), respectively, can be roasted successfully. Bone-in cuts cook faster than boned—this is especially true for lamb legs—because the bone helps spread the heat throughout the meat more quickly.

Whatever cut you decide on, check its marbling before you buy it. Marbling refers to the streaks of fat that run through the meat, which help keep it moist. The more marbling, the more tender and juicy the beef, lamb, or pork. This streaking is also an indication that the meat is of a superior grade. Look for several small flecks or thin "streams" of fat, rather than large deposits or broad white "rivers."

Leaner meats, which have less marbling, usually need added moisture. You can accomplish this by a few different methods. Barding, covering lean meat with bacon slices or a thin sheet of pork fat, is one way. This classic technique is employed to keep the meat loaf on page 187 moist and flavorful. You can cover the meat with a flavorful coating, as in Pork Tenderloin with Whole-Grain Mustard (page 221); slather it with butter, as in Venison Loin with Wild Blueberry Sauce (page 230); or brine it, as in Pork Chops with Cranberry-Orange Stuffing (page 225) or Caribbean-Brined Pork Chops (page 222).

These methods of adding moisture to lean meats have the advantage of also contributing flavor. But a number of other excellent ways to add flavor also exist. You can treat the meat to a marinade, for example, allowing the seasonings to penetrate it for a time before roasting, as in Lamb Chops with Mint, Tomato, and Garlic Sauce (page 206).

You can also apply seasonings to the exterior of meat. The chateaubriand on page 174 calls for a simple rub of ground dried shiitake mushrooms, the Leg of Lamb with Garlic and Rosemary (page 195) is studded with garlic cloves and rosemary sprigs, and the Slow-Roasted Pork Shoulder (page 208) is coated with a garlic-spice mixture.

Building a "rack" of vegetables to hold the meat not only imparts flavor to the roast, but also seasons the pan juices, which can be made into a sauce later. The beef tenderloin on page 171 uses onion slices for its roasting rack, while the pork loin chops on page 226 are placed on a bed of onion and rhubarb. Or you can surround the roasting meat with vegetables, creating an easy side dish at the same time, as in Cross-Rib Roast with Roasted Root Vegetables (page 168).

FLAVORING WITH STUFFING AND CRUSTS

Stuffing both large and small cuts of meat is yet another means of enhancing flavor. You can cut "pockets" into veal breasts or pork chops to accommodate fillings, or you can hollow out a "tunnel" in the center of a roast, a technique used for Pork Loin with Armagnac-Soaked Dried Plums (page 212). Other cuts can be rolled around a stuffing, such as the boneless leg of lamb encasing a vegetable stuffing on page 199.

Various crusts, from a layer of kosher salt for the porterhouse steak on page 182 to the bread crumb and herb mixture that coats the lamb on page 196, heighten flavor, too. So do basting mixtures, such as the sherry and balsamic vinegar blend brushed on the baby back ribs on page 219.

When the roasts are done, the pan juices that remain can be turned into wonderful sauces to accompany the meat. Eye of Round with Béarnaise Sauce (page 167) and Veal Loin Chops with Tarragon-Wine Sauce (page 193) are two fine examples of this classic finish to roasted meats.

Roasting Meats

Roasting is not limited to meat, of course, but arguably these recipes for beef, veal, pork, lamb, and venison show off the technique at its best. The burnished brown crusts, the meaty-sweet flavors, and the enticing aromas are all part of roasting meats.

All meat sold in the United States must be inspected by the United States Department of Agriculture (USDA). Grading, however, is voluntary, and much of the meat on the market is sold ungraded. While a higher grade of meat means better flavor after cooking, tenderness is mainly decided by the cut. Charts mapping the different cuts of beef, pork, and lamb appear on pages 288 to 293.

So-called natural meats have become more common in the marketplace in response to consumer concerns about environmentally responsible meat production and hormonal residues in food. To be labeled *natural*, meats must be minimally processed and contain no preservatives or artificial colorings, flavorings, or other artificial ingredients. Most fresh meat products meet these criteria, so be sure to look for additional labeling, such as claims of no hormones or growth stimulants, even though the expression of such statements is not presently covered by law.

Although the USDA has established standards for use of the term *organic* for many foods, it has not yet put together enforceable rules to govern organic meat products. Nonetheless, many meat processors follow the standards of California law, which state that the animals must have been raised without the use of steroids or antibiotics and fed only pesticide-free fodder, and they promote their products as organic.

ABOUT BEEF AND VEAL

Beef remains America's favorite red meat. In addition to natural and organic beef, some brands are labeled grass-fed. Most beef is corn-fed, a diet that brings larger, fatter cattle to the market more quickly. Grass-fed beef, which is promoted as an environmentally sustainable method of raising cattle, has about one-third less fat than corn-fed. To keep this leaner beef from drying out in the heat of the oven, roast it to no more than medium-rare.

Only three grades of beef, prime, choice, and select, are available to the home cook; the five lesser grades of beef are turned into processed foods. Most prime beef, the highest quality of the system, ends up in restaurant kitchens, but it can also be found at top-notch butcher shops. Most of the beef available to consumers is choice grade. Select grade beef is often used as a market's house brand and is sometimes misleadingly labeled with names like "super select."

Lamb, pork, and beef such as this chateaubriand should have just enough marbling, or streaks of fat, to keep the meat moist during roasting.

Veal loin chops are very lean. The meat is trimmed of any visible fat before roasting and should not be overcooked.

All beef is aged before selling, a process that can improve the flavor and texture of the meat. There are two primary aging methods, dry-aging and wet-aging. Dry-aging exposes unwrapped beef to refrigerated air during a period of three weeks or more. This condition releases tenderizing enzymes and evaporates juices to concentrate flavor, considerably raising the price. Dry-aged beef is not easy to find, but worth the search for its superior taste. Some beef is wet-aged in vacuum packaging for about two weeks, which develops tenderizing enzymes but does not evaporate juices for improved flavor.

When you buy beef, look for flesh that is cherry to brownish red, with clearly visible marbling. Graining should be tight with no gaps, and the fat should be creamy white.

Before roasting, trim away as much remaining external fat as you wish, keeping a thin layer of surface fat on roasts, but leave the internal marbling alone. Some meats, such as pork and beef tenderloin, are enclosed in a thin membrane, the silver skin, which must be removed. This is easily done: slip a thin, flexible knife under the membrane and run the knife down the length of the roast, being careful not to cut away the flesh.

The most delicate veal comes from calves that have been fed only a milk-based formula or their mother's milk. Grass- or range-fed veal has a slightly stronger flavor and is sometimes labeled "calf." Few processors grade their veal (which is voluntary) and prefer to use proprietary brand names to indicate quality. Of the veal that is graded, most prime cuts go to restaurants, and choice and select grades reach the consumer via markets and butchers.

Because veal is a popular meat in many European cuisines, excellent veal can usually be found at butcher shops in Italian neighbor-

A leg of lamb can be boned, flattened, and rolled around a stuffing to form a cylindrical roast (page 199). Tying the roll helps hold the stuffing and maintain a uniform shape.

hoods. Milk-fed veal should have pale pink flesh with visible intramuscular, white fat. Grass-fed veal will have rosy pink flesh and fat that may have an ivory cast.

Veal is almost austerely lean and is seldom cooked rare. The flavor of most veal does not fully develop unless the meat is cooked to medium. This is not a problem with tougher cuts, like shoulder and breast, but extra care should be taken with veal loin, as overcooking leads to dryness. Loin chops, for instance, are roasted briefly to medium-rare.

ABOUT LAMB

Most lamb is from relatively young (less than a year old) animals with mild-flavored flesh. During the holidays, you may be able to find delicate baby (milk-fed) or spring (under five months old and actually raised year-round) lamb. These are usually roasted whole and require special techniques and roasting pans.

Widely exported New Zealand lamb is processed from smaller, but not necessarily younger or more tender animals than most

domestic American lamb, and a leg from New Zealand will be noticeably smaller. Obviously, racks of lamb (the eight or nine rib chops from one side of the animal) are also smaller. Some cooks feel that New Zealand lamb, as well as Australian, is less strongly flavored than U.S. lamb. You may want to sample various cuts to determine your preference.

Lamb is subject to only four grades, with choice making up the bulk of what is available to the consumer. The meat should be red with smooth, white fat. You do not need to be concerned about whether the meat has sufficient marbling. Lamb does not need much intramuscular fat to be tender after cooking.

Use a sharp knife to trim away as much fat as possible from the surface of lamb. Underneath the fat on a leg of lamb is the fell, a thin, papery membrane. Some cooks remove the fell because they believe it gives the flesh a gamy flavor; others warn that it holds the meat together, and they do not find a taste difference. If you choose to trim off the fell, do so with a sharp, thin-bladed knife.

ABOUT PORK

Pork is a chameleon in the kitchen, able to handle a broad variety of flavors. The majority of pork in the market has been processed into smoked or cured products or has been turned into sausages, but fresh pork is the best candidate for roasting. The four numerical grades of fresh pork, from top grade number 1 through the commercial grade 4, are determined by the ratio of meat to fat. Only the top grade is sold fresh to the home cook.

Fresh pork is ideally pink with a slight tinge of red. The meat should be finely grained, although larger cuts of pork may look somewhat coarser. The fat should be pink and well trimmed from the surface. Much has been made of the healthfulness of today's lean pork, but some marbling markedly improves the moistness and flavor of the cooked meat. Some farmers still raise well-marbled pork by old-fashioned methods. You can seek out this full-flavored product at farmers' markets and specialty butcher shops. Your butcher may be able to order it for you.

Because nowadays pork is typically lean, you must be particularly careful not to overcook it to an unpalatable dryness. In the past,

After long roasting at low temperature, the meat on spareribs is meltingly tender (page 216). A spicy sauce is brushed on the ribs during their final hour in the oven.

cooks had to be concerned about the trichinosis parasite, which was occasionally found in fresh pork. While the USDA does not use microscopic or immunological testing for the trichinosis parasite, very few cases occur every year, and the ones that do are usually traced to wild boar or home-raised pork that has not been inspected. Trichinae are killed at temperatures above 137°F (58°C). Perfectly roasted pork is cooked to an internal temperature of about 150°F (65°C) and will have a hint of

pink when carved. Large, collagen-rich cuts, such as shoulder or fresh ham, are often cooked to higher temperatures for melt-in-your-mouth tenderness.

As is the case with most meats, pork needs little preparation for roasting. Trim any excess surface fat with a sharp knife, leaving a thin layer to act as a form of natural basting as it melts in the heat of the oven. The silver skin of boneless pork tenderloin can be peeled away with a sharp, flexible-bladed knife.

DONENESS TEMPERATURES FOR MEAT

The internal temperature of roasted meats rises 5° to 10°F (3° to 6°C) after they are removed from the oven and allowed to rest for 5 or 10 minutes or longer, depending on their size, shape, and weight. The figures below reflect the temperatures that roasted meats need to reach prior to the resting period. Be sure to allow meats to stand as directed in recipes so that the temperature will rise to the level of optimum doneness.

TYPE	RARE	MEDIUM-RARE	MEDIUM	MEDIUM-WELL	WELL
BEEF	120°–125°F (49°–52°C)	125°–130°F (52°–54°C)	135°–140°F (57°–60°C)	140°–150°F (60°–65°C)	150°F (65°C)
VEAL	___	125°–130°F (52°–54°C)	135°–140°F (57°–60°C)	140°–150°F (60°–65°C)	___
LAMB	120°–125°F (49°–52°C)	125°–130°F (52°–54°C)	135°–140°F (57°–60°C)	140°–150°F (60°–65°C)	150°F (65°C)
PORK	___	___	135°–140°F (57°–60°C)	140°–150°F (60°–65°C)	150°F (65°C)

TEMPERATURE AND TIMING

The recipes in this chapter provide specific amounts for ingredients and yields and exact numbers for temperature and timing. These calculations are based on the following guidelines, which can also be applied to any recipes that you create on your own.

For each serving, allow about $^1/_2$ pound (250 g) uncooked boneless meat or $^3/_4$ pound (375 g) uncooked bone-in meat. These amounts may sound large, but the meat will likely need trimming before it goes in the oven and will shrink during roasting.

In the past, recipes for roasting meats usually arrived at cooking times by specifying a certain number of minutes per pound (500 g) to reach the desired temperature, a method that considers only the meat's weight. The new thinking includes two additional factors: the size and the shape of the meat. The greater the ratio of surface area to weight, the more quickly the food cooks. In other words, an elongated, cylindrical beef tenderloin will cook faster than a rectangular rib roast, even if they weigh the same. Consider this example: Take

For an accurate reading, a thermometer should be inserted into the centermost portion of the meat without touching bone, which holds more heat.

two pork tenderloins, one 6 inches (15 cm) long and one 12 inches (30 cm) long, and both 2 inches (5 cm) in diameter. Because they are the same diameter, they will take the same amount of time to roast. But if you stack and tie a pair of 2-inch (5-cm) tenderloins together to make one thick roast, they will take twice as long to roast as single tenderloins because the combined pieces are twice as thick. Bones, which conduct heat and cook the meat from the inside, will also affect timing.

TESTING FOR DONENESS

Perhaps the most important factor in determining doneness is residual heat, which continues to cook meat outside the oven. Therefore, always remove the meat from the oven when it is 5° to 10°F (3° to 6°C) shy of its optimum doneness temperature. Large cuts retain more heat. If a roast is larger than 8 pounds (4 kg), you may want to allow a 15°F (7°C) window, especially if you prefer rare meat.

There is no substitute for a good meat thermometer (page 16). A roast cooks from the outside in, with the center the last to cook, so the tip of the thermometer must reach the center of the meat. The stem should not touch a bone or any fatty areas. It is sometimes difficult to determine the doneness of odd-shaped or fatty meats. Heat will not penetrate all areas of an irregularly shaped roast at the same rate. Fat heats quickly and can make one section of a roast hotter than another. If necessary, take two readings in different places and average the temperatures.

Doneness temperatures vary for different cuts and types of meat. Most lean meats, such as beef eye of round and tenderloin, should never be cooked beyond medium-rare, or they will dry out and toughen. On the other hand, veal and pork do not develop flavor until they

Beef roasted to medium-rare will have pinkish red flesh and, like other meats, should rest before being carved and served.

are cooked to the medium or medium-well stage, at which point they taste good and not overcooked. Stuffed meat has more layers for the heat to penetrate, which means it needs a longer stay in the oven than unstuffed meat. Different types of stuffings also affect roasting times. Moist, compact stuffings call for longer roasting than a loosely layered filling of ham and cheese does.

All roasted meat will be juicier and more evenly cooked after a resting period. While the time required for resting depends on the size of the roast, typically it is best to allow at least 10 minutes for the juices to redistribute themselves and for the internal temperature to equalize. If a roast is carved before a sufficient resting, the juices will rush out of the meat, taking the meat's natural moistness with them.

If meat is undercooked, do not panic. It is much easier to fix an undercooked roast than an overcooked one (in fact, the latter situation is impossible to remedy). Continue to roast the meat in 8- to 10-minute increments, using a meat thermometer to check the progress, until the meat reaches the desired doneness.

Eye of Round with Béarnaise Sauce

The eye of round is a robust cut of meat, not as tender as a rib eye, but wonderful when roasted medium-rare and thinly sliced. Refrigerating the seasoned meat for a few hours before roasting helps develop flavor. The tarragon-perfumed béarnaise sauce can be served at room temperature and has excellent staying power in the refrigerator. If it is cold, bring it back to room temperature and whisk it before serving. The beef can also be served at cool room temperature, making it excellent picnic fare.

Using a sharp knife, trim away the silver skin and most of the fat from the roast. Season the roast on all sides with salt and pepper, and refrigerate, uncovered, for 3–4 hours. Remove from the refrigerator at least 1 hour before roasting.

Preheat the oven to 400°F (200°C). Oil a flat roasting rack and place it in a roasting pan just large enough to hold the roast.

Preheat a large, heavy ovenproof frying pan over high heat until very hot. Add the oil and then the meat. Sear the meat on all sides, 3–4 minutes total. Transfer the meat to the rack. Roast until a thermometer (page 16) inserted into the center of the meat registers 125°F (52°C) for medium-rare (page 164), about 50 minutes.

Remove the roast from the oven and tent with aluminum foil. Let rest for 10–15 minutes.

While the roast is resting, make the sauce: In a small saucepan over medium-high heat, combine the vinegar, the vermouth, the shallot, and $1^1/2$ teaspoons of the fresh tarragon. Bring to a boil and cook until reduced to about 2 tablespoons, 3–4 minutes. Remove from the heat and allow the mixture to cool slightly. In another saucepan over medium-low heat, melt the butter until it begins to foam; keep warm.

In a blender, process the egg yolks on high speed until the yolks thicken, about 2 minutes. Add the vinegar mixture and process to combine. With the motor running and the lid in place, gradually add one-half of the hot butter, pouring it through the hole in the lid. The sauce will thicken. Pour the mixture into a bowl and gradually whisk in the remaining hot butter. Add the remaining $4^1/2$ teaspoons fresh tarragon and the *demi-glace* and tomato paste, if using, then season to taste with salt and white pepper. Taste the sauce, and if it does not seem to have enough tarragon flavor, stir in the $^1/2$ teaspoon dried tarragon. Allow the sauce to stand at room temperature until the meat has been sliced. (If you are making it more than 1 hour ahead, cover and refrigerate for up to 1 day, but bring to room temperature and whisk briefly before serving.)

Transfer the roast to a carving board and cut across the grain into slices $^1/4$ inch (6 mm) thick. Arrange 2 or 3 slices on each warmed, individual plate, or arrange slices on a platter. Spoon a little of the sauce over each slice and pass the remainder at the table.

1 eye of round roast, about 3 lb (1.5 kg)

Kosher salt and freshly ground black pepper

2 teaspoons extra-virgin olive oil

For the Sauce

$^1/4$ cup (2 fl oz/60 ml) tarragon wine vinegar

$^1/4$ cup (2 fl oz/60 ml) dry vermouth or dry white wine

1 tablespoon minced shallot

2 tablespoons minced fresh tarragon

1 cup (8 oz/250 g) unsalted butter

3 large egg yolks

$^1/2$ teaspoon beef *demi-glace* (page 295) (optional)

$^1/2$ teaspoon tomato paste (optional)

Kosher salt and freshly ground white pepper

$^1/2$ teaspoon dried tarragon, if needed

Cross-Rib Roast with Roasted Root Vegetables

1 boneless cross-rib roast, about 3¹/₂ lb (1.75 kg), tied

Extra-virgin olive oil for coating

Kosher salt and freshly ground pepper

2 cups (16 fl oz/500 ml) reduced-sodium beef broth

1 cup (8 fl oz/250 ml) dry red wine

5 or 6 fresh thyme sprigs

2 bay leaves

1 lb (500 g) carrots (about 5), peeled and cut into 1¹/₂-inch (4-cm) lengths

¹/₂ lb (250 g) shallots (about 6 large), unpeeled

1 lb (500 g) Yukon gold or red new potatoes (3 or 4 potatoes), peeled and cut into 1¹/₂-inch (4-cm) chunks

6 large cloves garlic, unpeeled

For this classic "Sunday dinner roast," carrots, shallots, and potatoes are roasted with the meat and served on the side. The soft roasted garlic cloves are delicious squeezed over the meat and vegetables, and a *jus* adds moistness and flavor. The cross-rib shoulder roast, also known as a shoulder clod, needs to be cooked well done to soften the connective tissue and produce a more tender result. It usually comes tied or in a net stocking, ready to cook.

Remove the roast from the refrigerator 1 hour before roasting. Preheat the oven to 350°F (180°C). Brush the roast on all sides with olive oil and season with salt and pepper. Preheat a large, deep ovenproof sauté pan over high heat until very hot. Add the meat and sear all sides, first turning it to sear the round surfaces and then the large flat end, 2–3 minutes total. Add the broth, wine, thyme, and bay leaves, cover with aluminum foil, and place in the oven.

Roast the meat for 1 hour. Carefully remove the pan from the oven, remove the foil, and add the carrots. Top with the shallots, potatoes, and garlic, and, using tongs, stir the vegetables so they will cook evenly in the liquid. Continue to roast, uncovered, until a thermometer (page 16) inserted into the center of the meat registers 150°F (65°C) and a fork goes into the meat easily, about 1 hour longer.

Remove the pan from the oven, transfer the meat to a platter, and tent with aluminum foil. Let rest for 15 minutes. Using a fork, check the vegetables to make sure they are tender. If they are not, return the pan to the oven for 5–10 minutes longer while the roast is resting, then spoon the vegetables into a large warmed serving bowl and cover with aluminum foil to keep warm. Remove the thyme sprigs and bay leaves from the pan and discard.

To make the *jus*, use a large spoon to skim off any surface fat from the pan juices and discard. Place the pan over high heat and bring the juices to a boil. Add any juices that have accumulated on the platter and cook until reduced to about 1¹/₄ cups (10 fl oz/310 ml), about 5 minutes. Season to taste with salt and pepper; keep warm.

Transfer the roast to a carving board and carve into slices ¹/₂ inch (12 mm) thick (page 286). Arrange on a warmed platter or individual plates. Spoon a little *jus* over the meat. Pass the remaining *jus* and the vegetables at the table.

Beef Tenderloin with Madeira Sauce

A whole roasted beef tenderloin is an ideal centerpiece for an easy and elegant company dinner. After trimming, a 6-pound (3-kg) tenderloin will yield about 4 pounds (2 kg) meat, which will serve ten people generously. The roast is done in a relatively short time, so the sweet onions are first cooked on top of the stove, then cooled slightly before being used as a roasting rack. A sweet, amber Bual Madeira provides complexity and flavor to the classic sauce. A tawny port can be substituted if the Madeira is unavailable. Accompany the tenderloin and sauce with oven-roasted fingerling potatoes (page 241).

Using a sharp, thin-bladed knife, remove the chain muscle, the long, thin side muscle with connective tissue and fat that runs almost the length of the beef tenderloin. Reserve for another use, such as stir-frying or ground beef, or discard. Then, remove the silver skin and most of the surface fat from the tenderloin. Next, make a shallow cut about halfway through the meat across the narrow tail 5–6 inches (13–15 cm) from the end, and fold this narrow end piece under to make a uniformly thick cylinder. Secure the cylinder with kitchen string by tying it at 1$\frac{1}{2}$-inch (4-cm) intervals along the length of the tenderloin. Place the tenderloin on a platter. Brush or rub the meat on all sides with 2 tablespoons of the olive oil, and season generously with salt and pepper, firmly pressing the seasonings in with your fingertips. (At this point, the roast can be refrigerated uncovered for up to 24 hours. Remove it from the refrigerator about 1 hour before roasting.)

In a large frying pan over low heat, warm the remaining 2 tablespoons olive oil. Add the onions, stir to coat with the oil, and season to taste with salt and pepper. Cook for 2–3 minutes, then add $\frac{1}{4}$ cup (2 fl oz/60 ml) water, the thyme, and the balsamic vinegar. Cover and cook over low heat, stirring occasionally, until the onions are very soft but not browned, about 15 minutes. Uncover and, if any liquid remains in the bottom of the pan, raise the heat to medium-high and cook just until the liquid evaporates. Again, do not let the onions color.

Position a rack in the upper third of the oven and preheat to 425°F (220°C). Arrange the onions down the center of a shallow roasting pan just large enough to hold the tenderloin (or on the diagonal if you have a larger roast) to form a platform for the roast. Place the tenderloin on the onions.

Roast the tenderloin until a thermometer (page 16) inserted into the thickest part registers 125°F (52°C) for medium-rare (page 164), about 45 minutes. The roast will vary somewhat in doneness depending on the thickness of its sections.

(continued on page 173)

1 whole beef tenderloin, about 6 lb (3 kg) before trimming

4 tablespoons (2 fl oz/60 ml) extra-virgin olive oil

Kosher salt and freshly ground pepper

2$\frac{1}{2}$ lb (2.25 kg) large Vidalia or other sweet onions (about 5), cut into slices $\frac{1}{4}$ inch (6 mm) thick

2 fresh thyme sprigs

1 tablespoon balsamic vinegar

(Beef Tenderloin with Madeira Sauce, continued)

Remove the pan from the oven, transfer the meat to a platter, and tent with aluminum foil. Let rest for 10–15 minutes.

While the meat is resting, make the sauce: In a saucepan over medium-high heat, bring the ¹/₂ cup Madeira to a boil and cook until reduced to ¹/₄ cup (2 fl oz/ 60 ml). Pour about ¹/₂ cup (4 fl oz/125 ml) of the pan juices from the roasting pan through a fine-mesh sieve into the saucepan. Discard the thyme and reserve the onions in the pan until serving. Add the beef broth to the saucepan, bring to a boil, and cook for 2–3 minutes to reduce slightly and blend the flavors. Reduce the heat to medium-low and stir in the *demi-glace* and red wine vinegar. Season to taste with salt and pepper and 2–3 tablespoons more Madeira, if desired.

Meanwhile, place the butter and flour in a small bowl and mix together with a fork until well combined, to make a beurre manié. Reduce the heat under the sauce to low, whisk the beurre manié into the liquid a little at a time (page 24), and simmer until the sauce reaches the desired consistency, 2–3 minutes. Keep the sauce warm.

Transfer the tenderloin to a carving board. Remove the strings and cut the roast into slices ¹/₂ inch (12 mm) thick. Place a spoonful of the onions on each warmed individual plate and top with a slice of tenderloin. Spoon a little of the sauce over the meat and pass the remaining sauce at the table.

For the Sauce

¹/₂ cup (4 fl oz/125 ml) Bual Madeira (see note), or as needed

3 cups (24 fl oz/750 ml) reduced-sodium beef broth

2–3 tablespoons beef *demi-glace* (page 295)

1 tablespoon red wine vinegar

Kosher salt and freshly ground pepper

2 tablespoons unsalted butter, at room temperature

2 tablespoons all-purpose (plain) flour

Chateaubriand with Shiitake Mushroom Rub

1 chateaubriand, 1–1¹/₄ lb (500–625 g)

6 dried shiitake mushrooms, about ¹/₄ oz (7 g) total weight

¹/₄ teaspoon peppercorns

Kosher salt

2 tablespoons extra-virgin olive oil

1 tablespoon dry Marsala, or as needed

For the Sauce

2 tablespoons unsalted butter

¹/₂ lb (250 g) fresh shiitake mushrooms, brushed clean, stems removed, and caps cut into slices ¹/₄ inch (6 mm) thick (about 2 cups/ 6 oz/185 g)

3 or 4 green (spring) onions, white part only, thinly sliced

¹/₄ cup (2 fl oz/60 ml) dry Marsala

2 teaspoons beef *demi-glace* (page 295)

Kosher salt and freshly ground pepper

1 teaspoon fresh lemon juice

White truffle oil for drizzling (optional)

Remove the chateaubriand from the refrigerator about 30 minutes before roasting. Preheat the oven to 450°F (230°C). Oil a flat roasting rack and place it in a roasting pan just large enough to hold the chateaubriand.

Remove the silver skin and most of the surface fat from the chateaubriand. Using kitchen string, tie at 2-inch (5-cm) intervals along the length of the chateaubriand. Break each dried mushroom into 2 or 3 pieces, and remove and discard the hard stems. In a spice grinder, combine the mushrooms and peppercorns and process until finely ground. Pour into a small bowl and add ¹/₄ teaspoon salt, the olive oil, and the 1 tablespoon Marsala. Stir well to form a paste. If needed, add a little more Marsala to make the mixture stick together. Press the mushroom mixture evenly over the surface of the chateaubriand. Transfer to the prepared pan.

Roast the meat until a thermometer (page 16) inserted into the center of the meat registers 125°–130°F (52°–54°C) for medium-rare (page 164), 30–35 minutes. If the mushroom crust seems to be overbrowning, place a small piece of aluminum foil over the top of the roast for the last few minutes of roasting time.

Remove the pan from the oven, transfer the meat to a warmed platter, and tent with aluminum foil. Let rest for 10 minutes.

Meanwhile, make the sauce: In a frying pan over medium-high heat, melt the butter. When it begins to foam, add the fresh mushrooms and sauté until they release their liquid, 2–3 minutes. Reduce the heat to medium-low, add the green onions, and cook for 2 minutes. Add the Marsala, *demi-glace*, and salt and pepper to taste, stirring to combine. Cook for 2 more minutes to blend the flavors. When ready to serve, add any accumulated juices from the platter and the lemon juice, and heat through gently.

Transfer the chateaubriand to a carving board and remove the strings. Cut across the grain into slices ¹/₂ inch (12 mm) thick. Fan the slices on a warmed platter or warmed individual plates and drizzle with a few drops of truffle oil, if using. Spoon the mushrooms and sauce alongside the meat, and serve at once.

The chateaubriand, a thick steak cut from the beef tenderloin, makes an elegant main course for a dinner for two. Here, it is coated with a simple rub of dried shiitake mushrooms before it is briefly roasted in a hot oven. The flavors in the rub are echoed in a sauce of fresh shiitakes and onions. If you wish, substitute fresh cremini or button mushrooms for the fresh shiitakes. Just a drizzle of white truffle oil provides a luxurious accent to the finished dish. Marsala, a fortified wine from Sicily, has a rich, almost smoky character that complements the earthy mushrooms.

Standing Rib Roast with Yorkshire Pudding

A standing rib roast is an impressive main course. It is full of flavor, juicy, and tender, and extremely easy to cook. Look for a roast with a thick layer of white fat and marbling through the meat. Ask the butcher for the "first cut," which comes from the loin end and has the biggest eye, and have him or her tie the roast to keep the fat from pulling away from the meat. Yorkshire pudding, a cross between a popover and a soufflé, bakes into a puffy shell. If there is not enough fat from the roasting pan to put 1 teaspoon in each cup, use vegetable oil to make up the balance. Serve the puddings the moment you remove them from the oven, while they still have their full height. Doubling the Horseradish Cream recipe on page 178 will yield 2 cups (16 fl oz/500 ml).

Remove the roast from the refrigerator about 1 hour before roasting. Preheat the oven to 450°F (230°C). Rub the roast on all sides with the softened butter, and season generously with salt and pepper.

To make the Yorkshire pudding, begin preparing the batter when you remove the roast from the refrigerator so that the batter has time to rest before baking. In a blender, combine the eggs and milk, then add the flour and 1 1/4 teaspoons salt. Process until the batter is smooth, about 30 seconds. Cover the blender beaker and place it in the refrigerator until you are ready to bake the pudding.

Place the roast, rib bones down, in a large roasting pan. Roast for 20 minutes. Reduce the oven temperature to 300°F (150°C). Continue to roast until a thermometer (page 16) inserted into the thickest part away from the bone registers 125°–130°F (52°–54°C) for medium-rare (page 164), about 1 1/4 hours longer. Remove the pan from the oven, transfer the roast to a warmed platter, and tent with aluminum foil. Let rest for 30 minutes. Deglaze the roasting pan as directed on page 23, using the broth and reserving the fat spooned from the pan liquid for the pudding. Then pour the pan liquid into a measuring pitcher. You should have 1/4 cup (2 fl oz/60 ml). Reserve the pan juices for making a *jus*.

Position an oven rack in the upper third of the oven and raise the oven temperature to 450°F (230°C). Put 1 teaspoon of the reserved fat in each of 12 nonstick standard muffin cups (see note). Place the muffin pan in the oven to heat for 5 minutes. Pour 3–4 tablespoons of the batter into each hot cup, filling about two-thirds full. Return the pan to the oven and reduce the oven temperature to 425°F (220°C). Bake the pudding until puffed and golden and a knife inserted into the center of one of the puddings comes out clean, about 30 minutes.

While the pudding is baking, prepare the *jus*: Pour the reserved pan juices through a medium-coarse sieve into a saucepan. Place over high heat, bring to a boil, and cook until reduced by about one-third, about 5 minutes. Season to taste with salt and pepper; keep warm.

Transfer the roast to a carving board. Remove the strings and cut along the rib bones to release the meat in a single large piece. Cut across the grain into thick slices. Serve on warmed individual plates and spoon a little *jus* over each slice. Remove the muffin pan from the oven and lift out each pudding with the tip of a knife. Place a pudding on each plate. Pass the horseradish sauce at the table.

4-rib standing rib roast, about 8 lb (4 kg), tied

2 tablespoons unsalted butter, at room temperature

Kosher salt and freshly ground pepper

For the Yorkshire Pudding

3 extra-large eggs

1 1/2 cups (12 fl oz/375 ml) whole milk

1 1/2 cups (7 1/2 oz/235 g) all-purpose (plain) flour

Kosher salt

2 cups (16 fl oz/500 ml) reduced-sodium beef or chicken broth

2 cups (16 fl oz/500 ml) Horseradish Cream (page 178)

New York Strip Steak with Horseradish Cream

2 boneless New York strip steaks, each about ³/₄ lb (375 g) and 1 inch (2.5 cm) thick

Extra-virgin olive oil

Kosher salt and freshly ground pepper

For the Horseradish Cream

¹/₂ cup (4 fl oz/125 ml) heavy (double) cream

2 tablespoons prepared horseradish

¹/₂ teaspoon Dijon mustard

Kosher salt

3 or 4 drops hot-pepper sauce

Using a sharp knife, trim most of the surface fat from the steaks. Brush or rub the steaks on both sides with olive oil and season them with salt and pepper. Allow the steaks to stand at room temperature for 30 minutes before roasting. Preheat the oven to 450°F (230°C).

To make the cream, in a small bowl, whisk the heavy cream until soft peaks form. Fold in the horseradish, the mustard, ¹/₄ teaspoon salt, and the hot-pepper sauce. Spoon the sauce into a serving bowl and refrigerate until serving.

Preheat a large, heavy ovenproof frying pan over high heat until very hot. Add the steaks and sear for 2 minutes on the first side. Turn the steaks and sear for 1 minute on the second side. Immediately place the pan in the oven and roast the steaks until a thermometer (page 16) inserted into the center of the meat registers 125°–130°F (52°–54°C) for medium-rare (page 164), 6–7 minutes. Remove the pan from the oven, transfer the steaks to a warmed platter, and tent with aluminum foil. Let rest for 3–4 minutes.

Transfer the steaks to a carving board. Cut each steak across the grain into slices ¹/₂ inch (12 mm) thick. Fan the slices on warmed individual plates, and pour the accumulated juices from the platter and carving board over the steaks. Pass the horseradish cream at the table.

Boneless New York strip steaks, a restaurant-menu favorite, are easily pan-roasted at home for a special dinner. This cut, also known as Delmonico, Kansas City, or shell steak, is from the porterhouse minus the bone and tenderloin. A zesty sauce of horseradish, mustard, and cream accompanies the meat and can also serve as dressing for a baked potato or cooked asparagus spears. You can make the sauce up to 3 hours in advance and refrigerate it until carving.

Rib-Eye Steaks Marchands de Vin

Here, rib-eye steaks, sometimes called prime rib steaks, are paired with the classic *marchands de vin* (wine merchants) sauce made with shallots and red wine and finished with a little butter. A small amount of *demi-glace* adds extra flavor to the sauce. Prepare the sauce first, then keep it warm while the steaks are roasting. Accompany the steaks with oven-roasted fingerling potatoes (page 241) and a green vegetable. Each steak will serve two people.

Remove the steaks from the refrigerator 30 minutes before serving. Preheat the oven to 450°F (230°C).

To make the sauce, in a small saucepan over medium-high heat, combine the shallot, wine, and peppercorns. Bring to a boil and cook until reduced to about ¹/₃ cup (3 fl oz/80 ml), including the shallot, 5–6 minutes. Remove from the heat and pour through a medium-coarse sieve into a small bowl. Discard the contents of the sieve. Return the sauce to the pan and stir in the *demi-glace*. (The sauce can be made to this point up to 30 minutes in advance.) Just before the steaks are ready, place the pan over medium heat and whisk in the butter a little at a time. Add the parsley and season to taste with salt and pepper; keep warm.

Using a sharp knife, trim away most of the surface fat from the steaks. Brush or rub both sides with olive oil and season with salt and pepper. Preheat a large, heavy ovenproof frying pan over high heat until very hot. Add the steaks and sear for 2 minutes on the first side. Turn the steaks and sear for 1 minute on the second side. Immediately place the pan in the oven and roast until a thermometer (page 16) inserted into the center of the meat away from the bone registers 125°–130°F (52°–54°C) for medium-rare (page 164), about 5 minutes. Remove the pan from the oven, transfer the steaks to a warmed platter, and tent with aluminum foil. Let rest for 4–5 minutes.

Transfer the steaks to a carving board. Cut each steak across the grain into slices ³/₄ inch (2 cm) thick. Arrange the slices on warmed individual serving plates. Spoon an equal amount of the sauce over each portion, then serve.

2 bone-in rib-eye steaks, each about 1 lb (500 g) and 1 inch (2.5 cm) thick

For the Sauce

1 large shallot, minced (about ¹/₄ cup/1¹/₂ oz/45 g)

1 cup (8 fl oz/250 ml) dry red wine

3 or 4 peppercorns

1 teaspoon beef *demi-glace* (page 295) or tomato paste

¹/₄ cup (2 oz/60 g) cold unsalted butter, cut into ¹/₂-inch (12-mm) cubes

1 tablespoon minced fresh flat-leaf (Italian) parsley

Kosher salt and freshly ground pepper

Extra-virgin olive oil for coating

Kosher salt and freshly ground pepper

Porterhouse Steak with Creamed Spinach

1 porterhouse steak, 1³/₄–2 lb (875 g–1 kg) and 1¹/₄ inches (3 cm) thick, trimmed of surface fat

6 oz (185 g) baby spinach leaves

2 tablespoons unsalted butter

3 or 4 fresh cremini or button mushrooms, brushed clean, stems removed, and caps thinly sliced

1 small shallot, minced

3–4 tablespoons (1¹/₂– 2 fl oz/45–60 ml) heavy (double) cream

Kosher salt and freshly ground pepper

Pinch of freshly grated nutmeg

Remove the steak from the refrigerator about 30 minutes before roasting. Preheat the oven to 450°F (230°C). Bring a saucepan of water to a boil. Add the spinach, blanch for 30–45 seconds, and drain. Rinse with running cold water and drain again. Squeeze out as much water as possible, then coarsely chop. In a frying pan over medium heat, melt the butter. Add the mushrooms and sauté until softened, 3–4 minutes. Add the shallot and cook for 1–2 minutes. Add 3 tablespoons of the cream, bring to a boil, and cook for 1–2 minutes. Add the spinach, season with salt and pepper, and cook for 1–2 minutes. Remove from the heat and add the nutmeg and the remaining 1 tablespoon cream, if desired; keep warm.

Preheat a heavy ovenproof frying pan over high heat until very hot. Sprinkle about ¹/₄ teaspoon salt over the bottom of the pan. Pat the steak dry and add to the pan. Sear for 2 minutes. Turn the steak and place the pan in the oven. Roast until a thermometer (page 16) inserted into the center of the meat away from the bone registers 125°–130°F (52°–54°C) for medium-rare (page 164), 7–8 minutes. Transfer the steak to a warmed platter and tent with aluminum foil. Let rest for 5 minutes.

Cut the loin and tenderloin from the bone and cut into slices ³/₈ inch (1 cm) thick. Arrange an equal amount of loin and tenderloin on each warmed plate. Spoon the creamed spinach alongside.

When indulgence is on the menu, a juicy, thick porterhouse steak fills the bill. The thin layer of kosher salt on the bottom of the hot pan helps keep the steak from sticking and seasons the exterior. Creamed spinach is a classic accompaniment. The steak was named after the porterhouses (malt liquor purveyors) of the eighteenth and nineteenth centuries, where the cut was often served to travelers. It comes from the large end of the short loin and contains meat from both the tenderloin and the top loin, separated by the T-bone.

Matambre

**1 large flank steak, 1¹/₂–2 lb
(750 g–1 kg)**

**Kosher salt and freshly
ground pepper**

**1 tablespoon red wine
vinegar**

1 large clove garlic, minced

**1 teaspoon fresh thyme
leaves**

**1 tablespoon extra-virgin
olive oil**

For the Stuffing

Kosher salt

**2 large carrots, peeled and
cut in half lengthwise**

2 sweet Italian sausages

20–30 large spinach leaves

**2 cups (8 oz/250 g) coarsely
grated provolone cheese**

**1 large red bell pepper (cap-
sicum), roasted, peeled, and
seeded (page 294), then cut
lengthwise into strips ¹/₂ inch
(12 mm) wide**

Freshly ground pepper

Lay the steak on a cutting board and cut it almost in half horizontally, stopping within ¹/₂ inch (12 mm) of the opposite side. Open up the steak like a book. Using a meat pounder, lightly pound the steak to flatten it to an even thickness. Season with salt and pepper and sprinkle with the vinegar, garlic, and thyme leaves. Allow the meat to stand at room temperature for 30 minutes.

To make the stuffing, bring a saucepan of water to a boil. Salt lightly, add the carrots, and cook until tender, about 10 minutes. Drain and then transfer to paper towels. In a frying pan, pour water to a depth of ¹/₂ inch (12 mm). Bring to a simmer, add the sausages, cover, and poach until cooked through, about 10 minutes. Using a slotted spoon, transfer the sausages to paper towels to drain. Cut the sausages in half lengthwise.

Preheat the oven to 375°F (190°C). Position the flank steak on a work surface with the long open edge facing you. Starting 1 inch (2.5 cm) in from the edge closest to you and using about half of the spinach leaves, cover the surface of the steak, stopping about 3 inches (7.5 cm) short of the edge farthest from you. Distribute one-half of the cheese over the spinach leaves. Starting about 1¹/₂ (4 cm) inches in from the edge closest to you, arrange a row of carrots so that they run parallel to the grain of the meat. Leave about a ¹/₂-inch (12-mm) gap and then arrange a row of pepper strips. Leave another gap of ¹/₂ inch, and arrange 2 sausage halves. Repeat the rows of carrots, pepper, and sausage until the spinach leaves are covered. Distribute the remaining cheese evenly over the rows, and then cover with the remaining spinach leaves. Starting at the edge nearest to you, fold over the 1¹/₂-inch flap of steak and then roll up tightly into a cylinder. Using kitchen string, secure the cylinder at 2-inch (5-cm) intervals. Season the roll with salt and pepper.

In a heavy ovenproof frying pan just large enough to hold the meat roll, warm the olive oil over high heat. When it is very hot, sear the meat roll on all sides, rotating it a quarter turn every 1–2 minutes. Transfer to the oven and roast the roll until a thermometer (page 16) inserted into the center of the roll registers 135°–140°F (57°–60°C) for medium (page 164), about 40 minutes. Transfer the roll to a carving board and tent with aluminum foil. Let rest for 15–20 minutes. Remove the strings. Cut into ¹/₂-inch (12-mm) slices and arrange on a platter. Serve warm, at room temperature, or cold.

Matambre—"kill the hunger"—is a popular Argentinean beef roulade stuffed with a savory vegetable and meat filling. If you do not want to attempt to butterfly the steak yourself, ask your butcher to do it for you. A sprinkle of red wine vinegar seasons the meat before it is stuffed. The *matambre* can be served warm or cold, and it keeps well in the refrigerator for up to 4 days, with its flavors mellowing. When cut, the slices show off a mosaic vegetable pinwheel that looks attractive on a platter for a buffet. Use a pie server to serve the slices so that they do not fall apart in transport.

Bacon-Wrapped Meat Loaf

Put some russet potatoes into the oven at the same time you put this old-fashioned meat loaf in to roast and you will have the basics for a delicious, no-fuss dinner. The meat loaf is molded in a loaf pan and then turned out on top of a rack of thick onion slices that allows the excess fat to drain away as it cooks. Serve the loaf sliced, either hot or cold, with ketchup and Dijon mustard.

Preheat the oven to 375°F (190°C). Line a 11-by-7^1/$_2$-by-2-inch (28-by-19-by-5-cm) baking pan with heavy-duty aluminum foil. Cut 1 of the onions into slices ^{1}/$_3$ inch (9 cm) thick and arrange the slices in 2 rows down the center of the prepared pan, forming a rack for the meat loaf. Finely chop the remaining onion.

In a frying pan over medium-low heat, warm the olive oil. Add the chopped onion and celery and toss to coat with the oil. Cover and cook, stirring occasionally, until the vegetables are softened, 8–10 minutes; do not let them color. Uncover, add the garlic, and cook for 1 minute longer. Remove from the heat and let cool for a few minutes.

In a large bowl, combine the cooled onion mixture, beef, veal, pork, crumbs, tomato sauce, parsley, egg, Worcestershire sauce, vinegar, mustard, chili powder, hot-pepper sauce, 1 teaspoon salt, and ^{1}/$_4$ teaspoon pepper. Stir thoroughly until all the ingredients are evenly distributed. Line an 8^1/$_2$-by-4^1/$_2$-by-2^1/$_2$-inch (21.5-by-11.5-by-6-cm) loaf pan with plastic wrap. Lay the bacon slices side by side across the width of the pan, with the ends extending over the sides of the pan. Spoon the meat mixture into the bacon-lined pan, and press down on it to pack it firmly. Fold the ends of the bacon strips over the top. Invert the pan over the onion base in the baking pan, lift off the pan, and peel the plastic wrap from the meat mixture.

Roast the meat loaf until a thermometer (page 16) inserted into the center of the loaf registers 180°F (82°C), about 1^1/$_4$ hours.

Remove the pan from the oven and allow the meat loaf to rest in the pan for about 15 minutes.

Transfer the meat loaf to a carving board. Discard the contents of the pan. Cut into slices and arrange on warmed individual plates. Serve at once.

2 large yellow onions

2 tablespoons extra-virgin olive oil

^{1}/$_2$ cup (3 oz/90 g) finely chopped celery hearts

2 cloves minced garlic

1 lb (500 g) ground (minced) beef

^{1}/$_2$ lb (250 g) ground (minced) veal or turkey

^{1}/$_2$ lb (250 g) ground (minced) pork

^{1}/$_2$ cup (1^1/$_2$ oz/45 g) crushed soda cracker crumbs

^{1}/$_4$ cup (2 fl oz/ 60 ml) tomato sauce

^{1}/$_4$ cup (^{1}/$_3$ oz/10 g) chopped fresh flat-leaf (Italian) parsley

1 large egg

1 tablespoon Worcestershire sauce

1 tablespoon red wine vinegar

1 teaspoon dry mustard

1 teaspoon chili powder

^{1}/$_4$ teaspoon hot-pepper sauce, or to taste

Kosher salt and freshly ground black pepper

6 or 7 slices bacon

Veal Loin Roast
with a Mustard-Shallot Crust

1 boneless veal loin roast, 3–4 lb (1.5–2 kg)

1 teaspoon unsalted butter, plus 2 tablespoons at room temperature

1 tablespoon minced shallot

3 tablespoons Dijon mustard

1 tablespoon minced fresh flat-leaf (Italian) parsley

1 teaspoon chopped fresh marjoram

Freshly ground black pepper

1 cup (8 fl oz/250 ml) reduced-sodium chicken broth

¹/₂ cup (4 fl oz/125 ml) dry vermouth or dry white wine

For the Sauce

1 cup (8 fl oz/250 ml) reduced-sodium chicken broth

1 tablespoon cornstarch (cornflour)

2 tablespoons dry vermouth or dry white wine

¹/₂ cup (4 fl oz/125 ml) crème fraîche

Kosher salt and freshly ground white pepper

2 teaspoons white truffle oil (optional)

Remove the veal from the refrigerator about 30 minutes before roasting. Preheat the oven to 500°F (260°C). Oil a flat roasting rack and place it in a roasting pan just large enough to hold the roast.

In a small frying pan over low heat, melt the 1 teaspoon butter. Add the shallot, and sauté until softened but not browned, 2–3 minutes. Remove the pan from the heat, transfer the shallot to a bowl, and let cool. Add the mustard, 2 tablespoons butter, parsley, and marjoram and mix well.

Leave any fat on the veal, which will help baste it during roasting. Shape the roast into a uniform, compact cylinder and tie with kitchen string at 2-inch (5-cm) intervals. Then tie once lengthwise to help the roast keep its shape. Sprinkle the veal with black pepper and spread it evenly with the mustard mixture. If the butcher has provided extra fat (see note), tie it over the meat. Transfer the veal to the rack. Pour the broth and vermouth into the pan.

Roast the veal for 20 minutes. Reduce the oven temperature to 375°F (190°C) and continue to roast until a thermometer (page 16) inserted into the center of the cylinder registers 135°–140°F (57°–60°C) for medium (page 164), 20–25 minutes.

Remove the pan from the oven, transfer the veal to a carving board, and tent with aluminum foil. Let rest for 10–15 minutes. Pour the pan drippings through a coarse-mesh sieve placed over a wide saucepan. Using a large spoon, remove and discard the fat. There should be about ³/₄ cup (6 fl oz/180 ml) liquid.

To make the sauce, add the broth to the saucepan and place over high heat. Bring to a rapid boil and boil until reduced by one-fourth, 3–4 minutes. Meanwhile, in a small bowl, dissolve the cornstarch in the vermouth. Reduce the heat to medium and whisk in the cornstarch mixture (page 24). Cook, stirring, until the sauce thickens slightly, 2–3 minutes. Stir in the crème fraîche, season with salt to taste, and add ¹/₄ teaspoon white pepper. Heat the sauce for 1 minute longer, but do not allow it to boil. Remove from the heat.

Carve the meat into slices ¹/₂ inch (12 mm) thick (page 286), discarding the extra fat, if used. Arrange on a warmed platter or individual plates. Spoon the sauce over the veal. If using the truffle oil, drizzle it lightly over the top. Serve at once.

A boneless veal loin roast is a tender cut that cooks to perfection in less than an hour. It requires little preparation, has only a thin layer of fat, is easy to carve, and makes an elegant main course. Veal loins vary in weight depending on the age of the animal. A roast of the size used here comes from a formula-fed calf, a slightly older animal than the young milk-fed veal seen in many markets. The latter tends to be much smaller and is better thinly sliced and quickly cooked as in scaloppini. Ask the butcher for a thin piece of fat to use for barding the roast. A coating of shallot, butter, and mustard flavors the roast and the elegant pan sauce. A little white truffle oil adds a nice finishing touch.

Stuffed Breast of Veal

Breast of veal is usually braised, but in this recipe, it is covered and steam-roasted in the oven for 1 hour, and then roasted uncovered until browned and tender, with the bones forming a natural roasting rack. Ask the butcher to cut a pocket for the stuffing, starting from the narrow end so that only a small opening remains to be closed after stuffing. Serve the veal hot as a main course with a little wholegrain mustard, or at room temperature with some Aioli (page 77) or Salsa Verde (page 279). You can also store the stuffed breast in the refrigerator for up to 3 days. Bring to room temperature before serving.

Preheat the oven to 375°F (190°C). Lightly oil a roasting pan large enough to hold the veal breast.

In a large frying pan over medium heat, warm the olive oil. Add the onion and sauté until soft, about 10 minutes. Add the garlic, Swiss chard, carrot, and thyme and cook until the chard is wilted and any liquid has evaporated, 6–7 minutes. Transfer the mixture to a large bowl and let cool for 10 minutes. Add the egg, rice, ground veal, peas, olives, cheese, vinegar, 2 teaspoons salt, and $1/2$ teaspoon pepper and mix until all the ingredients are evenly distributed. Using a large spoon or your hands, place the stuffing into the veal pocket, massaging it from the top to spread it evenly all the way down to the end. Close the pocket with small trussing skewers.

Place the veal breast in the prepared pan, rib side down. Pour the broth and vermouth into the pan. Cover the pan tightly with aluminum foil. Cook the veal breast for 1 hour. Remove the pan from the oven and carefully remove the foil. Reduce the oven temperature to 300°F (150°C). Baste the veal with the pan liquid, return it to the oven uncovered, and continue to roast, basting 2 or 3 times, until the meat is pulling away from the bones, about 2 hours longer. Add water to the roasting pan if it begins to look dry.

Remove the pan from the oven, transfer the veal to a carving board, and tent with aluminum foil. Let rest for 10 minutes.

Slice the veal breast between the bones, arrange the slices on a warmed platter or individual plates, and serve at once.

2 tablespoons extra-virgin olive oil

1 large yellow onion, chopped

3 cloves garlic, minced

3 cups (6 oz/195 g) coarsely chopped, stemmed Swiss chard leaves

1 cup (3 oz/90 g) coarsely grated, peeled carrot

1 teaspoon fresh thyme leaves, minced

1 large egg

2 cups (10 oz/315 g) cooked medium-grain white rice

$1/2$ lb (250 g) ground (minced) veal

1 cup (5 oz/155 g) fresh or frozen shelled English peas

$1/2$ cup (2 oz/60 g) coarsely chopped, pitted Kalamata olives

$1/2$ cup (2 oz/60 g) grated Parmesan cheese

1 tablespoon red wine vinegar

Kosher salt and freshly ground pepper

1 veal breast, about $2^{1}/_2$ lb (1.25 kg), with pocket (see note)

$1/2$ cup (4 fl oz/125 ml) *each* chicken broth and dry vermouth or dry white wine

Veal Loin Chops
with Tarragon-Wine Sauce

Thick, meaty veal loin chops are the equivalent of beef porterhouse steaks and make an impressive main course. A basic sauce prepared from the pan drippings, white wine, and fresh tarragon complements the tender steaks. Veal loin chops are at their tender best when cooked only to medium-rare. Serve them with steamed basmati rice or mashed potatoes to soak up the sauce.

Remove the veal from the refrigerator about 30 minutes before roasting. Preheat the oven to 450°F (230°C).

Using a sharp knife, trim the chops, leaving just a thin layer of fat. Season the chops on both sides with salt and pepper. Preheat a large, heavy ovenproof frying pan over high heat until very hot. Add the olive oil, and then add the chops and sear for 2 minutes on the first side. Turn the chops and sear for 1 minute on the second side. Immediately place the pan in the oven and roast the chops until a thermometer (page 16) inserted into the thickest part away from the bone registers 125°–130°F (52°–54°C) for medium-rare (page 164), 6–7 minutes.

Remove the pan from the oven, transfer the chops to a warmed platter, and tent with aluminum foil. Let rest for 4–5 minutes.

Place the frying pan over low heat, add the flour to the drippings, stir to combine, and cook for 1–2 minutes. Raise the heat to high and gradually add the chicken broth and white wine, stirring constantly. Bring to a boil and cook until the sauce thickens slightly, 2–3 minutes. Reduce the heat to low, add any accumulated juices from the platter and the *demi-glace*, cream, and tarragon, and heat through. Season to taste with salt and pepper.

To serve, place the chops on warmed individual plates and spoon a little of the sauce over each chop. Pass the remaining sauce at the table.

2 veal loin chops, each about $^3/_4$ **lb (375 g) and 1 inch (2.5 cm) thick**

Kosher salt and freshly ground pepper

1 tablespoon extra-virgin olive oil

1 tablespoon all-purpose (plain) flour

$^3/_4$ **cup (6 fl oz/180 ml) reduced-sodium chicken broth**

$^1/_4$ **cup (2 fl oz/60 ml) dry white wine**

2 teaspoons veal *demi-glace* (page 295)

$^1/_4$ **cup (2 fl oz/60 ml) heavy (double) cream**

1 tablespoon finely chopped fresh tarragon

Leg of Lamb with Garlic and Rosemary

A whole bone-in leg of lamb is an easy main course for a company meal because it requires no basting and cooks in less than 2 hours. Before roasting, the leg is salted and allowed to rest in the refrigerator for at least 24 hours to develop flavor. Garlic slivers pushed into the meat and a savory rub of rosemary, juniper berries, and pepper add more flavor. The rosemary added to the rich brown sauce echoes the flavors of the rub. Serve with oven-roasted potatoes (page 241). Ask your butcher to remove the hipbone and tailbone for easier carving, but do not have him or her crack the shank, as it provides a convenient handle for holding the roast while carving.

Using a sharp knife, trim the leg of all but a very thin layer of fat. Using kitchen string, make 2 or 3 ties at the top of the leg where the hipbone has been removed, to hold the meat in a compact package. Rub 1 tablespoon salt all over the leg, transfer to a platter or pan, and place in the refrigerator to rest, uncovered, for 24–36 hours. Remove the lamb from the refrigerator about 2 hours before roasting.

Preheat the oven to 325°F (165°C). Oil a flat rack and place it in a roasting pan just large enough to hold the lamb. Using the tip of a sharp knife, cut small slits each about 3/4 inch (2 cm) deep all over the meaty part of the leg, spacing them 2–3 inches (5–7.5 cm) apart. Push a garlic slice into each slit. In a spice grinder, combine the peppercorns and juniper berries and grind to a medium coarseness. In a small bowl, stir together the pepper mixture, rosemary, and olive oil. Rub this mixture all over the lamb. Place the lamb in the prepared pan.

Roast the lamb until a thermometer (page 16) inserted into the thickest part away from the bone registers 125°–130°F (52°–54°C) for medium-rare (page 164), 1–1 1/2 hours. Remove the pan from the oven, transfer the lamb to a warmed platter, and tent with aluminum foil. Let rest for 20 minutes.

Meanwhile, make the sauce: In a saucepan over medium-low heat, warm the olive oil. Add the shallot and sauté until softened, 2–3 minutes. Add the rosemary and broth, raise the heat to medium-high, and simmer for 5–6 minutes. Remove from the heat and pour through a fine-mesh sieve placed over a bowl. Discard the contents of the sieve. Using a large spoon, skim off the fat from the surface, then return the sauce to the pan and place over medium heat. Add the *demi-glace* and Madeira and mix well. Place the butter and flour in a small bowl and mix together with a fork until well combined, to make a beurre manié. Reduce the heat to low, whisk the beurre manié into the liquid a little at a time, and simmer, stirring occasionally, until slightly thickened, 3–4 minutes (page 24). Season to taste with salt and pepper; keep warm.

Carve the lamb (page 287). Transfer the slices to a warmed platter or individual plates. Spoon a little sauce over the slices. Pass the remainder at the table.

1 bone-in whole leg of lamb, 6–7 lb (3–3.5 kg)

Kosher salt

3 cloves garlic, cut into slices 1/4 inch (6 mm) thick

1 teaspoon peppercorns

12 juniper berries

1 1/2 tablespoons finely chopped fresh rosemary

1 tablespoon extra-virgin olive oil

For the Sauce

2 teaspoons extra-virgin olive oil

1/3 cup (2 oz/60 g) minced shallot (about 2 large)

1 teaspoon finely chopped fresh rosemary

3 cups (24 fl oz/750 ml) reduced-sodium beef broth

2 teaspoons beef *demi-glace* (page 295)

3 tablespoons dry Madeira or Port

2 tablespoons unsalted butter, at room temperature

2 tablespoons all-purpose (plain) flour

Kosher salt and freshly ground pepper

Leg of Lamb
with Bread Crumb Crust

1 bone-in, butt-end half leg of lamb, 4–5 lb (2–2.5 kg)

Extra-virgin olive oil for coating

Kosher salt and freshly ground pepper

For the Topping

1¹⁄₂ cups (3 oz/90 g) fresh bread crumbs

3 tablespoons plain yogurt

1 clove garlic, finely chopped

1 tablespoon extra-virgin olive oil

1 tablespoon finely chopped flat-leaf (Italian) parsley

1 teaspoon herbes de Provence

A bone-in half leg of lamb weighs 4 to 5 pounds (2 to 2.5 kg) and is the perfect size to serve six. When purchasing a half leg, ask for the butt end; it yields more meat than the shank end. Roasting the lamb on the bone adds extra flavor, and the meat cooks more rapidly than a boneless leg. Here, the leg is started at a high temperature, and then a crust of yogurt and bread crumbs is applied, and the lamb finishes roasting at a moderate temperature.

Remove the lamb from the refrigerator 1 hour before roasting. Preheat the oven to 425°F (220°C). Line a roasting pan just large enough to hold the lamb with heavy-duty aluminum foil. Oil a flat roasting rack and place it in the prepared pan. Using a sharp knife, trim most of the surface fat from the lamb. Rub on all sides with olive oil, and season with salt and pepper. Place the lamb, rounded side up, on the rack.

Roast the lamb for 30 minutes. Meanwhile, make the topping: In a small bowl, stir together the bread crumbs, yogurt, garlic, olive oil, chopped parsley, and herbes de Provence.

Remove the pan from the oven. Using a large spoon, firmly press the topping over the rounded top of the leg. Reduce the oven temperature to 350°F (180°C) and continue to roast the lamb until a thermometer (page 16) inserted into the thickest part away from the bone registers 125°–130°F (52°–54°C) for medium-rare (page 164), 50–60 minutes.

Remove the pan from the oven, transfer the lamb to a carving board, and tent with aluminum foil. Let rest for 15–20 minutes.

Carve the lamb (page 287). Transfer the slices to a warmed platter or individual plates. If serving on plates, make sure that each portion includes some of the flavorful crust.

Leg of Lamb Stuffed with Roasted Peppers and Onions

A boned leg of lamb is easy to carve and can be stuffed with vegetables or with herbs and bread crumbs. You can purchase the leg already boned, or you can ask your butcher to do it for you. It is important to trim most of the fat from any cut of lamb. This takes a little time and patience, but it reduces the risk of a roast with a gamy taste. Seasoning the lamb with a rub and refrigerating it for 24 hours heightens the flavor of the meat. Brushing the meat with olive oil and balsamic vinegar a couple of hours before roasting also adds flavor.

Using a sharp knife, trim away most of the fat from the surface of the roast. Then lay the roast out flat, boned surface up, and trim away any large pockets of fat. Cut several shallow slashes through the thicker muscles to make the roast a more even thickness.

In a small bowl, stir together the garlic, the cumin, 2 teaspoons salt, and $^1/_2$ teaspoon pepper. Rub the spice mixture over both sides of the meat. Place the meat on a large plate and refrigerate uncovered for 24 hours.

About 2 hours before roasting, in a small bowl, stir together the olive oil and balsamic vinegar. Brush over both sides of the meat. Return to the refrigerator. Remove the lamb from the refrigerator about 1 hour before roasting.

To make the stuffing, in a frying pan over medium heat, warm the olive oil. Add the onion slices and sauté until softened, 2–3 minutes. Add 2 tablespoons water, cover, reduce the heat to low, and cook until the onion is very tender, 8–10 minutes. Do not let the onion color. Remove the pan from the heat, uncover, and let cool completely.

Preheat the oven to 375°F (190°C). Oil a flat roasting rack and place it in a roasting pan just large enough to hold the lamb.

Place the lamb on a work surface, boned surface up. Place the onion and bell peppers in a line down the center of the length of the meat. Starting from a long side, roll up the meat tightly around the vegetables, forming a cylinder. Using kitchen string, secure the cylinder at 2-inch (5-cm) intervals along its length. Center a 30-inch (75-cm) long piece of kitchen string lengthwise under the roast. Place a 4-inch (10-cm) square of aluminum foil over each end of the roast to hold the stuffing in place, and then tie the string securely, but not too tightly, around the roast to help keep its shape.

Roast the lamb until a thermometer (page 16) inserted into the center of the cylinder registers 135°–140°F (57°–60°C) for medium (page 164), about 1 $^1/_4$ hours.

Remove the pan from the oven, transfer the lamb to a warmed platter, and tent with aluminum foil. Let rest for 20 minutes. Transfer the lamb to a carving board or platter. Carve into slices $^1/_2$–$^3/_4$ inch (12 mm–2 cm) thick (page 286) and arrange on warmed individual plates. Serve at once.

1 boneless leg of lamb, about 5 lb (2.5 kg)

1 teaspoon granulated garlic

$^1/_2$ teaspoon ground cumin

Kosher salt and freshly ground pepper

2 tablespoons extra-virgin olive oil

2 tablespoons balsamic vinegar

For the Stuffing

1 tablespoon extra-virgin olive oil

1 large yellow onion, cut into slices $^1/_2$ inch (12 mm) thick

2 red or yellow bell peppers (capsicums), roasted, peeled, and seeded (page 294), then cut lengthwise into strips $^1/_2$ inch (12 mm) wide

Lamb Shoulder Roast with Herbs and Black Olives

1 lamb shoulder roast, with round bone and blade, 3–4 lb (1.5–2 kg)

Kosher salt and freshly ground pepper

1 large carrot, peeled and finely diced

1 celery stalk, finely diced

1 small yellow onion, chopped

4 cloves garlic, thinly sliced

5 or 6 fresh flat-leaf (Italian) parsley sprigs, plus 2 tablespoons chopped

2 or 3 fresh oregano sprigs

Extra-virgin olive oil for coating

2 cups (16 fl oz/500 ml) reduced-sodium beef broth

$^1/_2$ cup (4 fl oz/125 ml) dry red wine

10–12 Kalamata olives, pitted and coarsely chopped (about $^1/_3$ cup/$1^1/_2$ oz/45 g)

2 tablespoons capers, rinsed and coarsely chopped

1 tablespoon tomato paste

1 teaspoon red wine vinegar

1 tablespoon cornstarch (cornflour)

Using a sharp knife, trim away all but a thin layer of fat from the lamb. Rub the meat all over with salt and pepper, place on a plate, and refrigerate uncovered for 12–24 hours. Remove from the refrigerator about 1 hour before roasting.

Preheat the oven to 400°F (200°C).

Select a heavy ovenproof frying pan just large enough to hold the lamb. Add the carrot, celery, onion, garlic, parsley sprigs, and oregano to the pan. Lightly brush or rub the lamb with olive oil and place, fat side up, on the vegetables. Pour in the broth and wine.

Roast the lamb for 1 hour. Remove from the oven and, using tongs or 2 thick pads of paper towels, turn the roast. Reduce the oven temperature to 325°F (165°C). Continue to roast the lamb for 30 minutes, then remove the pan from the oven and turn the roast again fat side up. Continue to roast until a thermometer (page 16) inserted into the thickest part away from the bone registers 180°F (82°C), 20–30 minutes longer. The meat should be brown and pulling away from the bone.

Remove the pan from the oven, transfer the lamb to a warmed platter, and tent with aluminum foil. Let rest while preparing the sauce.

Pour the contents of the frying pan through a coarse-mesh sieve placed over a measuring pitcher. Using the back of a spoon, press on the contents of the sieve to extract as much liquid as possible. Discard the contents of the sieve. Using a large spoon, remove as much fat from the surface of the pan juices as possible. You should have about 1$^1/_2$ cups (12 fl oz/375 ml) liquid. Pour into a small, wide saucepan and place over medium-high heat. Bring to the boil, add the olives, capers, tomato paste, vinegar, and chopped parsley, and reduce the heat to low. In a small bowl, dissolve the cornstarch in 2 tablespoons water and whisk into the simmering sauce. Cook, stirring, until slightly thickened, 2–3 minutes (page 24). Season to taste with salt and pepper; keep the sauce warm.

Transfer the lamb to a carving board. Cut the meat off the bone into slices $^3/_4$–1 inch (2–2.5 cm) thick and arrange on warmed individual plates. Spoon a little of the sauce over the meat. Pass the remaining sauce at the table.

This is comfort food for when you have a couple hours to devote to roasting. The lamb is seasoned at least 12 hours in advance to improve its flavor. It is cooked until well done to allow the connective tissue to soften and the fat to render, and then served with a pan sauce that includes vegetables, olives, and capers. Have your butcher remove the rib bones, leaving the round shoulder bone and blade in place. Accompany the lamb with polenta and a spoonful of the zesty sauce.

Rack of Lamb with Mustard and Thyme

2 racks of lamb, each 7 or 8 ribs and 1¹/₂–2 lb (750 g–1 kg)

1 tablespoon Dijon mustard

1 tablespoon whole-grain mustard

2 teaspoons fresh thyme leaves

Extra-virgin olive oil for coating

Kosher salt and freshly ground pepper

¹/₂ cup (4 fl oz/125 ml) reduced-sodium chicken broth

¹/₂ cup (4 fl oz/125 ml) dry white wine

Remove the lamb from the refrigerator about 30 minutes before roasting. Preheat the oven to 500°F (260°C). Place a flat rack in a roasting pan large enough to hold the lamb racks.

Using a sharp knife, trim away as much of the surface fat from the lamb as possible. If desired, french the bones (page 284). In a small bowl, stir together the Dijon and whole-grain mustards and the thyme. Brush or rub the racks on all sides with olive oil and season with salt and pepper. Preheat a large frying pan over high heat until very hot, 4–5 minutes. Place the lamb racks, meat side down, in the pan and sear for 1–2 minutes on the first side. Turn the racks upright and sear for 1 minute on their ends. Transfer the lamb, meat side up, to the roasting pan. Spread the mustard mixture evenly over the meat side of each rack. If desired, wrap the bare bones in aluminum foil to prevent them from charring. Pour the broth, the wine, and ¹/₂ cup (4 fl oz/125 ml) water into the roasting pan.

Roast the lamb racks until a thermometer (page 16) inserted into the thickest part away from the bone registers 125°–130°F (52°–54°C) for medium-rare (page 164), 12–14 minutes.

Remove the pan from the oven, transfer the lamb to a warmed platter, and tent with aluminum foil. Let rest for 10 minutes.

Pour the juices from the roasting pan into a small saucepan. Using a large spoon, remove as much fat from the surface ot the pan juices as possible. Bring to a boil and boil until reduced by about half, 3–4 minutes. Add any juices accumulated on the platter, and season to taste with salt and pepper; keep warm.

Transfer the racks to a carving board. Carve the racks into single chops or, if they are small, into double chops (page 286). Divide among warmed individual plates and spoon an equal amount of the sauce over each serving. Serve at once.

Succulent roasted racks of lamb make a dinner special. Allow 1 rack (the 7 or 8 rib chops from one side of the lamb) for two people. Be sure to trim the lamb well, which may include sacrificing a small, thin piece of the loin that hides a long strip of interior fat. Two sizes of lamb racks are generally available. The smaller racks are usually from Australia or New Zealand, and are of excellent quality, relatively lean, and particularly tender and delicately flavored. Racks from U.S. lambs weigh slightly more, have a stronger flavor, and require a few exra minutes to render the fat better. The butcher can french the bones for you, which involves trimming away the thin pieces of meat that line them. Ask the butcher to crack the chine on the racks so you can carve between the chops more easily.

Rack of Lamb with Goat Cheese and Rosemary Topping

Here, racks of lamb are coated with a savory bread-crumb mixture that flavors the lamb and helps keep it moist in the high heat of the oven. The creamy goat cheese provides flavor and moistness to the topping and helps it adhere to the meat. Serve with Roasted Root Vegetables (page 247) or with Asparagus with Shallots and Lemon (page 257). Either dish can be prepared before you cook the roast and kept warm while the lamb is in the oven.

Remove the racks of lamb from the refrigerator about 30 minutes before roasting. Preheat the oven to 500°F (260°C). Line a rimmed baking sheet with heavy-duty aluminum foil. Using a sharp knife, trim away as much of the surface fat from the lamb as possible. If desired, french the bones (page 284). Cut each lamb rack in half, yielding 4 or 5 rib pieces.

In a bowl, combine the bread crumbs, goat cheese, 1 tablespoon olive oil, garlic, parsley, and rosemary and season to taste with salt and pepper. Stir to combine well. The mixture should stick together when pressed between your thumb and forefinger; if it does not, add a little more olive oil. Brush or rub the lamb with olive oil, and season with salt and pepper. Preheat a large frying pan over high heat until very hot. Place the halved racks, meat side down, in the pan and sear for 1 minute. Turn the racks on end and sear for 1 minute. Transfer the lamb, meat side up, to the prepared pan. Firmly press an equal amount of the topping onto each rack. Roast the lamb until a thermometer (page 16) inserted into the thickest part away from the bone registers 125°–130°F (52°–54°C) for medium-rare (page 164), 14–16 minutes.

Remove the pan from the oven and tent the lamb with aluminum foil. Let rest for 8–10 minutes. Carve the racks into single chops (page 286). Serve at once.

2 racks of lamb, each 7 or 8 ribs and 1¹/₂–2 lb (750 g–1 kg)

1 cup (2 oz/ 60 g) fresh bread crumbs

3 tablespoons crumbled fresh goat cheese

1 tablespoon extra-virgin olive oil, or as needed, plus oil for coating

1 large clove garlic, minced

2 tablespoons minced fresh flat-leaf (Italian) parsley

1 teaspoon finely chopped fresh rosemary

Kosher salt and freshly ground pepper

Lamb Chops with Mint, Tomato, and Garlic Sauce

8 thick-cut bone-in lamb loin chops, each 1¹/₂ inches (4 cm) thick, 2–2¹/₂ lb (1–1.25 kg) total weight

Extra-virgin olive oil for coating, plus 1 tablespoon

Kosher salt and freshly ground pepper

2 tablespoons chopped fresh flat-leaf (Italian) parsley

2 tablespoons chopped fresh basil

For the Sauce

1 tablespoon extra-virgin olive oil

1 small shallot, minced

2 cloves garlic, minced

3 tomatoes, peeled, seeded, and coarsely chopped

2 teaspoons balsamic vinegar

Kosher salt and freshly ground pepper

6–8 fresh basil leaves, cut into narrow strips

6–8 fresh mint leaves, cut into narrow strips

¹/₄ cup (2 fl oz/60 ml) dry red wine

Chops cut from the loin are the most costly of the various types of lamb chops, but they are also the tastiest and most tender. This recipe calls for double loin chops, which are simply cut twice as thick as a typical loin chop. While the chops are resting, a quick pan sauce of tomatoes, garlic, basil, and mint that was started in a saucepan is finished in the roasting pan. Roasted potatoes (page 240), couscous, or basmati rice would round out the plate.

Using a sharp knife, trim away as much of the surface fat from the lamb as possible. Brush or rub the chops on both sides with olive oil, and season generously with salt and pepper. Press the parsley and basil firmly into both sides of each chop. Let stand at room temperature for 20–30 minutes before roasting.

Preheat the oven to 450°F (230°C).

Meanwhile, start making the sauce: In a small saucepan over medium-low heat, warm the olive oil. Add the shallot and sauté until softened, 3–4 minutes. Add the garlic and cook for 1 minute longer. Raise the heat to medium-high, add the tomatoes, and cook, stirring frequently, until the tomatoes soften and release their liquid, 3–4 minutes. Add the vinegar, and season with salt and pepper. Cook until most of the liquid has evaporated, 3–4 minutes longer. Remove from the heat, stir in the basil and mint, and set aside until the lamb chops are roasted.

Preheat a large, heavy ovenproof frying pan over high heat until very hot. Add the 1 tablespoon olive oil, and then add the lamb chops and sear for 2 minutes on the first side. Turn the chops and sear for 1 minute on the second side. Immediately place the pan in the oven and roast the lamb until a thermometer (page 16) inserted into the thickest part away from the bone registers 125°–130°F (52°–54°C) for medium-rare (page 164), 5–6 minutes.

Remove the pan from the oven, transfer the chops to a warmed platter, and tent with aluminum foil. Let rest while you finish the sauce.

Deglaze the pan as directed on page 23, using the wine. Add the tomato sauce and any juices that have accumulated on the platter and bring to a boil over medium-high heat. Remove from the heat.

Divide the chops among warmed plates. Divide the sauce evenly among them, spooning it over the top. Serve at once.

Slow-Roasted Pork Shoulder

1 boneless pork shoulder roast, 4¹/₂–5 lb (2.25–2.5 kg)

For the Rub

2 teaspoons ancho chile powder

1 teaspoon ground cumin

¹/₂ teaspoon granulated garlic

¹/₂ teaspoon dry mustard

Kosher salt and freshly ground pepper

For the Sauce

2 cups (16 fl oz/500 ml) tomato sauce

¹/₃ cup (3 fl oz/80 ml) cider vinegar

3 tablespoons firmly packed brown sugar

1 tablespoon chili powder

1 tablespoon granulated onion

2 teaspoons granulated garlic

2 teaspoons Worcestershire sauce

1 teaspoon dry mustard

¹/₂ teaspoon chipotle chile sauce, or to taste

Kosher salt and freshly ground pepper

Lay the pork roast flat, boned surface up, on a cutting board and, using a sharp knife, trim away any large pockets of fat.

To make the rub, in a small bowl, stir together the ancho chile powder, cumin, granulated garlic, mustard, 1 tablespoon salt, and ¹/₄ teaspoon pepper. Sprinkle about half of the rub mixture evenly over the inside of the roast. Roll up and, using kitchen string, tie at 2-inch (5-cm) intervals to secure the roast in a compact shape. Rub the remaining spice mixture over the outside of the roast. Transfer the roast to a plate, cover with plastic wrap, and refrigerate overnight.

Remove the roast from the refrigerator about 1 hour before roasting. Preheat the oven to 300°F (150°C). Oil a flat roasting rack and place it in a roasting pan just large enough to hold the roast. Place the pork on the rack. Roast the pork until a thermometer (page 16) inserted into the center of the meat registers 190°F (88°C), about 4 hours. Remove the pan from the oven, transfer the pork to a warmed platter, and tent with aluminum foil. Let rest for 20 minutes.

Meanwhile, make the sauce: In a saucepan over high heat, combine the tomato sauce, vinegar, brown sugar, chili powder, granulated onion and garlic, Worcestershire sauce, dry mustard, chipotle chile sauce, ¹/₂ teaspoon salt, and ¹/₄ teaspoon pepper. Bring to a boil, then reduce the heat to medium-low and simmer for 15 minutes to blend the flavors. Remove the pan from the heat. You should have about 2 cups (16 fl oz/500 ml). The sauce can be served warm or at room temperature.

Thinly slice, chop, or "pull" the pork into shreds using 2 forks or your fingers, discarding any large pieces of fat. Arrange the meat on individual plates with a little sauce spooned over the top. Serve at once.

A boneless pork shoulder roast, often called Boston butt, has generous amounts of internal connective tissue and fat that melt and release their flavors when roasted at a low temperature. Here, it is served sliced with an easy and flavorful barbecue sauce spooned over the top, but it can also be used for pulled pork sandwiches, tacos, and other similar preparations. If making sandwiches, mix the meat with some of the sauce, serve hot on buns, and accompany with coleslaw or slices of pickled jalapeño chile. Warm any leftover meat in the sauce before serving.

Fresh Ham with Pineapple-Jicama Salsa

A whole leg of pork, also called fresh ham, weighs 18–20 pounds (9–10 kg), but your butcher can cut it in half to make a roast of a more manageable size. The butt end (top end) is more compact, but the shank end (bottom of the leg) is easier to carve, so the choice is yours. Leave the skin and fat intact because they slow the cooking and help keep the meat moist. The leg is roasted initially at a high temperature for a short time, then the oven temperature is reduced and the ham is roasted for an additional 4 hours until meltingly tender and succulent. Leftovers make great sandwiches or can be moistened with the barbecue sauce that accompanies roasted pork shoulder on page 208.

Using a sharp knife, score the skin of the leg at 1-inch (2.5-cm) intervals, forming a diamond pattern. Rub the meat generously with salt and pepper. Allow the meat to rest at room temperature for 1 hour before roasting.

Preheat the oven to 425°F (220°C). Select a roasting pan just large enough to hold the pork and line with heavy-duty aluminum foil. Oil a flat rack and place it in the prepared pan. Transfer the roast, skin side up, to the rack.

Roast the pork for 20 minutes. Reduce the oven temperature to 325°F (165°C) and continue to roast until a thermometer (page 16) inserted into the thickest part away from the bone registers 165° (74°C), about 4 hours longer. Remove the pan from the oven and tent the pork with aluminum foil. Let rest for 20 minutes.

Meanwhile, make the salsa: Grate the zest from the orange and set aside. Using a sharp knife, cut a slice off both ends of the orange to reveal the flesh. Place the orange upright on the cutting board and, using the knife, cut downward to remove the remnants of the peel and the white membrane and pith, following the contours of the orange. Holding the orange over a bowl, cut along each side of the membrane between the sections, letting the freed sections drop into the bowl. Dice the sections and return them to the bowl. Add the pineapple, jicama, onion, chile(s), lime juice, lemon juice, cilantro, 1 teaspoon salt, and pepper to taste, and toss to combine. (The salsa can be made 3 or 4 hours ahead, covered, and refrigerated.)

Transfer the roast to a carving board. Using a sharp knife, remove the skin and top layer of fat. Cut the ham across the grain into very thin slices and arrange on a warmed platter. Pass the salsa at the table.

1 bone-in fresh leg of pork roast, 8–10 lb (4–5 kg)

Kosher salt and freshly ground pepper

For the Salsa

1 navel orange

3 cups (18 oz/560 g) diced pineapple ($^1/_2$-inch/12-mm dice)

2 cups (12 oz/375 g) diced, peeled jicama ($^1/_2$-inch/ 12-mm dice)

$^3/_4$ cup (3 oz/90 g) finely diced sweet onion such as Vidalia, rinsed briefly under running cold water

1 or 2 small red or green jalapeño chiles, seeded and minced

3 tablespoons fresh lime juice

2 tablespoons fresh lemon juice

$^1/_2$ cup ($^3/_4$ oz/20 g) chopped fresh cilantro (fresh coriander)

Kosher salt and freshly ground pepper

Pork Loin with Armagnac-Soaked Dried Plums

1 boneless center-cut pork loin roast, about 3–3¹/₂ lb (1.5–1.75 kg)

Kosher salt and freshly ground pepper

2 tablespoons extra-virgin olive oil

For the Stuffing

12–15 pitted dried plums, cut in half

¹/₄ cup (2 fl oz/60 ml) Armagnac

2 tablespoons unsalted butter

1 small yellow onion, coarsely chopped

1 teaspoon grated orange zest

¹/₂ teaspoon ground allspice

Kosher salt and freshly ground pepper

For the Sauce

1¹/₂ cups (12 fl oz/375 ml) reduced-sodium chicken broth

2 teaspoons cornstarch (cornflour)

Kosher salt and freshly ground pepper

Remove the roast from the refrigerator about 1 hour before roasting. Using a sharp knife, trim the roast, leaving only a thin layer of surface fat. Insert the blade of a long, narrow knife into the center of one end of the roast and carefully push the knife about halfway through the length of the roast. Turn the knife and enlarge the opening to about 1 inch (2.5 cm) wide. Start at the opposite end of the roast and again insert the knife blade, this time to meet the first cut. Widen the second opening by turning the knife, as you did with the first cut. Enlarge the cuts until each opening is about 1¹/₂ inches (4 cm) wide all the way through the roast. Preheat the oven to 350°F (180°C).

To make the stuffing, in a small bowl, combine the dried plums and Armagnac and let stand for 10–15 minutes, stirring 1 or 2 times. In a frying pan over low heat, melt the butter. Add the onion, cover, and cook, stirring occasionally, until soft, 8–10 minutes. Do not let the onion color. Drain the plums, reserving the Armagnac, and add the plums to the pan with the onions. Add the orange zest and allspice, season to taste with salt and pepper, and stir to combine. Remove the pan from the heat and let the stuffing cool for 5–10 minutes. Using a small spoon or spatula, stuff the pork loin with the onion-plum mixture, pushing the stuffing in from both ends. Close both ends with small trussing skewers to hold the stuffing in place. Season the roast with salt and pepper.

Preheat a large, heavy ovenproof frying pan over high heat until very hot. Add the olive oil and then add the pork loin. Sear the meat on all sides, about 2 minutes on each side. Immediately transfer the pan to the oven and roast the pork until a thermometer (page 16) inserted into the center of the meat registers 150°F (65°C) for well done (page 164), 1–1¹/₄ hours. Remove the pan from the oven, transfer the pork to a warmed platter, and tent with aluminum foil. Let rest for 15 minutes.

To make the sauce, deglaze the frying pan as directed on page 23, using the broth. Pour the liquid through a medium-mesh sieve into a saucepan, place over high heat, bring to a boil, and cook until reduced by one-third, 4–5 minutes. Pour any juices accumulated on the platter into the sauce. In a small bowl, dissolve the cornstarch in the reserved Armagnac and whisk into the sauce. Simmer until slightly thickened, 1–2 minutes (page 24). Season to taste with salt and pepper. Transfer the roast to a carving board. Cut the roast into slices ³/₄ inch (2 cm) thick and arrange on a warmed platter. Spoon the sauce over the slices and serve.

Boneless center-cut pork loin, the equivalent of a boneless strip loin roast of beef, yields tender succulent meat. Here, it is stuffed by cutting a tunnel through the center and filling it with dried plums, or prunes, and sautéed onion, which contribute moisture and flavor to the meat. Armagnac, a French brandy from Gascony, is used for soaking the dried plums and is later added to the pan sauce. Accompany the roast with oven-roasted sweet potatoes, and serve a Pinot Noir or fruity Merlot.

Crown Roast of Pork with Wild Rice Stuffing

A regal crown roast of pork makes a splendid centerpiece for a holiday or other special dinner. It is made up of 2 or 3 whole pork loin racks (the rib portion of the loin) tied together to form a circle, with the ribs pointing up. The roast usually consists of a minimum of 14 chops (7 chops in each rack), but your butcher can make it with as many as 21 chops. You will need to special-order a crown roast and ask the butcher to french the rib bones.

Remove the pork from the refrigerator 1 hour before roasting. Preheat the oven to 325°F (165°C). Select a roasting pan just large enough to hold the roast and line with heavy-duty aluminum foil. Oil a flat rack and place it in the prepared pan. Pour 1 cup (8 fl oz/250 ml) water into the pan. Rub the roast with salt and pepper. Crumple aluminum foil into a ball large enough to fill the center of the roast. Lightly oil the foil ball and push it firmly into the center to help the roast keep its circular shape. Wrap the exposed end of each rib bone with a small piece of foil to prevent burning. Transfer the crown roast to the rack. Roast the pork until a thermometer (page 16) inserted into the thickest part away from the bone registers 150°F (65°C) for well done (page 164), 2 1/2–3 hours.

While the pork is roasting, make the stuffing: In a large saucepan over high heat, bring 4 cups (32 fl oz/1 l) water to a boil. Add the rice and parboil, uncovered, for 10 minutes. Drain the rice and discard the water. Return the rice to the saucepan; set aside. In a frying pan over low heat, melt the butter. Add the onion, carrot, and celery and cook uncovered, stirring occasionally, until soft, about 10 minutes. Add the broth to the saucepan holding the rice and then add the vegetables. Bring to a boil over high heat, reduce the heat to low, cover, and cook until the rice is tender, 40–45 minutes. Add the apricots during the last 10 minutes of cooking. Taste and adjust the seasoning with salt, pepper, and the pinch of nutmeg. Cover to keep warm until ready to serve; stir in the pecans just before serving. If needed, reheat the stuffing over low heat.

When the roast is done, remove the pan from the oven, transfer the roast to a warmed large platter, and tent with aluminum foil. Let rest for 20 minutes. Remove the foil ball and foil pieces from the rib ends. Spoon some of the stuffing into the center of the roast and present the roast to your guests before carving. Then, transfer the roast to a carving board. Using a sharp knife, cut between the bones to separate the roast into chops, and serve 1 chop per person. Spoon a little wild rice stuffing on the side. Serve at once.

1 crown roast of pork with 14–18 loin ribs, 8–9 lb (4–4.5 kg)

Kosher salt and freshly ground pepper

For the Stuffing

1 1/2 cups (10 1/2 oz/345 g) wild rice

2 tablespoons unsalted butter

1/4 cup (1 1/2 oz/45 g) finely diced yellow onion

1/4 cup (1 1/2 oz/45 g) finely diced, peeled carrot

1/4 cup (1 1/2 oz/45 g) finely diced celery

3 cups (24 fl oz/750 ml) reduced-sodium chicken broth

1 cup (6 oz/185 g) chopped dried apricots

Kosher salt and freshly ground pepper

Pinch of freshly grated nutmeg

1 cup (4 oz/125 g) coarsely chopped pecans, toasted

Low Country–Style Spareribs

6 bone-in country-style spareribs, each about 1 inch thick (2.5 cm), about 5 lb (2.5 kg) total weight

Canola oil for coating

For the Rub

1 tablespoon firmly packed brown sugar

1 teaspoon granulated garlic

1 teaspoon granulated onion

1 teaspoon Hungarian sweet paprika

2 teaspoons ground cumin

1/2 teaspoon dry mustard

1/4 teaspoon cayenne pepper

Kosher salt and freshly ground black pepper

For the Basting Sauce

1 cup (8 fl oz/250 ml) cider vinegar

3 tablespoons firmly packed brown sugar

1 tablespoon tomato paste

1 teaspoon Worcestershire sauce

1/4 teaspoon hot-pepper sauce, or to taste

Kosher salt

Barbecue sauce (see note)

Using a sharp knife, trim away most of the surface fat from the ribs. Lightly brush or rub the ribs on both sides with the canola oil.

To make the rub, in a small bowl, stir together the brown sugar, granulated garlic and onion, paprika, cumin, mustard, cayenne pepper, 2 teaspoons salt, and 1 teaspoon black pepper. Sprinkle the rub mixture evenly over both sides of each rib and gently massage it into the meat. Place the ribs in a large pan, cover with plastic wrap, and refrigerate for at least 12 hours or for up to 24 hours. Remove the ribs from the refrigerator 30 minutes before roasting.

Preheat the oven to 300°F (150°C). Select a roasting pan just large enough to hold the spareribs and line with heavy-duty aluminum foil. Oil a flat rack and place it in the prepared pan. Arrange the ribs on the rack, meaty side up. Pour 1 cup (8 fl oz/250 ml) water into the pan and cover tightly with aluminum foil. Roast the ribs for 1 1/2 hours.

Meanwhile, make the basting sauce: In a small bowl, stir together the vinegar, brown sugar, tomato paste, Worcestershire sauce, 1/4 teaspoon hot-pepper sauce, and 1 teaspoon salt. Taste and adjust with more hot-pepper sauce to taste. Cover and set aside until needed.

When the ribs have roasted for 1 1/2 hours, remove the pan from the oven and remove the foil. Brush the ribs with the basting sauce, then turn the ribs. Continue to roast uncovered, turning the ribs 2 or 3 more times during roasting and brushing with the basting sauce each time they are turned, until the meat starts to pull away from the bones and is tender, 1–1 1/2 hours longer.

Remove the pan from the oven and brush the ribs again with the basting sauce. Place a rib on each warmed individual plate and serve at once with a little barbecue sauce, if desired.

Low Country cooking, centered in South Carolina, uses a sauce on pork that is vinegar and hot pepper based and includes very little tomato, unlike other barbecue sauces. Thick, meaty country-style spareribs are the pork equivalent of beef short ribs. Here, they are slowly roasted until the meat practically falls from the bones. A spicy rub is spread over the ribs, which are then refrigerated overnight before roasting to maximize flavor. A second layer of flavor is added near the end of cooking, with a generous brushing of a vinegar and hot-pepper sauce. Serve the ribs with your favorite purchased barbecue sauce or the sauce that accompanies the roast pork shoulder on page 208. Leftover meat from the ribs can be coarsely chopped, heated in some barbecue sauce, and served on a bun or made into taco filling.

Baby Back Ribs with Sherry and Balsamic Basting Sauce

Back ribs, sometimes called baby back ribs, are larger and meatier than spareribs. Removing the membrane from the back of the ribs allows the flavor of the spices to penetrate the meat and permits more of the fat to cook away. If not serving the ribs immediately, you can let them cool completely, cover them, and refrigerate for up to 3 days. To serve the ribs, place them on a baking sheet lined with aluminum foil, brush them with a little basting sauce, and heat in a preheated 400°F (200°C) oven until piping hot. Brush them again with the sauce just before serving.

Using a sharp knife, trim away most of the surface fat from the ribs. Working with one slab of ribs at a time, lay it bone side up on a work surface. Use the knife to make a vertical slit into the thin membrane near the center of the slab. Lift a corner of the membrane and, using a paper towel to get a good grip, pull the membrane back toward the end of the slab. Repeat to remove the membrane from the other side of the slab.

To make the rub, in a small bowl, stir together the paprika, mustard, coriander, garlic, cumin, 1 teaspoon salt, and $1/2$ teaspoon pepper. Sprinkle the rub mixture evenly over both sides of the ribs and gently massage it into the meat. Place the ribs in a large pan, cover with plastic wrap, and refrigerate for 3–4 hours, or let stand at room temperature for 1–2 hours. If the ribs have been refrigerated, remove them about 30 minutes before roasting.

Preheat the oven to 325°F (165°C). Line a large rimmed baking sheet with heavy-duty aluminum foil. Place the ribs, meaty side up, on the foil. Pour $1/3$ cup (3 fl oz/80 ml) water into the pan. Cover the ribs with another sheet of foil.

Roast the ribs for 1 hour. Reduce the oven temperature to 300°F (150°C). Remove the foil, turn the ribs, and continue to roast the ribs, uncovered, for 30 minutes. Spoon off any accumulated fat from the pan and turn the ribs again. Continue to roast until the meat is very tender and starting to pull away from the bone, about 1 hour longer.

Meanwhile, make the basting sauce: In a small bowl, stir together the cream sherry, vinegar, $1/4$ teaspoon hot-pepper sauce, and $1/2$ teaspoon salt. Taste and adjust with more hot-pepper sauce if needed. Set aside.

When the ribs are ready, remove the pan from the oven and spoon off any fat from the pan. Raise the oven temperature to 400°F (200°C). Brush the ribs with the basting sauce, return the ribs to the oven, and heat for 10 minutes to crisp the outside of the meat, basting 1 or 2 times more with the sauce.

To serve, cut the slabs into individual ribs. Serve warm with lots of napkins.

4 lb (2 kg) baby back ribs, in 2 slabs

For the Rub

1 tablespoon Hungarian sweet paprika or mild New Mexico chile powder

1 tablespoon dry mustard

1 tablespoon ground coriander

1 tablespoon granulated garlic

1 tablespoon ground cumin

Kosher salt and freshly ground pepper

For the Basting Sauce

$1/3$ cup (3 fl oz/80 ml) cream sherry

2 tablespoons balsamic vinegar

$1/4$ teaspoon hot-pepper sauce, or to taste

Kosher salt

Pork Tenderloin
with Whole-Grain Mustard

Pork tenderloin is a particularly tender cut with little fat, and it roasts quickly for an easy and delicious weeknight dinner. Whole-grain mustard is mild and grainy with flecks of mustard seed that add texture and an appealing appearance. Here the mustard is used to coat the pork, keeping it moist during the high-heat roasting. Serve the roast as a main course with warm cinnamon applesauce, or let it cool, slice it thinly, and use for sandwiches.

Preheat the oven to 425°F (220°C). Line a small roasting pan with heavy-duty aluminum foil. Oil a small flat rack and place in the pan.

Using a sharp knife, trim away the silver skin and most of the fat from the tenderloin. Brush or rub the mustard evenly over the pork, then sprinkle evenly with $1/2$ teaspoon pepper. Place the pork on the rack.

Roast the pork until a thermometer (page 16) inserted into the thickest part registers 140°–150°F (60°–65°C) for medium-well done (page 164), about 40 minutes. Remove the pan from the oven, transfer the roast to a platter, and tent with aluminum foil. Let rest for 15 minutes.

Transfer the meat to a carving board and cut into slices $1/2$ inch (12 mm) thick. Arrange on a warmed platter or individual plates and serve at once.

1 pork tenderloin, 1–1$1/4$ lb (500–625 g)

3 tablespoons whole-grain mustard

Freshly ground pepper

Caribbean-Brined Pork Chops

For the Brine

¹/₄ cup (2 oz/60 g) firmly packed brown sugar

¹/₄ cup (2 oz/60 g) kosher salt

6–8 whole allspice, lightly crushed in a mortar with a pestle

6–8 peppercorns

1 serrano chile, quartered lengthwise

1 lime

4 bone-in pork loin chops, each 10–12 oz (315–375 g) and about 1¹/₄ inches (3 cm) thick

2 teaspoons canola oil

For the Basting Sauce

2 tablespoons dark rum

2 teaspoons firmly packed brown sugar

Grated zest and juice of 1 lime

3 or 4 drops hot-pepper sauce

Kosher salt and freshly ground pepper

These pork chops are soaked for a few hours in a brine flavored with lime juice and chiles to make them moist and flavorful, then are seared on the stove top and briefly roasted in a hot oven. Rum, a popular Caribbean spirit, flavors a simple sauce that is both used as a basting sauce and spooned over the cooked chops.

To make the brine, in a large, nonreactive bowl, combine the brown sugar, salt, and 5 cups (40 fl oz/1.25 l) room-temperature water and stir until the sugar and salt dissolve. Add the allspice, peppercorns, and chile. Cut the lime in half, squeeze the juice from each half into the bowl, and add the spent halves. Stir to mix all the ingredients well. Add the pork chops, making sure the brine covers the meat. If it does not, add water as needed. Cover and refrigerate for 3–4 hours.

Preheat the oven to 450°F (230°C).

To make the basting sauce, in a small bowl, stir together the rum, sugar, lime zest and juice, hot-pepper sauce, and salt and pepper to taste. Set aside.

Remove the chops from the refrigerator about 30 minutes before roasting. Rinse briefly under running cold water. Pat dry with paper towels. Brush or rub the chops on both sides with the canola oil. Preheat a large, heavy ovenproof frying pan over high heat until very hot. Add the chops and sear for 2 minutes on the first side. Turn and sear for 2 minutes on the second side. Brush with the basting sauce, and immediately place the pan in the oven. Roast until a thermometer (page 16) inserted into the center of the meat away from the bone registers 140°–150°F (60°–65°C) for medium-well done (page 164), about 8 minutes.

Transfer the chops to individual plates. Deglaze the frying pan as directed on page 23, using the remaining basting sauce. Bring to a boil and cook for 1 minute. Spoon the sauce over the chops, dividing it evenly, and serve.

Pork Chops with Cranberry-Orange Stuffing

When purchasing pork chops, look for pinkish gray meat surrounded by a thin layer of creamy white fat. The sweetness and acidity of apples have long made them a preferred pairing with pork. In this recipe, the chops are soaked in an aromatic apple juice brine, then are filled with a flavorful stuffing of dried cranberries, orange zest and juice, onion, and bread crumbs. It is easy to cut a pocket in the chops, or you can ask the butcher to cut the pockets for you.

In a large, nonreactive bowl, combine the apple juice, vinegar, salt, brown sugar, peppercorns, bay leaf, and 1^1/$_2$ cups (12 fl oz/375 ml) room-temperature water, and stir to dissolve the salt and sugar completely. Place the chops in the brine. It should cover them. If it does not, add water as needed. Cover and refrigerate for 4–6 hours. Remove the chops from the refrigerator about 30 minutes before roasting. Rinse briefly under running cold water. Pat dry with paper towels.

To make the stuffing, in a small bowl, combine the cranberries and orange juice and let soak for 10 minutes. In a small frying pan over medium-low heat, melt the butter. Add the onion, cover, and cook, stirring occasionally, until softened, 8–10 minutes. Uncover, raise the heat to medium-high, add the bread crumbs and rosemary, and sauté until the crumbs are lightly browned, 3–4 minutes. Season with salt and pepper. Drain the cranberries, reserving the orange juice. Add the cranberries and orange zest to the pan and toss to combine. Remove from the heat and let cool completely. Preheat the oven to 375°F (190°C).

To cut a pocket in each pork chop, insert a sharp, thin-bladed knife into the middle of the meat on the side away from the bone, cutting all the way to the bone. Move the blade toward one side of the chop without cutting completely through the meat, then turn the knife and enlarge the pocket in the opposite direction. Try to keep the initial knife opening no more that 1 inch (2.5 cm) wide so the stuffing will not spill out. Using a teaspoon, place the stuffing in the pockets, dividing it evenly, then secure each pocket closed with a trussing skewer or toothpick. Lightly brush or rub both sides of the chop with the olive oil.

Preheat a large, heavy ovenproof frying pan over high heat until very hot. Add the chops and sear for 2 minutes on the first side. Turn the chops and sear for 1 minute on the second side. Immediately place the pan in the oven and roast the chops until a thermometer (page 16) inserted into center of the meat away from the bone registers 140°–150°F (60°–65°C) for medium-well done (page 164), 20–25 minutes. Transfer the chops to individual plates, remove the skewers, and tent with aluminum foil. Let rest while making the sauce. Deglaze the frying pan as directed on page 23, using the reserved orange juice and the broth. Raise the heat to high and cook until reduced by one-third, 6–8 minutes. In a small bowl, dissolve the cornstarch in 1 tablespoon water. Add to the sauce and continue to cook, stirring occasionally, until slightly thickened, 1–2 minutes (page 24). Spoon the sauce over the chops and serve.

1^1/$_2$ cups (12 fl oz/375 ml) apple juice

1 tablespoon cider vinegar

^{1}/$_4$ cup (2 oz/60 g) kosher salt

3 tablespoons firmly packed brown sugar

4–6 peppercorns

1 bay leaf

4 bone-in pork rib chops, each about ^{3}/$_4$ lb (375 g) and 1^1/$_2$–1^3/$_4$ inches (4–4.5 cm) thick

For the Stuffing

^{1}/$_3$ cup (1^1/$_2$ oz/ 45 g) dried cranberries

Grated zest and juice of 1 large orange

2 tablespoons unsalted butter

1 small yellow onion, coarsely chopped

^{3}/$_4$ cup (1^1/$_2$ oz/45 g) fresh bread crumbs

^{1}/$_2$ teaspoon finely chopped fresh rosemary

Kosher salt and freshly ground pepper

1 tablespoon extra-virgin olive oil

1 cup (8 fl oz/250 ml) chicken broth

1 teaspoon cornstarch (cornflour)

Pork Loin Chops
with Roasted Rhubarb

For the Rhubarb

1 lb (500 g) rhubarb (see note), trimmed and cut into slices ³/₄ inch (2 cm) thick

1 large yellow onion, thinly sliced

2 tablespoons extra-virgin olive oil

¹/₄ cup (2 fl oz/60 ml) reduced-sodium chicken broth

¹/₂ teaspoon whole allspice, ground

Kosher salt and freshly ground pepper

¹/₄ cup (2 oz/60 g) firmly packed brown sugar

6 pork loin chops, each 8–10 oz (250–315 g) and 1 inch (2.5 cm) thick

2 tablespoons extra-virgin olive oil

Kosher salt and freshly ground pepper

1 cup (8 fl oz/250 ml) apple juice

1 teaspoon cornstarch (cornflour)

Pork loin chops, like beef porterhouse steaks, have both the loin and the tenderloin, separated by the rib bone. In this good springtime dish, they are roasted on a bed of onions and rhubarb that provides a fruity, slightly tart accent. Select firm rhubarb stalks—red or green will do—with bright, glossy skin. Avoid very thick or very thin stalks; both are sometimes stringy. Discard the leaves, which are toxic and should not be consumed.

Preheat the oven to 375°F (190°C). Butter the bottom of a roasting pan just large enough to hold the chops in a single layer.

To roast the rhubarb, combine the rhubarb, onion, olive oil, broth, allspice, and a sprinkle each of salt and pepper in the prepared pan. Toss to combine and spread the mixture out in an even layer. Cover the pan with aluminum foil. Roast the rhubarb mixture until the rhubarb and onion are tender, about 30 minutes. Remove the pan from the oven, uncover, and sprinkle the rhubarb mixture with the brown sugar. Stir to distribute the sugar evenly and spread the mixture out again in an even layer.

Remove the chops from the refrigerator 20 minutes before roasting. Brush or rub the pork chops on both sides with the olive oil and season with salt and pepper. Preheat a large, heavy ovenproof frying pan over high heat until very hot. Working in batches if necessary, add the chops to the pan and sear for 2 minutes on the first side. Turn the chops and sear for 1 minute on the second side. Transfer the chops to the roasting pan, arranging them in a single layer on top of the rhubarb. Place the pan in the oven and roast until a thermometer (page 16) inserted into the center of the meat away from the bone registers 150°F (65°C) for well done (page 164), about 7 minutes.

Remove the pan from the oven, transfer the chops to warmed plates, and tent with aluminum foil. While the chops are resting, deglaze the frying pan as directed on page 23, using the apple juice. Bring to a boil and cook until reduced to about ¹/₃ cup (3 fl oz/80 ml), 4–5 minutes. Add any liquid from the rhubarb mixture in the roasting pan to the frying pan and reduce the heat to low. In a small bowl, dissolve the cornstarch in 1 tablespoon water. Whisk the cornstarch mixture into the frying pan a little at a time, and simmer until the sauce thickens slightly, 2–3 minutes (page 24). Add the rhubarb mixture, mix well, and heat through. Spoon some of the rhubarb mixture over each chop. Serve at once.

Rack of Venison
with Pomegranate Glaze

The term *venison* is correctly applied to the meat of both deer and antelope, but it is most often thought of as deer meat. Venison is lean, with very little interior fat when compared with other red meats, making it a healthful choice. Because it lacks fat, you must be careful not to overcook it, or it will toughen. It should always be roasted at high heat to guard against drying out, and is cooked rare, medium-rare as in this recipe, or medium (see chart, page 164). Ask the butcher to crack the chine bone for easier carving.

Remove the venison from the refrigerator 30 minutes before roasting. Preheat the oven to 425°F (220°C).

Using a sharp knife, trim away any silver skin and most of the surface fat from the venison rack. Lightly sprinkle the venison on all sides with salt. To make the glaze, in a small saucepan, combine the pomegranate molasses, Port, olive oil, juniper berries, and 1/2 teaspoon pepper and mix well. Place the venison rack, meat side up, in a roasting pan just large enough to hold it. Brush the venison generously with some of the glaze.

Roast the venison for 30 minutes. Remove from the oven and brush the rack with more of the glaze. Continue to roast until a thermometer (page 16) inserted into the thickest part away from the bone registers 125°–130°F (52°–54°C) for medium-rare, 10–12 minutes longer. Remove the pan from the oven, transfer the venison to a warmed platter, brush again with the glaze, and tent with aluminum foil. Let rest for 15 minutes. Place the saucepan with the glaze over medium-low heat, bring to a boil, and cook for 2–3 minutes to thicken slightly.

To serve, cut the venison into individual chops and place 2 chops on each warmed individual plate. Spoon an equal amount of the hot glaze over each chop and serve at once.

1 rack of venison with 8 ribs, about 3 lb (1.5 kg)

Kosher salt

For the Glaze

1/2 cup (4 fl oz/125 ml) pomegranate molasses

1/2 cup (4 fl oz/125 ml) ruby Port

2 tablespoons extra-virgin olive oil

10–12 juniper berries, lightly crushed

Freshly ground pepper

Venison Loin with Wild Blueberry Sauce

1 venison strip loin roast, about 2 lb (1 kg)

4 tablespoons (2 oz/60 g) unsalted butter, at room temperature

Kosher salt and freshly ground pepper

For the Sauce

2 tablespoons sugar

$^1/_2$ cup (4 fl oz/125 ml) dry red wine

2 cups (16 fl oz/500 ml) reduced-sodium beef broth

2 tablespoons fresh lemon juice

$^1/_4$ cup (2$^1/_2$ oz/75 g) seedless red raspberry jam

1 teaspoon beef *demi-glace* (page 295)

1 tablespoon cornstarch (cornflour)

Kosher salt

$^1/_4$ teaspoon freshly ground white pepper

1 cup (4 oz/125 g) fresh or thawed, frozen wild blueberries

Remove the venison from the refrigerator about 30 minutes before roasting. Preheat the oven to 425°F (220°C).

Using a sharp knife, trim away the silver skin from the venison. Using kitchen string, tie the roast at 2-inch (5-cm) intervals along its length to make a compact roll. Smear the butter evenly over the whole roast, then season on all sides with salt and pepper. Place the venison in a roasting pan just large enough to hold it.

Roast the venison until a thermometer (page 16) inserted into the thickest part registers 125°–130°F (52°–54°C) for medium-rare, about 20 minutes.

While the meat is roasting, make the sauce: In a saucepan over medium heat, combine the sugar and $^1/_4$ cup (2 fl oz/60 ml) water and stir until the sugar dissolves. Raise the heat to high, add the wine, broth, and lemon juice, bring to a boil, and cook until the liquid has reduced by one-half, 8–10 minutes. Remove from the heat and stir in the raspberry jam and the *demi-glace*. Reduce the heat to medium-low, return the pan to the heat, and warm the sauce, stirring, until the jam dissolves. Remove from the heat; keep warm.

Remove the pan from the oven, transfer the venison to a warmed platter, and tent with aluminum foil. Let rest for 10 minutes.

Just before serving, pour the accumulated juices from the platter into the pan holding the sauce, place over medium heat, and bring to a simmer. In a small bowl, dissolve the cornstarch in 2 tablespoons water. Whisk the cornstarch mixture into the simmering sauce, and cook, stirring, until the sauce thickens slightly, 2–3 minutes (page 24). Season to taste with salt and add the white pepper. Stir in the blueberries and cook for 30 seconds just to heat through.

Transfer the venison to a carving board. Remove the strings. Cut across the grain into slices $^1/_2$ inch (12 mm) thick and arrange 2 slices on each warmed individual plate. Spoon an equal amount of the sauce over each serving and serve at once.

A venison strip loin is similar to a small, whole beef New York strip loin or strip roast. It is very lean and has no bone or fat, and it is easily carved into slices $^1/_2$ inch (12 mm) thick. If there is a long strip of silver skin on the side, remove as much of it as possible so the meat does not curl during roasting. The venison is lavishly coated with softened butter to prevent it from drying out during its short high-heat roasting. A wild blueberry sauce provides a dramatic color contrast and accent to the tender meat. Small, intensely flavored wild blueberries are sometimes sold fresh and are often available frozen, but any fresh or frozen blueberries may be used here.

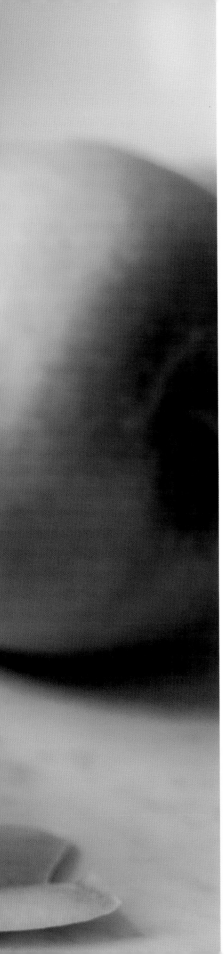

Vegetables and Fruits

About Vegetables and Fruits

Roasting concentrates the flavors of vegetables and fruits, caramelizes their natural sugars, and tenderizes their interiors. As the heat penetrates to the center of each piece, the flavor deepens and the texture is transformed, usually changing from firm and crisp to soft and yielding.

Some vegetables are better candidates than others for roasting, but many worthy contenders exist. Sturdy root vegetables and tubers, such as beets, carrots, onions, parsnips, potatoes, celery root (celeriac), and turnips, cook up beautifully in the dry heat of the oven. Gingered Baby Carrots (page 244), Herb-Roasted Fingerling Potatoes with Whole-Grain Mustard (page 241), and Curried Parsnips (page 245) are all stellar examples.

More delicate vegetables, such as mushrooms, are also roast-worthy. Full-flavored varieties—portobello, shiitake, porcino, and cremini—are the best choices. Look for specimens with fleshy caps of uniform size for preparing such dishes as Portobello Mushrooms with Parmesan and Basil (page 255).

Eggplant (aubergine) takes well to roasting, too, and requires considerably less oil than is needed when it is cooked by most other methods. Roasting also evaporates some of eggplant's mildly bitter juices. Two good examples are Vegetable Napoleon (page 263), which includes layers of eggplant and other colorful vegetables, and a roasted version of the French classic ratatouille (page 264).

TRANSFORMING TEXTURE

Roasting garlic, whether whole heads or individual cloves, mellows its potent aroma and turns its firm texture wonderfully smooth and creamy. The puréelike result is typically used to flavor other recipes, such as roast chicken (page 102) or turkey (page 130). Directions on how to roast garlic are in the Basic Recipes

section (page 279). In the same section, you will find a recipe for roasting one of garlic's close relatives, small cipolline onions, which soften nicely but still retain an appealing firmness. In this chapter, yet another family member, the long, slender, mild leek, is coated with bread crumbs, butter, and cheese and roasted until fork-tender (page 256).

Roasting changes the texture of tomatoes, too. Plum (Roma) tomatoes develop a somewhat chewy texture and a rich, concentrated flavor in the oven, making them ideal for adding to pasta sauces, omelets, and salads, or for serving on their own as a side dish. Directions for roasting the tomatoes appear on page 280 in the Basic Recipes section. You will also find a recipe for making a versatile sauce based on roasted tomatoes. Flash-Roasted Cherry Tomatoes (page 239) are lightly seasoned and drizzled with olive oil before they are cooked in a high-temperature oven just until their skins split, transforming them into a good side dish or a flavorful addition to a warm salad.

Summer squashes, usually found alongside tomatoes in the garden, are also delicious roasted, as in Summer Squash with Cilantro Pesto (page 258). When the weather cools, cooks turn to hard winter squashes for roasting. Brown Butter Winter Squash (page 248) works best with small varieties, such as butternut or acorn. The latter are also used for the Maple-Glazed Acorn Squash Rings (page 250).

Many vegetables are brushed or tossed with oil or melted butter before roasting to provide

a protective coating, then seasoned with herbs, spices, and aromatics such as onion and shallot. Other seasonings used before or during roasting include wine, vinegar, and fruit, as in Baby Beets with Orange Vinaigrette and Goat Cheese (page 253).

ROASTING FRUITS

Roasted fruits are also brushed or tossed with butter to flavor them and to prevent them from drying out. The bananas on page 277, inspired by the classsic dish bananas Foster, is a good example of this technique.

Fruits for roasting should be chosen carefully. Select firm fruits with cores, such as apples and pears, and stone fruits, including peaches and plums, because they hold their shape during roasting. Some varieties fare better than others. A Red Delicious is a wonderful apple for eating out of hand, but collapses when roasted. Golden Delicious or Granny Smith, in contrast, hold up in the oven heat.

Take extra care with recipes calling for delicate fruits like berries, which can soften too much in the oven. You will want to set your timer or keep a watchful eye on the Strawberry and Blueberry Compote (page 273), for example, which roasts only briefly.

Roasted fruits make good accompaniments to savory dishes, such as Apple Slices with Sage (page 281), which is delicious with meats, especially pork. Another classic pairing is Spiced Cherries (page 281) served with roast duck. Some recipes include variations that turn a savory dish into a dessert and vice versa. A sweet variation for the Apple Slices with Sage transforms the dish into a accompaniment to a dessert cheese course. The simple Roasted Pears (page 268) can be seasoned with cinnamon and liqueur for a dessert, or with sage or mint for a side dish to lamb.

Roasting Vegetables and Fruits

Roasting heightens the flavors of the sugars naturally present in vegetables and fruits, making them versatile beyond their usual roles. A platter of roasted vegetables can be a highly satisfying main dish, and roasted fruits shine in both homey desserts and savory condiments.

Cooking according to the season is a tenet of fine cuisine, but it is especially true when roasting produce. The local farmers' market is arguably the best place to find the vegetables and fruits that will inspire you in the kitchen year-round. Roasting cannot bring out flavors that are not already present, however, so select produce that is ripe and at the peak of flavor.

Always cut vegetables into uniform pieces, as a variety of shapes and sizes will yield unevenly cooked food. Smaller pieces are generally best for two reasons: they reduce the roasting time and they allow for more surface caramelization, which means fuller flavor. For consistently thin slices, imperative for Herbed Potato Chips (page 32), for example, use a mandoline or similar slicing tool, which will be more efficient and exacting than the steadiest hand with the sharpest knife.

Vegetables are typically roasted in a pan that is just large enough to hold them in a single layer without crowding. If they are too snugly packed, they will give off steam and not brown properly. A heavy-gauge, rimmed baking sheet, usually measuring 11 by 16 by 1 inch (28 by 40 by 2.5 cm), has a good-sized cooking surface and can be a better choice than a smaller roasting pan. Larger baking sheets, often called half-sheet pans, are available as well and are a good investment. Be sure to check that your oven will accommodate one of these larger pans before you purchase it.

Cutting vegetables into uniform pieces ensures that different varieties will roast evenly.

To roast vegetables along with meats, poultry, or fish, such as Chicken with Rosemary and Sweet Potatoes (page 106) or Cross-Rib Roast with Roasted Root Vegetables (page 168), choose a roasting pan that is just large enough to hold both items. Work out the roasting demands of each element so that both items are done at the same time. One might need to be in the oven longer than the other and will have to be started first. If you are serving roasted vegetables directly from the pan or dish in which they were cooked, have clean pot holders at the table to hold the hot vessel during serving. Even oiled vegetables can stick to cooking surfaces. A sturdy, flexible metal spatula is helpful for scraping up stubborn food from the pan.

Vegetables are nearly always coated with oil or melted butter before roasting to protect their surfaces from drying out and to encourage browning. Water should never be used for the same purpose, as it will create steam and prevent browning. Many recipes call for olive oil for its distinctive flavor, with high-quality green-hued extra-virgin oil delivering the most assertive taste. Regular olive oil, pale gold,

Vegetables need minimal preparation before roasting: just a light coating of oil or butter and seasoning with salt and pepper and perhaps a sprinkling of herbs.

milder in flavor, and less costly, is an excellent substitute for everyday cooking. A flavorless vegetable oil, such as canola, is used when olive oil may not be compatible with other seasonings in the recipe.

To better showcase their natural flavors, roasted vegetables often rely on a minimum of other ingredients. When a recipe is seasoned with only salt and pepper, it provides a chance for the cook to use seasonings that are out of the ordinary. For example, the highly prized *fleur de sel* from Brittany, a natural sea salt gathered in salt fields on the northwest coast of France, should be reserved for dishes where its unique flavor and texture can be noticed and appreciated. You might also fill your pepper mill with high-quality peppercorns, such as Tellicherry or Lampong.

ROASTING FRUITS

Like vegetables, fruits should be cut into uniform pieces to speed cooking and encourage caramelization. Their natural sugars can caramelize more quickly than you might think, so keep an eye on fruits during roasting, especially if the recipe includes additional sugar or other sweet ingredients. Toss fruits with melted unsalted butter or a flavorless oil before baking, or they may scorch and stick to the pan.

Many fruits are acidic, and during roasting their juices may react with uncoated metal roasting or frying pans, causing the fruits to discolor. To prevent this problem, use only heatproof glass or ceramic dishes or anodized or enameled aluminum pans.

If you use a steel-coated pan, the pan juices from particularly juicy fruits can be deglazed to make a sauce (page 23). Place the pan over medium heat and deglaze with heavy (double) cream, scraping up the caramelized juices with a wooden spatula or spoon. Bring to a boil,

Making a pan sauce is not restricted to savory foods. The pan used to roast fruit can be deglazed with cream (page 23) to make a flavorful accompaniment.

then cook until slightly thickened. If you wish, add a drop or two of vanilla extract (essence) to round out the flavor.

TESTING FOR DONENESS

To test roasted vegetables and fruits for doneness, first look at them. They should have an even golden to light brown patina, indicating that browning is complete. Insert the tip of a sharp knife or the tines of a fork into a piece. In general, it should yield easily, but not be too soft. Follow the cues in individual recipes indicating whether the vegetable or fruit

should be "just tender" or "soft." If the vegetables or fruits have browned sufficiently, but still need more roasting, loosely tent them with aluminum foil and continue cooking until tender. Some vegetables, such as broccoli (page 260) and cauliflower (page 261), are roasted until crisp-tender, which preserves their appealing texture.

Taste the food before serving to check for seasoning and sweetness. You may need a sprinkle of salt or sugar. The caramelized surfaces will be especially hot, so be careful that you do not burn your lips or tongue.

Flash-Roasted Cherry Tomatoes

Flash, or quick, roasting cherry tomatoes at high temperature allows them to retain their moisture and shape while deepening their natural flavors. You can substitute yellow tomatoes for all or part of the red cherry tomatoes. Grape tomatoes will also work well here. Chopped fresh rosemary, thyme, or tarragon can be used in place of the basil. Serve the tomatoes as a side dish, add them to a green salad, or toss them with just-cooked bowtie pasta along with additional oil and vinegar for a warm salad.

Preheat the oven to 450°F (220°C).

Combine the tomatoes and shallot in a shallow baking dish large enough to hold the tomatoes in a single layer. Season with salt and pepper, then drizzle evenly with the olive oil and stir to coat. Spread the tomatoes out evenly.

Roast the tomatoes, stirring once, for 10 minutes. Gently stir in the green onion, basil, and vinegar. Continue to roast the tomatoes until they are softened but still hold their shape, about 5 minutes longer.

Remove the baking dish from the oven and transfer the tomatoes to a serving bowl. Serve warm or at room temperature.

2 cups (12 oz/375 g) cherry or grape tomatoes

2 tablespoons thinly sliced shallot

Kosher salt and freshly ground pepper

3 tablespoons extra-virgin olive oil

1/4 cup (3/4 oz/20 g) sliced green (spring) onion, including tender green tops

1 1/2 tablespoons chopped fresh basil

1 1/2 tablespoons balsamic vinegar

Salt-and-Pepper-Roasted Potatoes

1¹/₂ lb (750 g) russet or other all-purpose baking potatoes

2 tablespoons extra-virgin olive oil

Kosher salt and freshly ground pepper

Malt vinegar for serving (optional)

Preheat the oven to 450°F (220°C).

Cut the potatoes lengthwise into slices ¹/₂ inch (12 mm) thick. Then cut each slice lengthwise into strips ¹/₂ inch (12 mm) wide. Arrange the potatoes in a single layer on a rimmed baking sheet. Drizzle with the olive oil, then toss to coat the potatoes evenly. Spread the potatoes out evenly. Sprinkle them with 1¹/₂ teaspoon each salt and pepper.

Roast the potatoes, turning them 1 or 2 times, until they are a rich gold and crisp, 18–22 minutes.

Remove the pan from the oven and transfer the potatoes to a napkin-lined bowl or basket. Drizzle with the malt vinegar, if desired, and serve at once.

Roasting at a high temperature is especially well suited to high-moisture russet or other baking potatoes. These are cut in the traditional french-fry shape, but you can instead slice them crosswise ¹/₄ inch (6 mm) thick or cut them into ¹/₂- to 1-inch (12-mm to 2.5-cm) cubes. For added flavor, you can sprinkle the potatoes with 1 teaspoon curry powder or Hungarian sweet paprika before roasting. The British serve their fried potatoes with malt vinegar. It is a good idea for roasted potatoes, too.

Herb-Roasted Fingerling Potatoes with Whole-Grain Mustard

A moderately high roasting temperature is ideal for waxy potatoes such as fingerlings, red, or Yukon gold, all of which need a little more time to cook through than baking potatoes. The most important advantage these potatoes have is that they hold their shape well and thus reheat nicely. Additionally, if you are roasting them along with meat or poultry and the oven temperature is 25°F (10°C) higher or lower to accommodate the meat, the potatoes will still roast fine.

Preheat the oven to 400°F (200°C).

If the potatoes are larger than 1¹/₂ inches (4 cm) in diameter, cut them in half. Arrange them in a single layer on a rimmed baking sheet. Sprinkle evenly with the rosemary. In a small dish, stir together the olive oil and mustard. Drizzle the mixture evenly over the potatoes, then sprinkle with salt and pepper. Toss to coat the potatoes evenly, then spread them out evenly in the pan.

Roast the potatoes, turning them 2 or 3 times, until the skin is golden and the flesh is tender when pierced with a fork, 40–45 minutes.

Remove the pan from the oven, transfer the potatoes to a warmed serving dish, and serve at once.

1 lb (500 g) fingerling or small red or Yukon gold potatoes, 1–2 inches (2.5–4 cm) in diameter, unpeeled

1 tablespoon chopped fresh rosemary

1 tablespoon extra-virgin olive oil

1 tablespoon whole-grain Dijon mustard

Kosher salt and freshly ground pepper

Sweet-and-Spicy Sweet Potatoes

1 lb (500 g) sweet potatoes, peeled, cut crosswise into slices ¹/₂ inch (12 mm) thick, and each slice cut in half to create half moons

3 tablespoons canola oil

1 tablespoon dark or light molasses

1 teaspoon chili powder

Kosher salt and freshly ground pepper

Preheat the oven to 450°F (230°C).

Arrange the sweet potatoes in a single layer on a rimmed baking sheet. In a small dish, stir together the canola oil and molasses. Drizzle the mixture evenly over the sweet potatoes. Sprinkle with the chili powder, then sprinkle generously with salt and pepper. Toss to coat the potatoes evenly, then spread them out evenly.

Roast the sweet potatoes, turning them 1 or 2 times, until they are browned and crisp, but still tender when pierced with a fork, 20–30 minutes.

Remove the pan from the oven and transfer the potatoes to a warmed serving dish. Serve at once.

Any variety of sweet potato is ideal for roasting because the natural sugars, especially when augmented with a little molasses, caramelize to a rich, deep color and flavor. The chili powder adds some heat to produce an appealing sweet-hot taste. You can substitute ground cumin for the chili powder for a milder result. Serve the sweet potatoes the moment they come out of the oven, while they are still crisp.

Gingered Baby Carrots

2 tablespoons unsalted butter

1 tablespoon honey

1 tablespoon finely chopped crystallized ginger

1 lb (500 g) small, thin carrots, peeled

Kosher salt and freshly ground pepper

2 tablespoons chopped fresh mint

2 teaspoons fresh lemon juice

1 bunch fresh mint

Preheat the oven to 400°F (200°C). Select a roasting pan just large enough to hold the carrots in a single layer.

Put the butter in the pan and place in the preheating oven. Watch carefully to prevent burning. When the butter has melted, remove the pan from the oven and stir in the honey and ginger. Add the carrots and stir to coat them evenly. Season with salt and pepper and sprinkle with 1 1/2 tablespoons of the chopped mint. Stir again, then spread the carrots out in a single layer.

Roast the carrots, stirring 2 or 3 times, until golden, glazed, and tender when pierced with a fork, 35–45 minutes.

Remove the pan from the oven and season the carrots to taste with salt and pepper. Sprinkle evenly with the remaining 1 1/2 teaspoons mint and the lemon juice and toss to coat. Make a bed of the mint sprigs on a platter and top with the carrots. Serve at once.

Baby carrots, seasoned with sweet and spicy crystallized ginger, glazed in butter and honey, and then served on a bed of mint, are a beautiful springtime accompaniment to roast lamb or chicken. Use a fragrant honey, such as orange blossom or thyme or tarragon. If you cannot find baby carrots, peel and cut slender full-sized carrots into 2-inch (5-cm) lengths.

Curried Parsnips

Parsnips are the forgotten root of the vegetable family. Relegated to "soup mix" status in the supermarket, they are typically left unchosen amid their flashier golden carrot and ruby beet cousins. However, when roasted with aromatic spices, as is the case here, they easily win new converts. The curry powder heightens the natural sweetness of the parsnips, to produce a side dish ideal for serving alongside roasted pork or chicken.

Preheat the oven to 400°F (200°C). Select a roasting pan just large enough to hold the parsnips in a single layer.

Put the butter in the pan and place in the preheating oven. Watch carefully to prevent burning. When the butter has melted, remove the pan from the oven, add the parsnip slices, and stir to coat them evenly. Sprinkle evenly with the curry powder and season with salt and pepper. Stir again, then spread the parsnips out in a single layer.

Roast the parsnips, stirring 2 or 3 times, until a rich gold and tender when pierced with a fork, 30–40 minutes.

Remove the pan from the oven and transfer the parsnips to a warmed serving bowl. Serve at once, and pass the lime wedges at the table for each diner to squeeze over his or her portion.

2 tablespoons unsalted butter

1 lb (500 g) parsnips, peeled and cut lengthwise into slices $1/4$ inch (6 mm) thick

1 teaspoon Madras curry powder

Kosher salt and freshly ground pepper

4 lime wedges

Roasted Root Vegetables

Despite their sturdy demeanor, root vegetables are rich in natural sugars, making them among the sweetest and gentlest in flavor of all the vegetables. They are harvested in late summer and autumn and are generally good keepers when properly stored in a cool, dry place, preferably a basket. An assortment of similarly cut root vegetables for roasting creates a particularly attractive dish. You can adjust the amounts given here by using more of one vegetable than another or using only a single vegetable. You can also substitute other herbs, such as sage or marjoram, for the thyme. The two-step roasting temperature results in caramelized tender vegetables with richly blended flavors.

Preheat the oven to 425°F (220°C).

Peel the carrots, parsnips, turnips, and celery root and cut into 1-inch (2.5-cm) chunks. Cut the unpeeled potatoes into 1-inch (2.5-cm) chunks. Combine all the cut vegetables and the garlic cloves in a large, shallow roasting pan or rimmed baking sheet. Drizzle evenly with the olive oil and sprinkle evenly with 1 1/2 tablespoons of the thyme. Season generously with salt and pepper. Toss to coat the vegetables evenly with the seasonings, then spread them out in a single layer.

Roast the vegetables for 10 minutes. Reduce the oven temperature to 350°F (180°C) and continue to roast the vegetables, stirring 1 or 2 times, until golden, caramelized, and tender when pierced with a fork, 35–45 minutes longer.

Remove the pan from the oven and season the vegetables to taste with salt and pepper. Transfer the vegetables to a serving bowl, then sprinkle with the remaining 1 1/2 teaspoons thyme. Serve at once.

1/2 lb (250 g) carrots

1/2 lb (250 g) parsnips

1/2 lb (250 g) small white turnips

1 celery root (celeriac), about 1/2 lb (250 g)

1/2 lb (250 g) small red potatoes

1 whole head of garlic, separated into cloves and peeled

1/4 cup (2 fl oz/60 ml) extra-virgin olive oil

2 tablespoons chopped fresh thyme

Kosher salt and freshly ground pepper

Brown Butter Winter Squash

2 small winter squashes, such as butternut or acorn, about 1 lb (500 g) each

1 tablespoon extra-virgin olive oil

Kosher salt and freshly ground pepper

2 tablespoons unsalted butter

1 tablespoon chopped fresh herb such as sage, thyme, rosemary, or marjoram

Small squashes are best for roasting in this manner. They cook more evenly than large squashes, and half of a squash is the perfect size for each serving. After the halves are baked cut side down for the first 20 minutes, they are turned and filled with a little butter and a fresh herb. Like a classic beurre noisette, the butter in the squash cavities turns light brown and develops a nutty fragrance. The squashes make an excellent accompaniment to roasted sausages or pork.

Preheat the oven to 400°F (200°C).

Lightly oil a rimmed baking sheet. Cut each squash in half lengthwise, then scoop out and discard the seeds and strings. Lightly brush both the skin and the cut sides of the squash halves with the olive oil. Season the cut sides generously with salt and pepper, then place the halves, cut side down, on the prepared pan.

Roast the squash halves until they are nearly tender when pierced with a knife, about 20 minutes. Remove the pan from the oven and, using a spatula, carefully turn each half cut side up. Divide the butter into 4 equal pieces and place a piece in each squash cavity. Sprinkle the cavity with the herb of choice, dividing it evenly. Continue to roast the squash halves until the butter is melted and begins to brown lightly, 5–10 minutes.

Remove the pan from the oven and divide the squash among warmed individual plates. Serve at once.

VARIATIONS

Winter Squash with Southwest Spices

Bake the squash for 20 minutes as directed. Meanwhile, melt the butter in a small pan over low heat, and add 1 teaspoon cumin seeds or chili powder. Stir for 30 seconds, then remove from the heat. When you turn the squash halves, add the seasoned butter to the cavities, dividing it evenly. Omit the herb and proceed as directed.

Winter Squash with Maple Syrup

Bake the squash for 20 minutes as directed. Meanwhile, melt the butter in a small pan over low heat, add 1 tablespoon maple syrup and $1/4$ teaspoon ground cinnamon, and remove from the heat. When you turn the squash halves, add the seasoned butter to the cavities, dividing it evenly. Omit the herb and proceed as directed.

Maple-Glazed Acorn Squash Rings

2 small acorn squashes, about 1 lb (500 g) each

Kosher salt and freshly ground pepper

1¹/₂ tablespoons unsalted butter

2 tablespoons maple syrup

1 tablespoon chopped fresh thyme, plus sprigs for garnish

2 teaspoons grated orange zest

2 tablespoons chopped cranberries

Preheat the oven to 400°F (200°C).

Oil a large rimmed baking sheet. Trim the ends from each squash and cut crosswise into slices ¹/₂ inch (12 mm) thick. Using a biscuit cutter slightly larger than the seeded center of each slice, cut out the seeds, leaving a neat circle in the center. Season the slices generously on both sides with the salt and pepper and arrange them in a single layer on the prepared pan. Roast the squash slices for 10 minutes.

Meanwhile, in a small saucepan, melt the butter. Stir in the maple syrup, chopped thyme, and orange zest and remove from the heat.

When the squash slices have roasted 10 minutes, remove the pan from the oven and brush the tops of the slices evenly with the butter mixture. Sprinkle evenly with the cranberries. Continue to roast the squash slices until glazed, browned, and tender when pierced with a fork, 10–15 minutes longer.

Remove the pan from the oven and transfer the squash rings to a platter. Garnish with thyme sprigs and serve at once.

Acorn squash, with its attractive shape, slices beautifully into scalloped rings. The maple syrup both complements the natural sweetness of the squash and lends a smoky edge. For a lighter, more golden glaze, substitute honey for the maple syrup or use only butter without any added sweetener. You can also use lemon zest in place of the orange zest. Serve the glazed rings as a side dish to roasted poultry.

Roasted Beets

Boiled beets have little character, but roasted beets are rich and sweet and have a smooth, creamy texture. Most recipes call for beets to be wrapped in aluminum foil before roasting, both to seal in juices and to keep the red juices from staining the pan. Other recipes simply coat the beets in oil and do not worry about the juices coloring the pan. This recipe uses the best of both methods, starting the beets in foil and then unwrapping them for the last half of roasting to evaporate some of the liquid and concentrate the sweet flavor.

Preheat the oven to 400°F (200°C).

If the beet greens are still attached, cut them off, leaving 1 inch (2.5 cm) of the stem intact; reserve the greens for another use. Brush the beets with the olive oil. Wrap each beet in a piece of heavy-duty aluminum foil and place the beets in a roasting pan just large enough to hold them.

Roast the beets for 1 hour. Remove the pan from the oven and unwrap the beets, but do not remove them from the foil. Instead, fold back the foil to expose the beets. Season the beets generously with salt and pepper. Continue to roast the beets until lightly caramelized and tender throughout when pierced with a knife, about 20 minutes.

Remove the pan from the oven and, when the beets are cool enough to handle, slip the skins off with your fingers. (To avoid stains, wear rubber gloves.) Slice the beets, if desired. Transfer the beets to a bowl and serve warm, or let the beets cool, cover, and refrigerate, then serve chilled.

4 red or orange beets, or a combination, about 5 oz (155 g) each

1 tablespoon extra-virgin olive oil

Kosher salt and freshly ground pepper

Baby Beets with Orange Vinaigrette and Goat Cheese

VARIATION

Roasted Baby Beets with Orange Vinaigrette, Goat Cheese, and Nuts

Sprinkle 1/4 cup (1 oz/30 g) walnut pieces or pine nuts, toasted, over the salads, dividing them evenly.

Baby beets take much less time to roast than larger beets, so they do not need to be wrapped in aluminum foil to keep them from drying out. The salad here showcases the flavor, texture, and colors of this beautiful root vegetable, which is available in a variety of hues, from red and gold to stripes of various colors. You can use crumbled blue cheese in place of the goat cheese, and two clementines in place of the orange. Beets are available year-round, but late summer through early autumn is prime time.

Preheat the oven to 400°F (200°C).

If the beet greens are still attached, cut them off, leaving 1 inch (2.5 cm) of the stem intact; reserve the greens for another use. Place the beets in a shallow baking dish just large enough to hold them in a single layer and season generously with salt and pepper. Drizzle with 1 1/2 tablespoons of the olive oil and toss to coat evenly, then spread the beets out evenly.

Roast the beets, stirring 1 or 2 times, until nearly tender when pierced with a fork, about 25 minutes. Remove the pan from the oven, add the orange chunks, drizzle with 1 1/2 teaspoons of the olive oil, and toss to coat evenly. Continue to roast until the orange chunks are softened and tinged with gold and the beets are fork-tender, about 10 minutes longer.

Remove the pan from the oven and, when the beets are cool enough to handle, slip the skins off with your fingers. (To avoid stains, wear rubber gloves.) In a small dish, whisk together the remaining 2 tablespoons olive oil, the vinegar, and the orange juice to make a vinaigrette. Drizzle the vinaigrette over the warm beets and orange chunks. Season with salt and pepper, toss well, and then taste and adjust the seasoning.

Divide the arugula among individual salad plates. Spoon the beets and orange chunks and then the vinaigrette left in the dish evenly over the arugula. Sprinkle with the goat cheese. Serve at once.

1 lb (500 g) baby beets in various colors (see note), each 1–2 inches (2.5–5 cm) in diameter

Kosher salt and freshly ground pepper

4 tablespoons (2 fl oz/60 ml) extra-virgin olive oil

1 navel orange, peeled and cut into 1-inch (2.5-inch) chunks

2 tablespoons red wine vinegar

2 tablespoons fresh orange juice

1 bunch arugula (rocket), tough stems removed

1/3 cup (1 1/2 oz/45 g) crumbled fresh goat cheese

Garlic Fennel Wedges

1 or 2 fennel bulbs, about 1 lb (500 g)

4 large cloves garlic, sliced

3 tablespoons extra-virgin olive oil

2 tablespoons reduced-sodium chicken broth or white wine

Kosher salt and freshly ground pepper

2 tablespoons chopped fresh marjoram, plus sprigs for garnish

Preheat the oven to 375°F (190°C).

Trim off the stems and fronds from the fennel bulb and reserve a few fronds for garnish. Trim away any bruised outer leaves. Cut the bulb lengthwise into wedges 1 inch (2.5 cm) wide. Cut out the tough core portions. Combine the fennel and garlic on a rimmed baking sheet. Drizzle with the olive oil and broth and toss to coat evenly. Season generously with salt and pepper. Spread the fennel wedges out in a single layer.

Roast the fennel, stirring 1 or 2 times, for 20 minutes. Remove the pan from the oven and sprinkle the fennel evenly with the chopped marjoram. Continue to roast until the fennel and garlic are tender when pressed with a fork and lightly browned at the edges, 25–30 minutes longer.

Remove the pan from the oven and transfer the fennel to a warmed serving bowl. Garnish with marjoram sprigs and fennel fronds. Serve at once.

Fennel has a strong anise flavor that pairs well with the assertive character of garlic. Because fennel can dry out easily during roasting, here it is drizzled with a little broth or wine to keep it moist while the edges caramelize. Thyme or oregano may be substituted for the marjoram. Serve this simple side dish with roasted pork or veal.

Portobello Mushrooms with Parmesan and Basil

With their rich flavor and dense texture, roasted portobello mushrooms make a satisfying vegetarian main course. You can also put the roasted caps between toasted slices of coarse country bread for a hearty sandwich, or slice them and stir them into a pan sauce for serving with roasted poultry or meats.

Preheat the oven to 450°F (230°C). Lightly oil a rimmed baking sheet. Trim off the stems from the mushrooms and reserve for another use or discard.

In a small bowl, whisk together 2 tablespoons of the olive oil and the garlic. Brush the mushrooms all over with the garlic oil. Season generously with salt and pepper. Place the mushroom caps, gill side down, on the prepared pan.

Roast for 10 minutes. Remove the pan from the oven, turn the mushrooms gill side up, and roast until tender when pierced with a fork, about 8 minutes longer. Meanwhile, in a small dish, stir together the slivered basil and the 2 tablespoons cheese. Remove the pan from the oven and sprinkle the cheese mixture evenly over the mushrooms. Continue to roast the mushrooms until the cheese begins to melt, about 2 minutes.

In a small dish, stir together the remaining 1 tablespoon oil and the vinegar. Remove the pan from the oven and place the mushrooms on individual plates. Leave whole or cut into thick slices. Drizzle with the vinegar mixture, garnish each serving with a basil sprig, and sprinkle with cheese, if desired. Serve at once.

4 large fresh portobello mushrooms, about 6 oz (185 g) each, brushed clean

3 tablespoons extra-virgin olive oil

1 large clove garlic, finely chopped

Kosher salt and freshly ground pepper

2 tablespoons slivered fresh basil, plus 4 fresh sprigs

2 tablespoons shaved Parmesan or Asiago cheese, plus extra for garnish (optional)

1 tablespoon balsamic or sherry vinegar

Leeks with Buttered Bread Crumbs

1 lb (500 g) leeks (about 4), each about 1 inch (2.5 cm) in diameter, halved lengthwise

1 tablespoon extra-virgin olive oil

3 tablespoons dry white wine

Kosher salt and freshly ground pepper

1/3 cup (3/4 oz/20 g) fresh French bread crumbs

2 tablespoons grated Parmesan cheese

2 tablespoons unsalted butter, melted

Leeks, mild members of the onion family, come in all sizes, from slender stalks 1/2 inch (12 mm) in diameter to stocky ones 2 inches (5 cm) in diameter. For the best flavor and prettiest presentation, choose medium-sized leeks about 1 inch (2.5 cm) in diameter. Leeks trap the sandy soil in which they are grown. The best way to clean them is to trim off both ends, then spread out the layers a bit and hold them under running cold water. Shake off the excess water, but do not dry the leeks before roasting them. The dampness helps keep them moist.

Preheat the oven to 400°F (200°C).

Place the leeks, cut side down, on a rimmed baking sheet. Brush with about 1 1/2 teaspoons of the olive oil. Turn the leeks cut side up, push close together, and brush with the remaining 1 1/2 teaspoons olive oil. Sprinkle with the wine and season generously with salt and pepper. In a small dish, toss together the bread crumbs, cheese, and butter until the crumbs are evenly moistened. Sprinkle evenly over the leeks.

Roast the leeks, without turning, until they are tender when pierced with a knife, their edges are browned, and the crumbs are toasted, 20–30 minutes.

Remove the pan from the oven and transfer the leeks to a platter or individual plates. Serve at once.

VARIATION

Leeks with Seasoned Buttered Bread Crumbs

Add 1 tablespoon minced fresh herb such as thyme or marjoram to the bread crumb mixture and toss to mix.

Asparagus with Shallots and Lemon

VARIATIONS

Asparagus with Shallots and Herbs

Sprinkle 1 tablespoon chopped fresh mint or chervil on the asparagus just before serving.

Asparagus with Shallots and Ham

Sprinkle 2 tablespoons finely cubed smoked ham or slivered prosciutto on the asparagus before roasting. Season lightly with salt and generously with pepper, then roast the asparagus as directed.

Choose asparagus of the same thickness, preferably somewhat slim, to ensure that all the spears will be done at the same time. To remove the tough end from each spear, bend the cut end of the spear until it breaks naturally. It will snap where the fibrous portion begins. You do not need to peel asparagus for roasting.

Preheat the oven to 400°F (200°C).

Place the asparagus close together on a rimmed baking sheet. Brush evenly with about 1 tablespoon of the olive oil. Turn the spears and brush evenly with the remaining 1 tablespoon oil. Sprinkle evenly with the shallot, then season generously with salt and pepper.

Roast the asparagus, without turning, until the spears are tender and the tips are browned, 12–15 minutes.

Remove the pan from the oven and transfer the asparagus to a platter. Top with the lemon juice and then sprinkle with the lemon zest. Serve warm or at room temperature.

1 lb (500 g) medium-slim asparagus, tough ends removed (see note)

2 tablespoons extra-virgin olive oil

2 tablespoons sliced shallot

Kosher salt and freshly ground pepper

2 teaspoons fresh lemon juice

1 teaspoon grated lemon zest

Summer Squash with Cilantro Pesto

For the Cilantro Pesto

3 cloves garlic

2 cups (2 oz/60 g) loosely packed fresh cilantro (fresh coriander) leaves

3 tablespoons pine nuts, lightly toasted

$1/2$ cup (4 fl oz/125 ml) extra-virgin olive oil

$1/2$ cup (2 oz/60 g) grated Parmesan cheese

2 zucchini (courgettes), about 6 oz (185 g) each, trimmed and halved lengthwise

2 yellow crookneck squashes, about 6 oz (185 g) each, trimmed and halved lengthwise

2 tablespoons extra-virgin olive oil

Kosher salt and freshly ground pepper

Summer squash, with its high moisture content and delicate soft skin, needs to be roasted at a moderate temperature to evaporate some of the liquid. Choose small, nicely shaped zucchini and crookneck squashes. Serve the squash over a bed of rice, as a vegetarian main course, or offer it as a side dish to grilled meat, poultry, or seafood. The pesto recipe, which can be made with basil in place of the cilantro, makes more than you will need for this recipe. It has many uses, however, from stirring into scrambled eggs to spreading on bread for a roast-chicken sandwich.

To make the pesto, engage the motor of a food processor and drop the garlic cloves through the feed tube. When the garlic is minced, turn off the motor and add the cilantro and pine nuts. Process until finely chopped. Then, with the motor running, pour in the oil in a slow, steady stream and process until a smooth, thick paste forms. Transfer the pesto to a small bowl and stir in the cheese. You will have about 1 cup (8 fl oz/250 ml). Measure out about $1/4$ cup (2 fl oz/60 ml) to use for the squash. Refrigerate the remainder for another use (see note).

Preheat the oven to 375°F (190°C). Lightly oil a rimmed baking sheet.

Scoop out any large seeds from the squash halves. Brush or rub the halves all over with the olive oil and then season generously with salt and pepper. Place the squashes, cut side up, on the prepared pan.

Roast the squash halves, without turning, until nearly tender, 20–25 minutes. Remove the pan from the oven and spread $1^1/2$ teaspoons of the pesto on the cut side of each half. Continue to roast until the pesto is bubbly, 4–5 minutes.

Remove the pan from the oven and transfer the squash to a platter or individual plates. Serve at once.

VARIATION

Tomatoes with Cilantro Pesto
Substitute 8 meaty tomato slices, each $1/2$ inch (12 mm) thick, for the zucchini and crookneck squashes. Roast for 15 minutes, top with the pesto, and then roast for 5 minutes longer.

Broccoli with Soy, Rice Vinegar, and Sesame Seeds

1 lb (500 g) broccoli spears, tough ends trimmed

Kosher salt and freshly ground pepper

2 tablespoons peanut oil

1 tablespoon Asian sesame oil

1 large clove garlic, finely chopped

1 tablespoon sesame seeds

1 tablespoon soy sauce

1 tablespoon rice vinegar

Roasting brings out the best in broccoli. The tips of the flowers char lightly while the stems stay nicely crisp. And best of all, roasting turns this strong-flavored vegetable into a mild, sweetly flavored flower stalk. The secret is high heat. For a particularly attractive presentation, serve the broccoli atop strips of roasted red bell pepper (capsicum) (page 294).

Preheat the oven to 475°F (245°C).

Arrange the broccoli spears in a single layer on a rimmed baking sheet. Season lightly with salt and pepper. In a small dish, stir together the peanut and sesame oils and the garlic. Brush the broccoli spears on all sides with the oil mixture.

Roast the broccoli, turning once, until the stems are nearly crisp-tender and the florets are beginning to brown, about 10 minutes. Remove the pan from the oven and sprinkle the broccoli evenly with the sesame seeds. Continue to roast until the seeds are toasted, the stems are crisp tender, and florets are browned, about 5 minutes longer.

Remove the pan from the oven and arrange the broccoli on a platter. Drizzle with the soy sauce and vinegar and serve warm or at room temperature.

VARIATION

Broccoli with Garlic Oil

Omit the peanut and sesame oils, sesame seeds, soy sauce, and rice vinegar. In a small bowl, stir together 3 tablespoons olive oil and the garlic. Arrange the broccoli on the baking sheet. Season with salt and pepper and brush with the garlic oil. Roast for about 15 minutes. Drizzle 2 teaspoons fresh lemon juice over the broccoli and serve.

Caramelized Cauliflower

VARIATION

Caramelized Curried Cauliflower

In a small bowl, stir together the olive oil, ¹/₂ teaspoon salt, 1 teaspoon curry powder, and ¹/₄ teaspoon cayenne pepper. Drizzle over the cauliflower, toss to coat evenly, and roast as directed. When the cauliflower is done, in a small bowl, stir together ¹/₂ cup (4 oz/125 g) plain yogurt and 1 tablespoon Dijon mustard. Pour over the hot cauliflower and serve.

When you roast cauliflower, it becomes tender and lightly caramelized and has none of the strong cabbagelike odors that usually develop when it is boiled or steamed. Cauliflower is a late-harvest vegetable. Choose snowy white or pale yellow heads free of blemishes.

Preheat the oven to 400°F (200°C).

Arrange the cauliflower florets in a single layer on a rimmed baking sheet. Drizzle the olive oil evenly over the florets, then sprinkle with ¹/₂ teaspoon salt. Toss to coat the cauliflower evenly, then spread the florets out evenly.

Roast the cauliflower, stirring 1 or 2 times, until golden brown and crisp-tender, 25–35 minutes. Remove the pan from the oven and transfer the cauliflower to a warmed bowl. Serve at once.

1 head cauliflower, about 1¹/₂ lb (750 g), cored and cut into florets about 1 inch (2.5 cm) in diameter

2 tablespoons extra-virgin olive oil

Kosher salt

Vegetable Napoleon

The classic napoleon is layers of puff pastry filled with pastry cream or whipped cream, but nowadays the definition has grown to embrace almost anything, sweet or savory, that is layered. Roasted vegetables, which are pliant and colorful, make a particularly wonderful napoleon. Eggplant, zucchini, onion, and tomato are the choices here, and the roasted yellow pepper purée makes an attractive—and easy—sauce. If you like, substitute basil or thyme for the mint.

In a food processor, combine the roasted pepper and 2 tablespoons of the olive oil and process to a coarse purée. Add the wine and process until nearly smooth. Season to taste with salt and pepper. Set aside.

Preheat the oven to 425°F (220°C).

Arrange the eggplant, zucchini, onion, and tomato slices in a single layer on a large rimmed baking sheet (or use 2 sheets). Brush with 1¹⁄₂ tablespoons of the olive oil. Turn the slices and brush with the remaining 1¹⁄₂ tablespoons oil. Season generously with salt and pepper. Sprinkle evenly with the garlic and oregano.

Roast the vegetables, turning once, until tender when pierced with a fork and tinged with brown, 12–15 minutes. Remove the pan from the oven and sprinkle the tops of the vegetables with the ¹⁄₂ cup feta cheese. Continue to roast until the cheese is softened, 2–3 minutes. Remove from the oven.

Using a spatula, place an eggplant slice on each individual plate. Then layer in the following order: a zucchini slice, an onion slice, and a tomato slice, placing 1 or 2 mint leaves and a few sprinkles of vinegar between each layer. Top with a second eggplant slice. Drizzle the roasted pepper sauce on top of the napoleons and garnish with the remaining mint leaves and feta cheese. Serve at once.

1 yellow bell pepper (capsicum), roasted, peeled, and seeded (page 294)

5 tablespoons (3 fl oz/80 ml) extra-virgin olive oil

¹⁄₄ cup (2 fl oz/60 ml) dry white wine

Kosher salt and freshly ground pepper

1 small eggplant (aubergine), about ³⁄₄ lb (375 g), trimmed and cut lengthwise into slices ¹⁄₄–¹⁄₂ inch (6–12 mm) thick (8 slices total)

1 zucchini (courgette), about ¹⁄₂ lb (250 g), trimmed and cut lengthwise into slices ¹⁄₄–¹⁄₂ inch (6–12 mm) thick (4 slices total)

1 yellow onion, about 6 oz (185 g), cut crosswise into slices ¹⁄₄ inch (6 mm) thick (4 slices total)

1 tomato, about 6 oz (185 g), cut crosswise into slices ¹⁄₄ inch (6 mm) thick (4 slices total)

1 large clove garlic, chopped

1 tablespoon chopped fresh oregano

¹⁄₂ cup (2¹⁄₂ oz/75 g) crumbled feta cheese, plus extra for garnish

¹⁄₃ cup (¹⁄₃ oz/10 g) fresh mint leaves

1 tablespoon red wine vinegar

Ratatouille

1 lb (500 g) plum (Roma) tomatoes, halved lengthwise

4 large cloves garlic, sliced

1 large yellow onion, cut crosswise into slices $^1/_4$ inch (6 mm) thick

1 small eggplant (aubergine), trimmed and cut into 1-inch (2.5-cm) chunks

1 small zucchini (courgette), trimmed and cut crosswise into slices $^1/_2$ inch (12 mm) thick

1 small yellow crookneck squash, trimmed and cut crosswise into slices $^1/_2$ inch (12 mm) thick

1 orange or green bell pepper (capsicum), seeded and cut into 1$^1/_2$-inch (4-cm) squares

5 tablespoons (3 fl oz/80 ml) extra-virgin olive oil

Kosher salt and freshly ground pepper

$^1/_4$ cup ($^1/_3$ oz/10 g) finely shredded fresh basil

2 tablespoons chopped fresh thyme

Ratatouille, a classic of Provence, is the quintessential summer garden dish. The vegetables are traditionally simmered together on the stove top, but here they are roasted, which gives the dish a new profile. Without liquid to dilute their colors and flavors, the ripe garden vegetables develop a more intense flavor. Serve them as a side dish, or toss them with $^3/_4$ pound (375 g) cooked linguine as a main dish for three or four people. You can also let the vegetables cool to room temperature and use them as a topping for brushetta or on an antipasto platter.

Preheat the oven to 425°F (220°C).

Arrange the tomatoes, garlic, onion, eggplant, zucchini, crookneck squash, and bell pepper in a single layer on a large rimmed baking sheet (or use 2 sheets if necessary). Drizzle the olive oil evenly over the vegetables and season generously with salt and pepper. Stir the vegetables to coat evenly with oil, then spread them out in a shallow layer.

Roast the vegetables, stirring 1 or 2 times, for 20 minutes. Remove the pan from the oven and sprinkle the vegetables evenly with the basil and thyme. Stir to distribute the herbs evenly, then spread the vegetables out again. Continue to roast the vegetables, stirring 1 or 2 times, until tender when pierced with a fork and tinged with brown, 5–10 minutes longer. Remove the pan from the oven and season the vegetables again with salt and pepper.

Transfer the vegetables to a serving bowl. Serve the ratatouille hot, warm, or at room temperature.

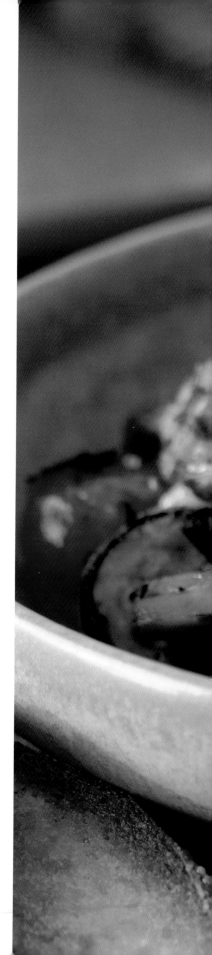

Apples with Crème Anglaise

VARIATION

Savory Roasted Apples

Omit the crème anglaise. Reduce the brown sugar to 3 tablespoons, the cinnamon and ginger to ¹/₄ teaspoon each, and the honey to ¹/₄ cup (3 oz/90 g). Proceed as directed. Serve with roasted pork, ham, or veal.

Medium-sized apples are ideal here, but if you can find only large apples, cut them in half crosswise. They must be tart and juicy, however; Jonathan, Cortland, Empire, and Granny Smith are all good choices. Bay leaves are particularly compatible with apples and work well whether the recipe is sweet or savory. If you are short of time, omit the crème anglaise and serve the apples with crème fraîche or whipped cream. You can also roast the apples an hour or so ahead of time and keep them warm in a 200°F (95°C) oven, basting occasionally with the juices, until serving.

To make the crème anglaise, in a saucepan over medium heat, warm the milk until small bubbles appear along the edges of the pan. Meanwhile, in a bowl, whisk together the egg yolks and sugar until pale and thick. Slowly add the hot milk to the egg mixture while whisking constantly. Return the mixture to the saucepan over medium heat and cook, stirring constantly, until it is thick enough to coat the back of a spoon and a finger drawn along the spoon leaves a trail, about 5 minutes. Pour through a sieve placed over a clean bowl and stir in the vanilla. Let cool, cover, and refrigerate until serving.

Preheat the oven to 375°F (190°C). Select a shallow baking dish just large enough to hold the apples and coat the bottom with 1¹/₂ teaspoons of the butter.

Cut a thin slice off the top and the bottom of each apple. Then, working from the top of the apple, peel the apple about halfway down. Stand the apples, peeled end up, in the prepared dish.

In a small bowl, stir together the brown sugar, cinnamon, ginger, cloves, and lemon zest. Sprinkle the mixture evenly over the tops of the apples. Cut the remaining 2 tablespoons butter into small pieces and divide among the tops of the apples. In a small saucepan over low heat, combine the honey, lemon juice, bay leaves, and 1 cup (8 fl oz/250 ml) water and heat, stirring, until the honey melts. Pour the liquid around the apples.

Roast the apples, basting 3 or 4 times with the juices in the dish, until they are just tender when pierced with a knife, 40–45 minutes. Remove the dish from the oven and let the apples cool slightly, about 10 minutes, spooning the juices over them as they cool to glaze them. Discard the bay leaves.

Divide the warm apples among individual plates. Spoon the crème anglaise around the apples and serve.

For the Crème Anglaise

1 cup (8 fl oz/250 ml) milk

4 large egg yolks

3 tablespoons sugar

³/₄ teaspoon vanilla extract (essence)

2¹/₂ tablespoons unsalted butter

4 tart apples (see note)

5 tablespoons (2¹/₂ oz/75 g) firmly packed golden brown sugar

¹/₂ teaspoon ground cinnamon

¹/₂ teaspoon ground ginger

¹/₄ teaspoon ground cloves

¹/₂ teaspoon grated lemon zest

¹/₃ cup (4 oz/125 g) honey

1 tablespoon fresh lemon juice

3 bay leaves, each broken in half

Roasted Pears

1¹/₂ tablespoons unsalted butter

2–4 tablespoons sugar

4 ripe but firm pears such as Bosc, Bartlett, or Anjou, unpeeled, halved lengthwise and cored

2 teaspoons fresh lemon juice

1 tablespoon chopped fresh sage or ¹/₂ teaspoon ground cinnamon

4 tablespoons (2 fl oz/60 ml) white wine

Preheat the oven to 425°F (220°C).

Choose a shallow baking dish just large enough to hold the pears in a single layer. Coat the bottom with 1¹/₂ teaspoons of the butter. Sprinkle with half of the sugar (use 1 tablespoon if making savory pears or 2 tablespoons if making sweet) and place the pear halves, cut side up, on the sugar. Brush the cut sides with the lemon juice, then sprinkle with the sage for savory pears or the cinnamon for sweet pears. Sprinkle with 1 tablespoon of the remaining sugar for savory pears or 2 tablespoons for sweet pears. Drizzle 2 tablespoons of the wine evenly over the pear halves. Cut the remaining 1 tablespoon butter into pieces and evenly dot the pears with them.

Roast the pears just until tender, 22–25 minutes. Remove the dish from the oven and drizzle the pears with the remaining 2 tablespoons wine and ¹/₄ cup (2 fl oz/60 ml) water. Continue to roast, basting 1 or 2 times with the liquid in the dish, until the pears are very tender and lightly browned, 12–15 minutes longer. Remove the dish from the oven. Serve the pears warm or at room temperature with the pan syrup spooned over the top.

This basic recipe for roasted pears can be made in both a sweet and a savory version. You simply increase or reduce the amount of sugar and change the spices depending on the intended use. Savory roasted pears are a wonderful holiday side dish for roasted meats or poultry, while sweet roasted pears are lovely drizzled with chocolate sauce. You can substitute mint for the sage for a good accompaniment to roasted lamb.

Amaretti Pears

Thickly sliced pears roasted in Amaretto and butter are a sophisticated ending to any Italian meal. Amaretti are crisp almond cookies from Italy, usually sold in tins with one or two cookies wrapped in colorful tissue. They make an appealingly crisp topping for the pears. For a less sweet dessert, substitute more dry white wine for the Amaretto. The pears are delicious accompanied by a dollop of crème fraîche or a tiny scoop of vanilla or almond gelato.

Preheat the oven to 400°F (200°C).

Coat a shallow 2-qt (2-l) baking dish with 1¹/₂ teaspoons of the butter. Sprinkle with 1¹/₂ teaspoons of the sugar. Arrange the pear slices, slightly overlapping them, to cover the bottom of the prepared dish. Sprinkle with the lemon juice and zest. Pour the white wine and Amaretto evenly over the pears. Cut the remaining 2 tablespoons butter into small pieces and evenly dot the pear slices with them. In a small dish, stir together the remaining 2 tablespoons sugar and the nutmeg. Sprinkle evenly over the pears, then top with the crumbled amaretti.

Roast the pears, basting 2 or 3 times with the pan juices, until they are tender and the amaretti are browned, 20–22 minutes.

Remove the dish from the oven. Divide the pears among individual bowls and spoon the dish juices over the top. Serve warm.

2¹/₂ tablespoons unsalted butter

2¹/₂ tablespoons sugar

4 ripe but firm pears such as Bosc or Anjou, halved, cored, peeled, and thickly sliced

1 tablespoon fresh lemon juice

1 teaspoon grated lemon zest

¹/₄ cup (2 fl oz/60 ml) dry white wine or pear nectar

2 tablespoons Amaretto

¹/₄ teaspoon freshly grated nutmeg

¹/₂ cup (1¹/₂ oz/45 g) crumbled amaretti

Apricot Crisp

4$^{1}/_{2}$ tablespoons (2$^{1}/_{2}$ oz/ 75 g) unsalted butter

1$^{1}/_{2}$ lb (750 g) apricots, pitted and thickly sliced

2 tablespoons Grand Marnier or other orange liqueur

1 tablespoon fresh lemon juice

$^{1}/_{4}$ teaspoon vanilla extract (essence)

6 tablespoons (3 oz/90 g) firmly packed golden brown sugar

$^{1}/_{4}$ cup (1 oz/30 g) coarsely chopped walnuts

1$^{1}/_{2}$ tablespoons all-purpose (plain) flour

$^{1}/_{2}$ teaspoon ground cinnamon

Apricots are usually picked early, while they are still firm, since the ripe fruits are delicate and bruise easily during shipping. If you live where apricots are grown, you are lucky. If you do not, roasting brings out the best flavor in any apricot. In the market, choose fruits that are firm but still yield to soft pressure. The relatively high roasting temperature promotes the "crisp" in the topping. The apricots are delicious plain, but they can also be garnished with a spoonful of heavy (double) cream or a small scoop of vanilla ice cream.

Preheat the oven to 475°F (245°C). Select a shallow baking dish just large enough to hold the apricots in a single or double layer. Coat the bottom with 1$^{1}/_{2}$ teaspoons of the butter.

Combine the apricots, liqueur, lemon juice, and vanilla extract in the prepared dish and toss to coat the apricots evenly. Spread the apricots out evenly.

Cut the remaining 4 tablespoons (2 oz/60 g) butter into small pieces. In a bowl, combine the butter, brown sugar, walnuts, flour, and cinnamon. Using your fingers, rub the ingredients together to make coarse crumbs.

Sprinkle the flour mixture evenly over the apricots. Roast the apricots until the topping is browned and crisp and the apricots are softened, 8–12 minutes. Remove the dish from the oven. Serve the crisp warm or at room temperature.

VARIATION

Apricot Crisp with Pernod and Almonds

Substitute Pernod or other anise liqueur for the orange liqueur, almonds for the walnuts, and almond extract for the vanilla extract. Add $^{1}/_{2}$ teaspoon aniseeds to the topping with the cinnamon. Proceed as directed.

Peaches and Cream with Raspberries

1 lb (500 g) ripe peaches

2 tablespoons unsalted butter

$^1/_3$ cup (3 oz/90 g) firmly packed golden brown sugar

$1^1/_2$ tablespoons fresh lemon juice

1 teaspoon grated lemon zest

$^1/_4$ teaspoon ground allspice

1 cup (8 fl oz/250 ml) heavy (double) cream, whipped to soft peaks

About 1 cup (4 oz/125 g) raspberries

Bring a saucepan three-fourths full of water to a boil. Working in batches, add the peaches and blanch for about 20 seconds, then lift out with a slotted spoon and immerse in very cold water. When the peaches are cool, using a small knife, peel off the skins. Halve, pit, and slice thickly. Set aside.

Preheat the oven to 450°F (230°C). Select a shallow baking dish just large enough to hold the peach slices in a single layer. Combine the butter and brown sugar in the dish and place in the preheating oven. Watch carefully to prevent burning. When the butter has melted, stir to dissolve the sugar. Remove the dish from the oven and stir in the peaches, lemon juice and zest, and allspice until evenly coated. Spread the peaches out evenly.

Roast the peaches, stirring 1 or 2 times, until they are softened but still maintain their shape, 7–10 minutes.

Remove the dish from the oven and let peaches cool slightly. Divide the peaches and pan juices among individual dishes or bowls. Top with the whipped cream and raspberries, dividing evenly. Serve at once.

Roasting brings out the lush aroma of the peaches in this recipe inspired by the classic peach Melba dessert. For variations on the same theme, try using unpeeled nectarines in place of the peaches or blackberries or blueberries in place of the raspberries.

Strawberry and Blueberry Compote

With only a brief roasting, strawberries and blueberries taste riper, look brighter, and have a fuller flavor. The fruits can be roasted separately, but together they are a brilliant pairing. Serve them just as they are or as an accompaniment to crisp sugar cookies, or spoon them over angel food cake or vanilla ice cream. You can roast the strawberries alone and serve them over split, buttered biscuits for a roasted strawberry shortcake.

Preheat the oven to 450°F (230°C).

Select a shallow baking dish just large enough to hold the berries in a shallow layer no more than 3 berries deep. Combine the strawberries, blueberries, sugar, Cognac, and orange juice in the dish and toss to coat the berries evenly. Spread the berries out evenly.

Roast the berries, stirring gently 1 or 2 times, just until they begin to soften and become glossy and the sugar melts into a syrup, 5–7 minutes.

Remove the dish from the oven. Divide the berries among individual bowls and serve at once.

2 cups (8 oz/250 g) straw-berries, stems removed and cut in half if large

1/2 cup (2 oz/60 g) blue-berries

1/4 cup (2 oz/60 g) sugar

2 tablespoons Cognac or other brandy

1 tablespoon fresh orange juice

Plum Crumble

VARIATIONS

Plum Crumble with Crystallized Ginger

Add 2 tablespoons chopped crystallized ginger to the plums with the brown sugar. Proceed as directed.

Plum Crumble with Cinnamon and Nutmeg

Omit the five-spice powder. Add ¹/₂ teaspoon *each* ground cinnamon and freshly grated nutmeg to the topping. Proceed as directed.

The best plums for roasting are small prune plums, also known as Italian plums, available in late summer. They have firm flesh and hold their shape in the oven. Any good plum can be roasted, however, and a combination of varieties gives the most interesting flavor. Serve this crumble for dessert or for breakfast on a lazy summer Sunday morning.

Preheat the oven to 400°F (200°C). Coat the bottom of a 9-inch (23-cm) pie dish with 1¹/₂ teaspoons of the butter.

Combine the plums, orange juice, vanilla, and 2 tablespoons of the brown sugar in the prepared dish and toss to coat the plums evenly. Then spread the plums out evenly.

Cut the remaining 3 tablespoons butter into small pieces. In a bowl, combine the butter, oats, flour, orange zest, five-spice powder, and remaining 3 tablespoons brown sugar. Using your fingers, rub the ingredients together until crumbly.

Sprinkle the mixture evenly over the plums. Roast the crumble until the topping is browned and crisp and the fruit is bubbly, 25–30 minutes. Remove the dish from the oven. Serve the crumble warm or at room temperature.

3¹/₂ tablespoons unsalted butter

1 lb (500g) plums (see note), pitted and thickly sliced

2 tablespoons fresh orange juice

¹/₂ teaspoon vanilla extract (essence)

5 tablespoons (2¹/₂ z/75 g) firmly packed golden brown sugar

¹/₃ cup (1 oz/30 g) quick-cooking rolled oats

¹/₃ cup (2 oz/60 g) all-purpose (plain) flour

1¹/₂ teaspoons grated orange zest

1 teaspoon five-spice powder

Gingered Rhubarb

1 lb (500 g) rhubarb, cut into ¹/₂-inch (12-mm) slices

¹/₂ cup (4 oz/125 g) sugar

3 tablespoons chopped crystallized ginger

¹/₄ cup (2 fl oz/60 ml) Grand Marnier or other orange liqueur or fresh orange juice

1 cup (8 fl oz/250 ml) heavy (double) cream, whipped to soft peaks, or 4 small scoops vanilla ice cream

Preheat the oven to 450°F (230°C).

Select a shallow baking dish just large enough to hold the rhubarb slices in a single or double layer. Combine the rhubarb, sugar, ginger, and liqueur in the dish and toss to coat the rhubarb evenly. Spread the rhubarb out evenly.

Roast the rhubarb, stirring 2 or 3 times, until it is very soft but still retains some of its shape, 25–30 minutes.

Remove the dish from the oven. Let the rhubarb cool to room temperature, divide among individual bowls, and top each serving with a dollop of whipped cream, or use as a filling for shortcake (see note). Alternatively, divide the scoops of ice cream among individual bowls and spoon the rhubarb evenly over the top.

Rhubarb is usually stewed in sugar to soften and sweeten the hard stalks, but roasting is an even better method. The rhubarb retains a bit of its firm texture, and its sweet-tart flavor is more concentrated. If you cannot find fresh rhubarb, which is available spring through summer, use sliced or chopped, frozen rhubarb. The rhubarb can be served on shortcake biscuits and garnished with whipped cream, or on its own with ice cream or whipped cream.

Bananas with Rum and Cinnamon

This is a roasted variation of the New Orleans classic, bananas Foster. The dessert originated in the 1950s at the famous Commander's Palace Restaurant and is named in honor of the owner's friend, Dick Foster. It is just as popular today in its flambéed frying pan version, but roasting the bananas is much easier than sautéing them, and the recipe can be doubled for a larger number of people, too. Be sure to use slightly underripe bananas with skins tinged with green.

Preheat the oven to 475°F (245°C). Select a shallow baking dish just large enough to hold the bananas in a single layer. Combine the butter and brown sugar in the dish and place in the preheating oven. Watch carefully to prevent burning. When the butter has melted, remove the dish from the oven and stir in orange juice, rum, orange and banana liqueurs, lemon juice, and cinnamon.

Place the bananas in the dish and stir gently to coat evenly with the liqueurs, juice, and other seasonings. Spread the bananas out in a single layer.

Roast the bananas, basting 2 or 3 times with the pan juices, until softened and tinged with gold, 8–10 minutes.

Remove the dish from the oven. Divide the ice cream among individual bowls. Top with the warm bananas and dish juices, dividing evenly. Serve at once.

2 tablespoons unsalted butter

2 tablespoons dark brown sugar

2 tablespoons fresh orange juice

1 tablespoon dark rum

1 tablespoon Grand Marnier or other orange liqueur

1 tablespoon banana liqueur

2 teaspoons fresh lemon juice

$1/2$ teaspoon ground cinnamon

4 slightly underripe bananas, halved lengthwise, then halved crosswise

4 scoops vanilla ice cream

Basic Recipes

A selection of herb-and-spice rubs and an Asian-inspired sauce offer ways to season meats, poultry, and fish before cooking. Savory accompaniments include salsas, a holiday relish, and roasted vegetables, as well as roasted fruits, which can also be made into delicious desserts.

Basic Herb Rub

1 tablespoon dried thyme

1 tablespoon dried basil

1 tablespoon dried oregano

2 teaspoons dried rosemary

Kosher salt and coarsely ground pepper

Extra-virgin olive oil or canola oil

In a small bowl, stir together the thyme, basil, oregano, rosemary, 1 teaspoon salt, and $1/2$ teaspoon pepper. Brush or rub the meat or poultry on all sides with oil, then rub the herb mixture on all sides of the meat or poultry.

Makes about $1/4$ cup ($1/3$ oz/10 g), enough to flavor 2–3 lb (1–1.5 kg) meat or poultry

VARIATION
To make a rub for meaty fish such as halibut, omit the basil and rosemary. Add 1 tablespoon paprika and $1^1/2$ teaspoons *each* granulated onion and celery seeds.

Dry Rub for Pork

2 teaspoons dried thyme

2 teaspoons ground allspice

1 teaspoon granulated onion

1 teaspoon sugar

$1/2$ teaspoon freshly grated nutmeg

$1/2$ teaspoon Madras curry powder

$1/4$ teaspoon ground cinnamon

$1/4$ teaspoon cayenne pepper

$1/8$ teaspoon ground cloves

Kosher salt

Extra-virgin olive oil or canola oil

In a small bowl, stir together the thyme, allspice, granulated onion, sugar, nutmeg, curry powder, cinnamon, cayenne, cloves, and $1/2$ teaspoon salt. Brush or rub the pork on all sides with oil, then rub the herb and spice mixture on all sides of the pork.

Makes about $3^1/2$ tablespoons, enough to flavor 2–3 lb (1–1.5 kg) pork

VARIATION
To make a rub for poultry, omit the allspice, sugar, nutmeg, curry powder, cinnamon, and cloves. Add 1 tablespoon *each* New Mexico or ancho chile powder and 1 tablespoon ground cumin.

Dry Rub for Lamb

1 tablespoon dried marjoram

1 tablespoon dried thyme

1 tablespoon dried summer savory

2 teaspoons dried lavender

2 teaspoons dried oregano

2 teaspoons dried rosemary

1 teaspoon dried sage

$1/2$ teaspoon lightly crushed fennel seeds

Kosher salt and coarsely ground pepper

Extra-virgin olive oil or canola oil

In a small bowl, stir together the marjoram, thyme, summer savory, lavender, oregano, rosemary, sage, fennel seeds, and $1/2$ teaspoon *each* salt and pepper. Brush or rub the lamb on all sides with oil, then rub the herb mixture on all sides of the lamb.

Makes abut $1/3$ cup ($1/2$ oz/15 g), enough to flavor 3 lb (1.5 kg) lamb

Miso-Sake Basting Sauce

1 cup (8 fl oz/250 ml) low-sodium chicken broth

$1/2$ cup (4 fl oz/125 ml) sake, mirin, or sweet sherry

2 tablespoons white or yellow miso

1 tablespoon finely chopped, peeled fresh ginger

$1/4$ cup ($3/4$ oz/20 g) chopped green (spring) onion, including tender green tops

$1^1/2$ teaspoons cornstarch (cornflour)

1 tablespoon soy sauce

In a saucepan, whisk together the broth, sake, miso, ginger, and green onion. In a small bowl, dissolve the cornstarch in the soy sauce. Bring the miso-sake mixture to a boil and cook until reduced by half. Remove the pan from the heat and whisk in the cornstarch mixture. Place the pan over low heat and cook the sauce until slightly thickened, 1–2 minutes. Remove from the heat and keep warm. The sauce is best used the day it is made.

Makes about $3/4$ cup (6 fl oz/180 ml)

SERVING TIP
Reserve half of the miso-sake sauce. Brush the remaining sauce on salmon, halibut, or tuna steaks or fillets before roasting. Using a clean brush, coat the fish again before serving with the reserved sauce.

Salsa Verde

$^1/_3$ cup ($^1/_2$ oz/15 g) chopped fresh flat-leaf (Italian) parsley

2 olive oil–packed anchovy fillets

6–8 fresh basil leaves, chopped

1 teaspoon capers, plus 2 teaspoons brine

$^1/_4$ cup (2 fl oz/60 ml) extra-virgin olive oil

3 tablespoons red wine vinegar

Place the parsley, anchovy fillets, basil, capers and brine, olive oil, and vinegar in a food processor. Pulse to combine, then process until the anchovies, basil, and capers are finely minced. Transfer to a small serving bowl, using a rubber spatula to scrape the sides of the processor bowl. Refrigerate for up to 3 days. Bring to room temperature before serving.

Makes about $^3/_4$ cup (6 fl oz/180 ml)

SERVING TIP

Serve with a range of roasted foods, including fish, meats, poultry, and vegetables such as potatoes and leeks.

Roasted Garlic

2 heads garlic

$^1/_4$ cup (2 fl oz/60 ml) extra-virgin olive oil

Kosher salt and freshly ground pepper

Preheat the oven to 300°F (150°C). Using a small, sharp knife, score each head of garlic around the middle, cutting through the papery skin but not into the cloves. Remove the top half of the papery skin and expose the cloves. Lightly oil a small roasting pan and set the garlic heads in the pan. Drizzle the olive oil evenly over the tops of the garlic heads, then sprinkle evenly with salt and pepper. Cover the pan with aluminum foil.

Roast the garlic heads for 1 hour. Remove the pan from the oven, remove the foil, and baste the garlic with the pan juices. Continue to roast the garlic until tender when pierced with a knife, 10–15 minutes longer. Remove the pan from the oven and let the garlic heads cool. Separate the cloves from the heads as needed and squeeze out the pulp. If not using the garlic immediately, store in the refrigerator for up to 3 days.

Makes 2 heads garlic

SERVING TIP

Slip the softened garlic pulp under the skin of chicken (page 106), turkey (page 130), or other poultry before roasting, or rub on the surface of meats. Just-roasted garlic can be set out for guests to squeeze the pulp onto slices of coarse country bread.

Vegetable Salsa

$^1/_2$ lb (250 g) tomatillos, husks removed, rinsed, and cut into $^3/_4$-inch (2-cm) chunks

2 tomatoes, seeded and cut into $^3/_4$-inch (2-cm) chunks

1 yellow onion, cut into $^1/_2$-inch (12-mm) dice

1 cup (6 oz/185 g) corn kernels

1 jalapeño chile, seeded and finely chopped

2 large cloves garlic, thinly sliced

1 teaspoon cumin seeds

Kosher salt

$^1/_4$ cup (2 fl oz/60 ml) extra-virgin olive oil

2 tablespoons chopped fresh cilantro (fresh coriander)

Preheat the oven to 450°F (220°C). On a rimmed baking sheet, stir together the tomatillos, tomatoes, onion, corn, chile, garlic, cumin seeds, and $^1/_2$ teaspoon salt. Drizzle with the olive oil, stir to coat the vegetables evenly with the other ingredients, and spread the vegetables out evenly.

Roast the vegetables, stirring often, until the tomatillos, tomatoes, and onion are soft when pierced with a fork and the corn is tinged with gold, 10–12 minutes. Remove the pan from the oven and transfer the salsa to a bowl. Stir in the cilantro, then taste and season with salt if necessary. The salsa will keep for up to 3 days in the refrigerator.

Makes 8–10 servings

SERVING TIP

Serve the salsa warm or at room temperature with corn tortilla chips as a starter. Or offer it as an accompaniment for roasted or grilled meats, poultry, or fish.

Sweet-and-Sour Cipolline Onions

1 lb (500 g) cipolline or pearl onions

3 tablespoons extra-virgin olive oil

1 tablespoon chopped fresh rosemary

1 teaspoon sugar, if using pearl onions

Kosher salt and freshly ground pepper

1 tablespoon red wine vinegar

Preheat the oven to 400°F (200°C). Bring a saucepan of water to a boil. Add the onions and boil for 1–2 minutes; drain. When they are cool enough to handle, slip off the skins.

Select a shallow baking dish just large enough to hold the onions in a single layer. Combine the peeled onions, olive oil, rosemary, and the sugar, if using pearl onions, in the pan.

Season generously with salt and pepper and toss to coat the onions evenly. Spread the onions out evenly. Roast the onions, stirring 2 or 3 times, until tender when pierced with a fork and a rich golden brown, 35–45 minutes. Remove the pan from the oven and transfer the onions to a warmed serving bowl. Drizzle with the vinegar and toss to coat evenly. Serve warm. The onions can be prepared up to 8 hours ahead and reheated in a low oven; add 1 or 2 tablespoons dry red wine, if needed, to prevent the onions from drying out.

Makes 4 servings

SERVING TIP

The onions make a delicious side dish for roasted or grilled meats and poultry.

Roasted Tomato Sauce

2 tablespoons extra-virgin olive oil

2 tablespoons unsalted butter

1 yellow onion, chopped

2 cloves garlic, finely chopped

2 lb (1 kg) plum (Roma) or other ripe, meaty tomatoes, halved, seeded, and diced

Kosher salt and freshly ground pepper

1/4 cup (1/3 oz/10 g) chopped mixed fresh herbs such as basil, thyme, oregano, and/or marjoram, in any combination

2 tablespoons red wine vinegar

1/4–1/2 cup (2–4 fl oz/60–125 ml) reduced-sodium chicken or vegetable broth or dry or full-bodied red wine, if needed

Preheat the oven to 400°F (200°C). Select a shallow baking dish just large enough to hold the tomatoes in a layer no more than 1 inch (2.5 cm) deep. Combine the olive oil and butter in the dish and place it in the preheating oven.

Watch carefully to prevent burning. When the butter has melted, stir in the onion and garlic and roast, stirring once, for 5 minutes.

Remove from the oven, stir in the tomatoes, spread them out evenly, and season with salt and pepper. Roast, stirring 1 or 2 times, until the tomatoes are very soft and a thick, chunky sauce forms, about 40 minutes. Stir in the herbs and vinegar and continue to roast for 5 minutes longer to blend the flavors. Remove the dish from the oven. If the sauce is too thick, stir in some broth. Taste and adjust the seasoning with salt and pepper. Use the sauce immediately, or let cool, cover, and refrigerate for up to 2 days, then reheat gently on the stove top.

Makes about 2 cups (16 fl oz/500 ml)

SERVING TIP

Use the sauce as you would any tomato sauce. It will serve 4 as a sauce for pasta.

Slow-Roasted Plum Tomatoes

2 lb (1 kg) plum (Roma) tomatoes, halved, or quartered if large, and seeded

2 large cloves garlic, sliced

3 tablespoons extra-virgin olive oil

Kosher salt and freshly ground pepper

Preheat the oven to 300°F (150°C). Arrange the tomatoes in a single layer in a shallow baking dish. Sprinkle evenly with the garlic, then drizzle evenly with the olive oil. Season lightly with salt and pepper. Stir the tomatoes to coat them with the oil, then spread them out evenly.

Roast the tomatoes, stirring gently 2 or 3 times, until they are richly tinged with brown and slightly chewy to the bite, 2–2½ hours. Remove the pan from the oven. Use the tomatoes immediately, or store them in an airtight container in the refrigerator for up to 2 days or in the freezer for up to 2 months.

Makes 6–8 servings

SERVING TIP

Serve the tomatoes as a side dish to accompany roasted meat or poultry. The tomatoes can also be cut into slivers and used as a filling for omelets. To make a simple pasta sauce, toss the tomatoes with about 1 tablespoon olive oil and 1/4 cup (2 fl oz/60 ml) dry red wine per serving.

Romesco Sauce

4 tablespoons (2 fl oz/60 ml) extra-virgin olive oil

2 slices coarse country bread, torn into pieces

1/4 cup (1½ oz/45 g) blanched almonds

1 cup (6 oz/185 g) peeled, seeded, and chopped fresh or canned tomatoes

1 clove garlic, minced

2 teaspoons Hungarian sweet paprika

1/4 teaspoon red pepper flakes

3 tablespoons red wine vinegar

Kosher salt and freshly ground pepper

In a frying pan over medium heat, warm 2 tablespoons of the olive oil. Add the bread and cook until golden on both sides, about 2 minutes total. Transfer to a food processor. Add the almonds to the oil remaining in the pan and sauté until golden, about 2 minutes. Transfer to the processor and add the tomatoes, garlic, paprika, and red pepper flakes.

In a small bowl, combine the red wine vinegar and the remaining 2 tablespoons olive oil. With the processor running, pour the oil mixture through the feed tube in a slow, steady stream and process until smooth. Season the sauce to taste with salt and pepper. Transfer the sauce to a serving bowl and let stand for 1 hour to blend the flavors. The sauce will keep for up to 5 days in the refrigerator.

Makes about 1 1/2 cups (12 fl oz/375 ml)

SERVING TIP
The sauce makes an excellent companion to roasted fish, poultry, and vegetables.

Cranberry, Pear, and Orange Relish

1 thin-skinned navel orange, skin intact

2 firm but ripe pears

3 cups (12 oz/375 g) cranberries

1/4 cup (6 oz/185 g) sugar, or to taste

1/2 teaspoon ground cardamom

Cut the orange into 8 wedges, then cut each wedge in half crosswise. Peel the pears, then cut into quarters, remove the cores, and finely chop the flesh; set aside. Place the orange pieces, cranberries, and sugar in a food processor and process until finely chopped. Transfer to a bowl. Add the pears and cardamom to the cranberry mixture and stir to mix well. Taste and add more sugar, if desired. Cover and refrigerate until well chilled before serving, about 1 hour. The relish will keep in the refrigerator for up to 3 days.

Makes about 4 cups (2 lb/1 kg)

SERVING TIP
Serve the relish alongside roasted turkey or goose at the holidays or with roasted poultry, pork, or venison anytime of the year.

Spiced Cherries

1/2 lb (250 g) sweet dark cherries, pitted

2/3 cup (5 fl oz/160 ml) hearty red wine such as Cabernet Sauvignon or Pinot Noir

1 tablespoon sugar

4 whole allspice

4 whole cloves

1 cinnamon stick, broken in half

Preheat the oven to 400°F (200°C). Select a baking dish just large enough to hold the cherries in a shallow layer. Combine the cherries, wine, and sugar in the dish, toss to mix evenly, and spread out evenly. Place the spices on a small square of cheesecloth (muslin) and tie into a bundle with kitchen string. Add to the dish.

Roast the cherries, stirring 1 or 2 times, until they are softened but still hold their shape and about half of the liquid has evaporated, 20–30 minutes. Remove and discard the cheesecloth bundle. Transfer the cherries to a bowl and serve warm. The cherries can be made 1 day ahead and reheated in a covered baking dish in a low-temperature oven.

Makes 4 servings

SERVING TIP
Spiced Cherries are a classic accompaniment to duck, but they are equally delicious with pork, veal, and goose.

VARIATION
For Sweet Spiced Cherries, increase the sugar to 1/4 cup (2 oz/60 g) and proceed as directed. Serve the warm cherries over vanilla ice cream.

Apple Slices with Sage

2 large or 3 medium tart apples such as Granny Smith, peeled, halved, cored, and cut into slices 1/2 inch (12 mm) thick

1/4 cup (2 fl oz/60 ml) apple juice

3 tablespoons sugar

1 tablespoon cider vinegar

1 tablespoon unsalted butter

1 tablespoon chopped fresh sage

Kosher salt and freshly ground pepper

Preheat the oven to 400°F (200°C). Arrange the apple slices in a baking dish just large enough to hold them in a shallow layer. In a saucepan over medium-low heat, combine the apple juice, sugar, vinegar, and butter and heat, stirring, just until the butter melts and the sugar dissolves. Stir in the sage and remove from the heat. Season the apples generously with salt and pepper, drizzle the apple juice mixture evenly over the top, and toss to coat evenly. Spread the apples out evenly.

Roast the apples, turning 2 or 3 times, until they are just tender and the liquid is nearly evaporated, 25–30 minutes. Remove from the oven and transfer the apples to a serving dish. Serve warm. The apples are best served the day they are made.

Makes 4 servings

SERVING TIP
Serve with roasted meats, particularly pork, and with duck, goose, or other poultry.

VARIATION
For Dessert Apple Slices with Sage, omit the vinegar and increase the sugar to 1/4 cup (2 oz/60 g). Serve with a selection of cheeses.

Basic Techniques

CUTTING AND BONING POULTRY

1 Using poultry shears, cut through the skin between the thigh and the body. Locate the leg joint by moving the leg, then cut through the joint to remove the leg. Repeat on the other side of the bird.

2 Turn the bird so a wing is easily accessible. Move the wing to locate the joint between the wing and the body. Cut through the joint to remove the wing from the bird. Repeat on the other side of the bird.

3 Holding the bird securely and beginning at the neck opening, cut along one side of the backbone, then the other side, to separate it from the breast section. Discard the backbone or reserve it for making stock.

4 Cut along the center of the breast to split it in half. If desired, separate the drumsticks from the thighs by cutting through the joints. If the breast is split and the legs and thighs are separated, a whole bird will yield 8 pieces.

5 To bone a breast half, insert a sharp knife between the bones and the meat, starting at the rib side. Cut the meat away from the bones, following the curve of the bones. Pull off the skin, if desired.

6 Trim away the tough membrane from the rib side of the breast meat. Locate the white tendon on the underside of the breast and scrape the meat away from the tendon. Trim any large bits of fat.

BONING A POULTRY DRUMSTICK AND THIGH

1 Pull off the skin from the drumstick and thigh, if desired. Without separating the drumstick and leg, use a knife to cut along the thigh bone to expose the bone, and then cut down the drumstick to expose the bone.

2 Use your fingers to push the meat away from the bones, beginning with the thigh. As you hold the thigh, let the meat fall away from the bone. Then let the meat fall away from the drumstick bone.

3 Place the leg on the cutting board, flesh side down, and spread out as much as possible to expose the bones fully. Following the line where the meat is still attached to the bones, cut it away.

BUTTERFLYING POULTRY

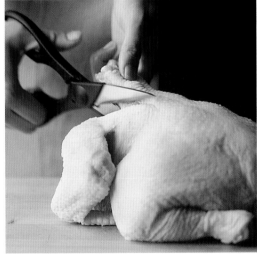

1 Place the bird breast side down on a cutting board. Using poultry shears or a large, sharp knife, cut along one side of the backbone.

2 Pull the bird open slightly and cut down the other side of the backbone to free it. Reserve for making stock or discard.

3 Turn the bird breast side up and open it as flat as possible. Press firmly to break the breastbone and flatten the bird.

Basic Techniques

TRUSSING POULTRY

1 Place the bird breast side up on a cutting board. Loop a long piece of kitchen string under the tail, cross it over once, then bring the ends up and around the legs, pulling tightly.

2 Pull the ends of the string toward the breast. Turn the bird breast side down and bring the string under each wing. Cross the ends and hold them securely to steady the bird.

3 Turn the bird breast side up on the cutting board and make sure that the shape of the bird is compact. Tie the strings securely at the top of the neck and trim them close to the knot.

FRENCHING MEAT BONES

1 Trim most of the fat from the lamb rack or roast. Then insert the blade of a sharp knife into the meat and tissue on each side of the bones to mark what should be cut away.

2 Use the knife and your fingers to cut and pull out the meat and tissue from between the bones, working up to 2–3 inches (5–7.5 cm) from the ends of the bones.

3 Using the back of the knife blade, scrape off any remaining meat or tissue to leave the bones nearly clean. Alternatively, use a kitchen towel to rub off the meat and tissue.

CARVING A CHICKEN OR OTHER SMALL BIRD

1 Using a carving knife, cut through the skin between the thigh and breast. Move the leg to locate the thigh joint, then cut through the joint to remove the leg. Use the same procedure to remove the wing from the breast by cutting through the shoulder joint.

2 If the bird is small, the leg, with both the drumstick and the thigh, may be served whole. If it is large, cut through the joint to separate the drumstick and thigh. Larger thighs may be cut into 2 pieces by removing the meat from the bone.

3 Just above the thigh and wing joints, make a deep horizontal cut toward the bone. Starting at the breastbone, carve downward along the bone toward the horizontal cut to remove the breast in a single piece, then thinly slice the breast if desired.

CARVING A TURKEY

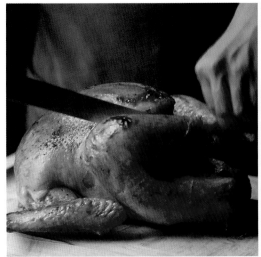

1 Cut through the skin between the breast and thigh. Move the leg to locate the thigh joint; cut through the joint to remove the leg. Use the same procedure to remove the wing from the breast by cutting through the shoulder joint.

2 Cut through the joint in the leg to separate the drumstick and thigh. Carve the drumstick into thin slices parallel to the bone. Repeat to cut thin slices of meat from the remaining drumstick and both thighs.

3 Just above the thigh and wing joints, carve a deep horizontal cut through the breast meat to the bone. Starting at the breastbone, carve downward toward the horizontal cut to yield long, thin slices of meat.

Basic Techniques

CARVING A WHOLE FISH

1 Starting near the center of the back of the fish, use a thin-bladed knife to cut carefully along the length of the back and loosen the top fillet from the backbone.

2 Using a spatula, or 2 spatulas if the fish is large, ease the spatula(s) under the top fillet, carefully lift the fillet, and transfer it to an individual plate.

3 Lift out the backbone and discard it. Discard any seasonings in the cavity, if used. With the spatula(s), transfer the bottom fillet to another plate.

CARVING A BONELESS ROAST

CARVING A RACK OF LAMB

1 Place the roast on a carving board. Leave the strings in place to hold the roast together. Insert a carving fork to secure the roast alongside where you will be slicing.

2 Using a carving knife, carve the meat across the grain into horizontal slices 1/4–1/2 inch (6–12 mm) thick, removing the strings from the roast as you reach them.

Steady the rack on the carving board with a carving fork. Insert a carving knife between the first and second ribs and cut to separate. Repeat to cut the rack into chops.

CARVING A BONE-IN LEG OF LAMB I

1 Place the leg on a carving board and, with a kitchen towel, hold it firmly by the end of the shank bone. Position the leg so the rounded, meaty side will be carved first.

2 Tilt the leg slightly upward and cut a slice about ¹/₂ inch (12 mm) thick from the meaty side, cutting away from you and parallel to the bone.

3 Continue carving the meat parallel to the first slice and to the bone. Rotate the leg to expose the flatter side and repeat to cut slices about ¹/₂ inch thick.

CARVING A BONE-IN LEG OF LAMB II

1 Holding the leg firmly with a kitchen towel, cut 1 or 2 slices from the flat side for stability, then turn the leg meaty side up. About 6 inches (15 cm) up from the shank end, remove a small, wedge-shaped piece of meat.

2 Starting at the wedge, cut slices about ¹/₂ inch (12 mm) thick, working perpendicular to the bone and cutting through the meat to the bone. Make a cut along the bone, starting at the wedge, to free all of the slices.

3 Cut down along each side of the bone and around the leg to release the remaining meat from the bottom side of the leg. Remove the meat in a single large piece. Cut it across the grain into slices ¹/₂ inch thick.

Beef Cuts

Butchers in the United States divide the steer into eight primary sections, illustrated below.
In general, cuts from the top of the steer are more tender than those from the bottom of the steer,
which benefit from the use of flavorings such as rubs and marinades.

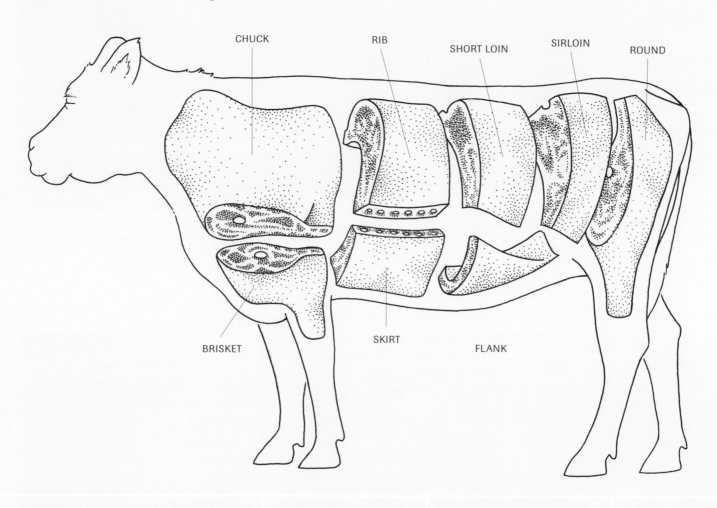

CHUCK · RIB · SHORT LOIN · SIRLOIN · ROUND

BRISKET · SKIRT · FLANK

RIB

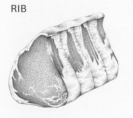

Rib Roast

Rib-Eye Steak

CHUCK

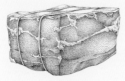

Cross-Rib Roast

FLANK

Flank Steak

ROUND

Eye of Round

BEEF CUTS FOR ROASTING

The cuts described here are those featured in the recipes in this book. For information on purchasing beef, see page 163.

Rib Roast

Cut from the prized rib portion of the steer, the standing rib roast is paired with Yorkshire pudding (see Standing Rib roast with Yorkshire Pudding, page 177). Although the rib roast can be cut from either the upper or the lower rib section of the steer, the back portion—the ribs closest to the loin end—is preferred because it has the largest eye. The roast can also be boned before roasting, but roasting the meat on the rib bones enhances both the flavor and the juiciness.

Rib-Eye Steak

Also known as the prime rib steak or club steak, the rib-eye steak is available boneless and sometimes on the bone. The meat benefits from seasoning before roasting and is also delicious when roasted only briefly after searing on the stove top (see Rib-Eye Steaks Marchands de Vin, page 181).

Cross-Rib Roast

The cross-rib roast is a boneless cut from the chuck, a part of the animal that has more connective tissue than other sections. Cooking the roast until well done allows the meat to soften and become tender (see Cross-Rib Roast with Roasted Root Vegetables, page 168).

Flank Steak

Cut from the underbelly, the thin, fibrous flank steak benefits from marinating to enhance the tenderness of the meat. This boneless steak can be butterflied and stuffed, another way to add flavor (see Matambre, page 184).

Eye of Round

Lacking the internal fat of other cuts, boneless eye of round is lean. Seasoning the meat and letting it stand in the refrigerator help develop the flavor before roasting it (see Eye of Round with Béarnaise Sauce, page 167).

Chateaubriand

Many cuts of beef are sold as chateaubriand. All are tender and sized to serve two. The most authentic cut comes from the tenderloin and averages 1–1 1/4 pounds (500–625 g). This boneless steak is appreciated for its tenderness and flavor (see Chateaubriand with Shiitake Mushroom Rub, page 174).

Strip Steak

The strip steak is the larger piece that is cut from the porterhouse. Searing the steak adds flavor prior to roasting it briefly at a high temperature (see New York Strip Steak with Horseradish Cream, page 178).

Porterhouse Steak

The porterhouse is from the short loin, the portion of the steer that yields the highest-quality steaks. It consists of a meaty strip steak and a succulent tenderloin attached to a T-shaped bone. Pan-roasting the steak ensures a juicy, flavorful result (see Porterhouse Steak with Creamed Spinach, page 182).

Tenderloin

The cylindrical shape and tenderness of this boneless cut from the short loin make it an easy roast to prepare. A 6-pound (3-kg) tenderloin roasted at a high oven temperature is done in less than an hour (see Beef Tenderloin with Madeira Sauce, page 171).

SHORT LOIN

Chateaubriand

Strip Steak

Porterhouse Steak

Tenderloin

Lamb Cuts

Lamb sold in the United States is divided into six primary cuts, shown below. The rib and loin, the less exercised parts of the animal, yield the most tender cuts, though the leg and shoulder yield moist, flavorful meat when roasted.

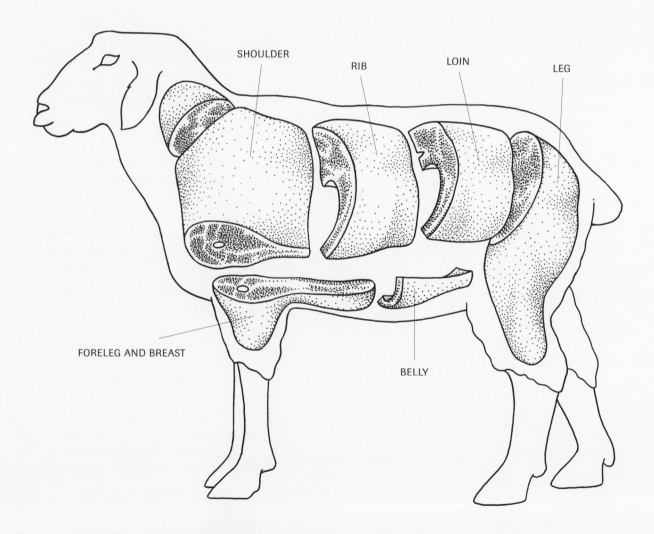

LEG

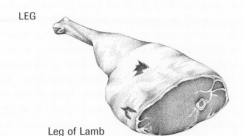

Leg of Lamb

Boneless Leg of Lamb

LOIN

Loin Chop

RIB

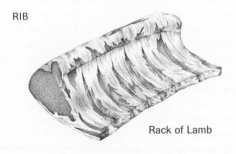

Rack of Lamb

SHOULDER

Shoulder Roast

LAMB CUTS FOR ROASTING

The cuts described here are those featured in the recipes in this book. For information on purchasing lamb, see page 163.

Leg of Lamb

A whole bone-in hind leg of lamb is a tender cut that is easy to roast and yields enough flavorful meat to serve eight. The meat can be seasoned prior to roasting with herbs, spices, and aromatics (see Leg of Lamb with Garlic and Rosemary, page 195). A half leg of lamb can be taken from the shank (bottom) end or butt (top) end, the latter of which offers more meat. Compared with a whole leg, which weighs 6 to 7 pounds (3 to 3.5 kg), the half leg is 4 to 5 pounds (2 to 2.5 kg) and serves six (see Leg of Lamb with Bread Crumb Crust, page 196).

Boneless Leg of Lamb

Not only is a boneless leg of lamb flavorful and tender, but it is very easy to carve. The meat can be flattened and trimmed, then rolled around a stuffing of vegetables or other ingredients to make a compact, cylindrical roast (see Leg of Lamb Stuffed with Roasted Peppers and Onions, page 199). A whole leg is easy to bone, but butchers will bone the leg on request.

Loin Chops

The most expensive of the lamb chops, the loin chops are also the most tender and flavorful. These chops have the T-shaped bone characteristic of the loin. Thick-cut loin chops, or double loin chops, are cut twice as thick as a typical chop. After a brief searing, the chops are roasted until medium-rare (see Lamb Chops with Mint, Tomato, and Garlic Sauce, page 206).

Rack of Lamb

A rack consists of the 7 or 8 ribs from one side of the lamb, which are cut into single or double chops after roasting (page 286). Ideal for a special occasion, this popular and elegant cut offers meat that is tender and full flavored. The ribs are often frenched, or trimmed, prior to roasting (page 284). The meat can be simply seasoned before cooking (see Rack of Lamb with Mustard and Thyme, page 202) or can be coated with a savory topping (see Rack of Lamb with Goat Cheese and Rosemary Topping, page 205). Roasted at a high temparature, racks are ready to serve in about a half hour.

Shoulder Roast

Although not as tender as other cuts of lamb, the shoulder develops a depth of flavor and succulence when roasted until well done, which softens the connective tissue and renders the fat. Seasoning the meat in advance of roasting, searing it before it goes into the oven, and roasting at two temperatures—an effective technique called hybrid roasting (page 13)—enhance the flavor and texture (see Lamb Shoulder Roast with Herbs and Black Olives, page 200). Shoulder roasts are available with the bone in and also boneless and tied, ready to roast.

Pork Cuts

Many U.S. butchers divide the pig into five primal sections, illustrated below. Some also divide the loin into the sirloin and center loin. The cuts range from the small, lean tenderloin and single-serving chops to the large, moist leg enveloped in a layer of fat and the elegant crown roast.

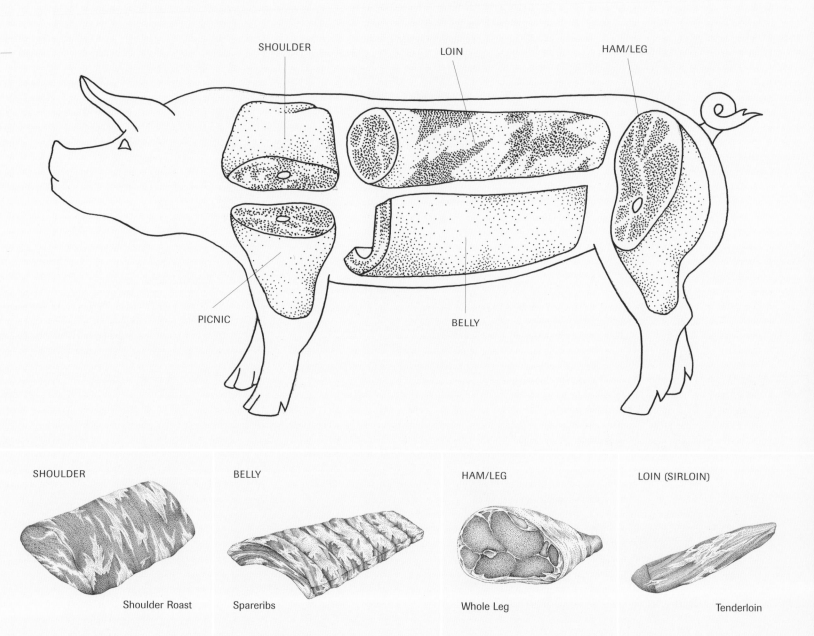

SHOULDER

LOIN

HAM/LEG

PICNIC

BELLY

SHOULDER

Shoulder Roast

BELLY

Spareribs

HAM/LEG

Whole Leg

LOIN (SIRLOIN)

Tenderloin

PORK CUTS FOR ROASTING

The cuts described here are those featured in the recipes in this book. For information on purchasing pork, see page 164.

Shoulder Roast

Cut from the top of the shoulder, this roast has an abundant amount of connective tissue and good supply of fat. The meat can be transformed into juicy, falling-apart shreds after long roasting at low temperature (see Slow-Roasted Pork Shoulder, page 208).

Spareribs

These ribs from the belly are meatier than back ribs. They can be seasoned with a rub and basted during a long, slow roasting (see Low Country–Style Spareribs, page 216).

Whole Leg

A large cut weighing up to 20 pounds (10 kg), the whole leg is roasted until very well done to ensure that the meat will be moist and tender (see Fresh Ham with Pineapple-Jicama Salsa, page 211). If you prefer a smaller roast, you can purchase a half leg. The butt, or top, end is more compact than the shank, or bottom, end, but the latter is easier to carve.

Tenderloin

The boneless tenderloin, averaging 1 pound (500 g), comes from the lower-middle back. Of all pork cuts, it is the most tender and most lean. A variety of seasonings can be used to flavor the meat (see Pork Tenderloin Canapés, page 40, and Pork Tenderloin with Whole-Grain Mustard, page 221).

Loin Chop

This lean chop has a T-shaped bone and contains part of the prized tenderloin. Soaking the chops in a brine (see Caribbean-Brined Pork Chops, page 222) helps keep them moist.

Searing the chops adds flavor (see Pork Loin Chops with Roasted Rhubarb, page 226).

Rib Chop

Cut from the loin after the loin chops have been removed, rib chops have only a small piece, if any, of the tenderloin attached to the T-bone. They are less expensive than loin chops, and the meat tends to be fattier. Like loin chops, rib chops can be brined to help them retain moisture (see Pork Chops with Cranberry-Orange Stuffing, page 225).

Baby Back Ribs

Often called back ribs, these are the rib bones remaining after the pork loin and tenderloin have been removed. A rub can be used to flavor the ribs prior to roasting, and a basting sauce can be brushed on during cooking to moisten and flavor the meat before it becomes falling-apart tender (see Baby Back Ribs with Sherry and Balsamic Vinegar Basting Sauce, page 219).

Boneless Loin Roast

The popular center-cut loin delivers succulent meat when roasted. Stuffing a boneless roast adds moisture and flavor (see Pork Loin with Armagnac-Soaked Dried Plums, page 212). The same cut is also available bone-in.

Crown Roast

To make this impressive and elegant roast, 2 or 3 rib sections of loin, known as the pork loin racks, are tied together to create a circle, with the ribs pointing up (see Crown Roast of Pork with Wild Rice Stuffing, page 215). The roast can contain from 14 chops to as many as 21 chops. The ends of the ribs are usually frenched (page 284).

LOIN (CENTER LOIN)

Loin Chop

Rib Chop

Baby Back Ribs

Loin Roast

Crown Roast

Glossary

BALSAMIC VINEGAR A dark brown, syrupy, aged vinegar that is sweet and mellow while still possessing a complex, lightly acidic tang. It adds rich flavor to marinades and glazes used on roasted foods and to pan sauces. Select a relatively young balsamic vinegar for these uses; long-aged vinegars should be used sparingly and never cooked.

BASMATI RICE A long-grain rice with a nutty flavor and perfumelike aroma. The cooked grains are sturdy, yet fluffy, perfect for a stuffing for roasted meats, poultry, or fish.

BELL PEPPERS Bell peppers (capsicums) become soft, meaty, and extra sweet when roasted and take on a smoky flavor that gives them a distinctive character.

To roast bell peppers, preheat the oven to 500°F (260°C). Arrange the peppers on a baking sheet and roast, turning as needed, until blackened and blistered on all sides, 20–30 minutes. Remove the peppers from the oven, drape them loosely with aluminum foil, and let them stand until cool enough to handle, about 10 minutes. Using your fingers, peel away the skins. Cut the peeled pepper in half lengthwise and remove the stems, seeds, and ribs before using.

BREAD CRUMBS Bread crumbs are a simple source of crisp toppings or crunchy coatings that add texture to roasted foods and also help keep them moist in the heat of the oven. French bread and baguettes, coarse country white breads, whole-wheat (wholemeal) breads, and egg breads all make good fresh crumbs.

To make fresh bread crumbs, lay the bread slices in a single layer on a work surface and leave overnight to dry. Remove and discard the crusts, tear the bread into large pieces, and process in a food processor to the desired con-sistency. Fresh bread crumbs will keep in a zip-pered plastic bag in the refrigerator for up to 1 month or in the freezer for up to 6 months.

CAPERS Capers are the unopened flower buds of bushes native to the Mediterranean. The buds, which are dried, cured, and then usually packed in a vinegar brine, add a pleasant tang to cooked dishes and salads. Capers are also sold packed in salt; rinse them thoroughly before using.

CHEESE Some types, such as Parmesan and ricotta, are used in stuffings for roasted meats and poultry. Others are sprinkled on foods just before or after they are removed from the oven to create a flavorful finish.

Asiago An Italian cow's milk cheese that comes in several forms: the ordinary semifirm variety has a medium sharpness, while fresh Asiago, also semifirm, is milder. Both semifirm types melt well. Aged Asiago is a hard grating cheese with a full, sharp flavor.

Feta Known primarily for its use in Greek cuisine, feta is a young cheese traditionally made from sheep's milk, although it is some-times made from goat's or cow's milk. Mild but with a distinctive sharpness, feta is aged vary-ing amounts of time in brine, which heightens its saltiness. This versatile, bright white cheese crumbles easily and melts into silky morsels.

Goat, fresh Also called chèvre and made from pure goat's milk or sometimes a blend of goat's and cow's milk. Fresh goat cheese is soft and has a mild, slightly tangy flavor and a pleas-antly coarse texture.

Gruyère This semifirm, dense, smooth cow's milk cheese is produced in Switzerland and France and is appreciated for its mild, nutty flavor and superior melting properties.

Manchego A Spanish cheese made from sheep's milk, Manchego is sold at various stages of maturity. The aged cheeses are hard and yellow and excellent for grating. Mild, slightly salty young Manchego, a premium melting cheese, has a pale yellow, almost white interior dotted with a few small holes.

Parmesan An aged, hard grating cheese made from partially skimmed cow's milk, with a salty flavor and a rich, assertive fragrance. The most prized version, produced in the Emilia-Romagna region of Italy, is always labeled with the trade-mark name Parmigiano-Reggiano.

Provolone Made from cow's milk, provolone is sold in young and aged versions. Both are smooth, dense, and lightly salty, and have a buttery essence; the latter has a spicier, sharper taste, is harder, and is used for grating.

Ricotta Traditionally made by further process-ing whey, the liquid left over from cheese making, although nowadays milk is sometimes added. White and mild, ricotta is soft and can be easily scooped from its container. Both whole-milk and part-skim cheeses are sold. Ricotta retains its moisture and flavor during long cooking and at fairly high temperatures, making it an ideal ingredient in roasted dishes.

Roquefort France's premier blue cheese is made from sheep's milk. The interior is streaked with the delicate network of blue veins for which all blue cheeses are named, the result of special mold cultures introduced during the ripening period. Pale, moist, and crumbly, Roquefort has a strong, salty, peppery flavor and a pleasing savory aroma when cooked.

Swiss A generic term for the category of cheeses typified by the classic cow's milk cheeses of Switzerland, such as Emmentaler. Easily distinguished by its network of small or large holes, Swiss is generally semifirm, shiny, and yellow, and is a good melting cheese.

CHILE POWDER A pure powder made by grinding a single specific variety of dried chile. Ancho and New Mexico chile powders are the most commonly available. Do not confuse these pure powders with chili powder, typically a blend of powdered dried chile, oregano, cumin, and sometimes other seasonings.

CHILES Fresh chiles range in size from tiny to large, in heat intensity from mild to fiery hot, and in use from seasoning to vegetable. Select firm, bright-colored chiles with blemish-free skins. To reduce the hotness of a chile, remove the membranes and seeds, where the heat-producing compound, called capsaicin, resides. When working with hot chiles, wear gloves to avoid burning your skin, then wash your hands and any utensils thoroughly with hot, soapy water the moment you finish.

Jalapeño The jalapeño measures from 2 to 4 inches (5 to 10 cm) long, has a generous amount of flesh, and ranges from mildly hot to fiery. Green jalapeños are widely available, but you can sometimes find red ones, the ripened form, which are slightly sweeter.

Serrano The serrano is similar to the familiar jalapeño in heat intensity and appearance, although it is smaller, usually about 2 inches (5 cm), and more slender. It can be green or red.

CRÈME FRAÎCHE This rich, cultured cream product makes a luxurious topping and can be purchased or made at home. To make crème fraîche, combine 1 cup (8 fl oz/250 ml) heavy (double) cream and 1 tablespoon buttermilk in a saucepan over medium-low heat. Heat just to lukewarm; do not allow to simmer. Remove from the heat, cover, and let stand at room temperature until thickened, which can take 8 to 48 hours. Chill before using.

CURRY POWDER Typical ingredients of this ground spice blend from South Asia include turmeric, cumin, coriander, pepper, cardamom, mustard, cloves, and ginger. Curry powders are usually categorized as mild, hot, and very hot. Madras curry powder is considered a well-balanced version with medium heat.

DEMI-GLACE The classic *demi-glace* is a rich brown sauce made by combining *espagnole* sauce, a basic brown sauce, with a reduced meat stock and flavoring it with Madeira or sherry. It is cooked slowly for many hours until it has thickened into a glazelike reduction and is then used as a base for many other sauces, contributing deep flavor and an attractive sheen. Look to specialty-food stores and mail-order suppliers for high-quality beef or veal *demi-glace* without unwanted ingredients such as hydrogenated oils.

FIVE-SPICE POWDER A common spice blend in southern China and Vietnam, often used for seasoning poultry for roasting. Purchase it at well-stocked markets or, for maximum freshness in aroma and flavor, make your own blend: Using a spice grinder or a mortar and pestle, grind together 1 star anise pod, 2 teaspoons Sichuan peppercorns, $1/4$ teaspoon fennel seeds, and $1/4$ teaspoon whole cloves, then stir in $1/4$ teaspoon ground cinnamon.

GARAM MASALA A mixture of toasted, ground spices used in South Asia. The blend may consist of as many as a dozen spices, including black pepper, cumin, cloves, cardamom, coriander, fennel, fenugreek, and mace. Traditionally it is added in a small quantity at the end of cooking or sprinkled over the finished dish just before serving to add a subtle flavor. It is also good for flavoring marinades or for using in dry rubs. Garam masala is available in Indian markets and many well-stocked supermarkets.

GINGER A refreshing combination of spicy and sweet in both aroma and flavor, ginger is a standard ingredient in most Asian cuisines and adds a lively note to many dishes, including sauces and marinades for roasted foods.

Crystallized Fresh ginger that has been cooked in sugar syrup and then coated with granulated sugar. Also called candied ginger.

Fresh Hard and knobby fresh ginger has thin, pale brown skin. Although called a root, it is actually a rhizome, or underground stem. Select fresh ginger that is firm and heavy with smooth, unbroken skin.

GOOSE FAT Geese are high in fat, but much of the fat can be rendered and put to good use in braised vegetable dishes, sauces, and stews. Use the crisp, tasty cracklings in the same way you would use crisply fried bacon, such as in salads and egg dishes.

To render goose fat and make cracklings, remove the lumps of fat from the goose cavity and set aside. Trim any fat from the neck. Cut the neck fat into $1/2$-inch (12-mm) pieces. Place in a deep-sided saucepan with 1 cup (8 fl oz/ 250 ml) water. Bring to a simmer over low heat and cook until the pieces of fat are crisp and golden brown, 20–30 minutes. Do not allow the cracklings to burn. Using a slotted spoon, transfer the cracklings to paper towels to drain. Return the saucepan with the liquid to the stove top, add the reserved fat from the body cavity, and cook over low heat until all of the water evaporates and the liquid fat stops spitting, about 20 minutes. Strain through a fine-mesh sieve into a clean jar. Let cool, then seal and refrigerate for up to 2 weeks. The cracklings will keep in the refrigerator in an airtight container for up to 5 days.

GRANULATED GARLIC Granulated garlic provides the flavor of garlic in a form that is easy to apply evenly to the surface of meat when using in spice rubs. It is preferred over powdered garlic for this purpose because the larger particles deliver a more concentrated flavor and noticeable texture.

GRANULATED ONION Granulated onion is useful for preparations that benefit from the flavor but do not require the vegetable itself. Like granulated garlic, it is ideal for spice rubs; the large grains blend evenly with other spices and contribute to a pleasing texture.

HERBES DE PROVENCE Available in specialty-food stores and well-stocked supermarkets, herbes de Provence is a mixture of dried herbs typical of those used in the Provence region of France. It usually contains lavender, thyme, basil, fennel seed, and summer savory.

HORSERADISH This spicy, bright-tasting root is only used raw. It is commonly grated, mixed with vinegar, and then sold in jars labeled "prepared horseradish" at the supermarket. Using fresh horseradish, which is becoming more widely available, ensures a purer flavor. Wash, peel, and trim any green areas from the root. Cut into slices and purée in a food processor. Add white vinegar to taste and pulse to make a paste. Refrigerate until ready to use.

JUNIPER BERRIES These dark blue berries from the evergreen juniper bush give gin its distinctive taste. They add pungency to a variety of preparations, including marinades, and are sometimes crushed before using.

KALAMATA OLIVES The black-purple Kalamata is a popular olive variety from Greece. Meaty and fairly large, Kalamatas are cured in brine, then packed in oil or vinegar. They have a rich flavor that is not too salty.

MOLASSES This thick syrup, a by-product of sugarcane processing, is used as a sweetener in sauces and glazes for roasted foods, as well as in baked goods. Light molasses has pure cane syrup added. Dark molasses is thicker and less sweet than its light counterpart.

MUSHROOMS, DRIED To reconstitute dried mushrooms, cover with warm water and let soak for 10–30 minutes. Drain, reserving the flavorful soaking liquid for use in the same recipe as the mushrooms or for another use.

Porcino Fresh porcino mushrooms, also called ceps, are difficult to find and relatively expensive outside the locations where they grow wild. The dried version is a good alternative. Porcini have a sweet fragrance, meaty texture, and full, earthy flavor.

Shiitake Dried shiitakes have meaty flesh and a delicate, complex flavor.

MUSHROOMS, FRESH The popularity of all types of mushrooms has resulted in the successful farming of many different varieties, blurring the distinction between cultivated and wild. A few species have resisted cultivation and are truly still wild, requiring foraging. Wild or farmed, mushrooms are delicious when roasted and contribute a deep earthiness to recipes.

Chanterelle Also known as *girolles*, these trumpet-shaped mushrooms are a bright golden yellow and have a vaguely fruity taste.

Cremini Also known as the common brown mushroom, this everyday mushroom is closely related to the white mushroom, but has a firmer texture and a slightly stronger flavor. Brown-capped cremini may be substituted for white mushrooms in most recipes.

Morel This wild mushroom has a hollow stem and an elliptical, spongelike cap. Unlike other mushrooms, morels should be rinsed before using, as the crevices may be filled with sand.

Oyster The ivory to pale gray oyster mushroom has a fan-shaped cap and takes its name from its subtle shellfish flavor. Select smaller, younger mushrooms, as older ones can be tough.

Portobello Portobello mushrooms are actually mature cremini that are allowed to grow until the caps are about 6 inches (15 cm) in diameter. They are dark brown and have a smoky flavor and meaty texture that makes them well suited to roasting.

Shiitake This widely cultivated, usually dark brown mushroom is the most popular variety in Japan. Purchase fresh shiitakes with smooth, plump caps and undamaged gills.

White The ubiquitous, versatile, smooth white mushrooms sold in supermarkets. The term *button mushrooms* is used for the same species, but only when the mushrooms are small, young, and tender, with closed caps.

NUTMEG, FRESHLY GRATED The seed of a tropical evergreen tree, a nutmeg is about $3/4$ inch (2 cm) long with a hard shell. This warm, piquant, just slightly sweet spice should be bought whole and then freshly grated on the extrafine rasps of a nutmeg or similar grater just before using.

OILS Before roasting, foods are often brushed, rubbed, or tossed in oil, which helps retain moisture and enhance browning. Oils such as olive or peanut add a distinctive flavor to recipes, while a neutral oil like canola is preferred when a more assertive variety might conflict with other seasonings called for in a recipe. Still other oils are used to garnish foods at the end of cooking, shortly before serving.

Asian sesame A deep amber-colored oil pressed from toasted sesame seeds with a rich, nutty flavor. It is used sparingly as a seasoning.

Canola A bland oil noted for its healthful monounsaturated fats and recommended for general cooking.

Olive Olive oil contributes a delicate, fruity flavor to dishes. Deeply flavorful extra-virgin olive oil is used to best advantage in dressings or as a seasoning. Virgin and pure olive oils are not as fragrant as extra-virgin, but are good, less-expensive cooking oils that add subtle flavor.

Peanut Pressed from peanuts, the mildly fragrant oil has a nutty flavor and does not smoke at high temperatures.

Walnut Ideally made from toasted nuts, walnut oil has a low smoke point and a delicate flavor that is easily destroyed by heat. It is typically used in salad dressings or on its own as a seasoning. Highly perishable, walnut oil must be refrigerated after opening.

White truffle oil Both black and white truffles, aromatic underground fungi, are rare, highly prized, and expensive. Truffle-infused olive oil captures their evocative fragrance, with the white truffle oil the more strongly scented of the two. To protect that fragile essence, the oil is sprinkled on foods just before serving.

PANCETTA Italian bacon made by seasoning belly pork with spices, rolling it into a tight cylinder, and then curing, rather than smoking, it for at least 2 months. It is used to flavor soups, sauces, meats, and vegetables.

PAPRIKA Red or orange-red ground spice made from dried peppers, used both as a seasoning and as a garnish. The finest paprikas come from Hungary and Spain in three basic grades: sweet, medium-sweet, and hot. The sweet types, which are mild but still pungent, are the most versatile.

POMEGRANATE MOLASSES This thick, deep red syrup, made by concentrating pomegranate juice, delivers the sweet-tart flavor of the fruit to sauces and marinades for roasting and grilling and to salad dressings.

POTATOES Roasting potatoes yields beautifully browned skins and tender centers, making these root vegetables ideal for use as starters and as delicious accompaniments to roasted poultry, meat, or fish.

Fingerling Small, white potatoes with waxy skins that get their name because of their long, narrow shape. Low in starch, they are good roasted, steamed, or boiled.

New Immature potatoes usually of the round red or white variety. Look for them in spring and early summer. Not all small potatoes are true new potatoes, which are freshly harvested and have thin, tender skins.

Red One of the best choices for roasting, smooth-skinned red potatoes are high in moisture and low in starch, with a waxy flesh that holds its shape well during cooking.

Russet Also called baking or Idaho potatoes, russets are the familiar large, oblong potatoes with dry brown skin. When cooked, they have a dry, fluffy texture that marries well with gravies and roasting juices.

Yukon gold These all-purpose, thin-skinned potatoes have golden yellow flesh, a dense texture, and a slightly buttery flavor. They hold their shape well when cooked.

PROSCIUTTO Famed Italian ham, cut from the rear leg of the pig, lightly seasoned, cured with salt, and then air-dried. Celebrated for its subtle but intense flavor, prosciutto is eaten raw or cooked as a flavoring agent.

RICE VINEGAR Vinegars made from fermented rice are widely used in Asian cuisine. They are mild and add a light acidity to cooked foods.

SALT, KOSHER Kosher salt is preferred for its large, coarse flakes that are easy to handle and because it is usually free of additives. In addition, kosher salt can be used more liberally

than regular table salt or sea salt because it does not taste as salty. Sea salt, which also rarely contains additives, is produced naturally by evaporation, and the taste of each variety is influenced by the location where it was made. Sea salt is available in coarse or fine grains that resemble hollow, flaky pyramids. By contrast, table salt is usually amended with iodine and with additives that prevent it from caking and enable it to flow freely.

SEMOLINA FLOUR This flour is ground from durum wheat, a hard, or high-protein, variety used primarily for making dried pasta. Look for it in Italian delicatessens.

SWEET POTATOES Sweet potatoes have either pale yellow skins and yellow flesh or reddish brown or purple skins and orange flesh. The latter type is often called a yam, although the true yam is actually a different species and is cultivated primarily in the tropics.

TOMATILLOS Literally "little tomatoes," tomatillos are actually not related to the tomato. Firm and green, the tomatillo has a tart, citrusy flavor when raw; roasting tempers the sharpness and sweetens the flesh. Choose firm specimens with tightly clinging husks; remove the sticky, papery husks and rinse before using.

VIDALIA ONIONS The Vidalia onion is one of a special category of fresh, mild onions that are notable for their natural sweetness. When roasted, Vidalia and other sweet onions, such as Maui and Walla Walla, caramelize deeply, becoming rich, tender, and even sweeter.

WILD RICE Wild rice is not a rice, but rather the seed of an aquatic grass. Almost black, with long, narrow, pointed grains, it has a chewy texture and pronounced nuttiness. Combine it with white or brown rice for a side dish or stuffing for roasted poultry and meats.

Index

OXMOOR HOUSE INC.

Oxmoor House books are distributed by Sunset Books
80 Willow Road, Menlo Park, CA 94025
Telephone: 650-321-3600 Fax: 650-324-1532
Vice President/General Manager: Rich Smeby
National Accounts Manager/Special Sales: Brad Moses

Oxmoor House and Sunset Books are divisions of
Southern Progress Corporation

WILLIAMS-SONOMA, INC.
Founder & Vice-Chairman: Chuck Williams

WELDON OWEN INC.
Chief Executive Officer: John Owen
President and Chief Operating Officer: Terry Newell
VP International Sales: Stuart Laurence
Creative Director: Gaye Allen
Publisher: Hannah Rahill
Associate Creative Director: Leslie Harrington
Series Editor: Jennifer Newens
Managing Editor: Judith Dunham
Copy Editor: Sharon Silva
Assistant Editor: Donita Boles
Editorial Assistant: Juli Vendzules
Designer: Charlene Charles
Production Director: Chris Hemesath
Color Specialist: Teri Bell
Production Coordinator: Todd Rechner
Proofreader: Carrie Bradley
Indexer: Ken DellaPenta
Photographer: Noel Barnhurst
Food Stylist: Sandra Cook
Assistant Food Stylists: Melinda Barsales
and Elisabet der Nederlanden

ACKNOWLEDGMENTS
Noel Barnhurst wishes to thank assistants Noriko Akiyama and Sara
Johnson for their invaluable help. Sandra Cook thanks Blake Howard
for her assistance, as well as Golden Gate Meats and Mission Market
for supplying essential ingredients.

   Weldon Owen thanks Vené Franco for providing the chapter intro-
ductions; Carrie Bradley for writing the glossary text; Karen Kemp,
for production assistance; and Maren Caruso for the technique
photographs on page 284.

THE ESSENTIALS SERIES
Conceived and produced by
WELDON OWEN INC.
814 Montgomery Street, San Francisco, CA 94133
Telephone: 415-291-0100 Fax: 415-291-8841

In Collaboration with Williams-Sonoma, Inc.
3250 Van Ness Avenue, San Francisco, CA 94109

A WELDON OWEN PRODUCTION
Copyright © 2004 Weldon Owen Inc.
and Williams-Sonoma, Inc.

First printed in 2004
10 9 8 7 6 5 4 3 2

ISBN 0-8487-2889-0

Printed by Midas Printing Limited
Printed in China